Raised with
PRAISE

How My Parents Made Me
a Happy Soul

Written and Published by
William J. Callaghan

*Cover photograph taken in Daytona Beach, Florida
January 1967 by Coyne Callaghan (Bill's father)*

*Backcover photograph taken in Palm Coast, Florida
March 2009 by Joe Callaghan (Bill's son)*

Graphic Design by Kathleen Casey O'Leary

VISIT: **www.raisedwithpraise.com**

ISBN 1449963080

Printed in the Unites States of America

Contents

About the Book

I recently overheard Dad talking on the phone to a steel supplier and the guy said, "How are you, Coyne?"

"Still in the race!" Dad said.

"What race?"

"The human race. I heard the first 100 years are the toughest". That's my Dad – filled with rare Irish blarney.

This book is a tribute to my parents, Martha and Coyne Callaghan. I felt compelled to write this book because I believe their approach to raising children is something special and should be shared with the world. Writing this book with my parents has been one of the most gratifying and enjoyable experiences of my life. It is a story about my experiences growing up and how my parents shaped my life!

I was raised with praise from the day I was born. I'm not an expert on parenting, and I don't have a PhD in child psychology, but I know that I was definitely raised in a positive light. As a result, I can't help but approach life with a positive attitude and instill that positive outlook in my family and everyone I meet.

I guess I don't know how to be any other way; it's the way I was raised.

Aristotle wrote, *"Praise invariably implies a reference to a higher standard."*

1

Divine Inspiration

In May of 2000, our company was exhibiting at the Powder & Bulk Solids Tradeshow and Conference in Chicago. While I was sitting by myself in the hot tub at the Embassy Suites, the thought came to me to write a book about the way my parents raised their 11 children. The idea landed in the whirlpool like a cannon ball, complete with the title of the book.

My brother, Tom, and I had breakfast that morning with a man named Muhammad, who was a solids technology professor and happened to be one of the keynote speakers at the conference. I was so excited and inspired about this book idea that I told them, "I'm going to write a book." Mr. Fayed said in a strong Middle Eastern accent, "Really, and what is the name of this book?" "Raised with Praise," I said. He looked at me with a big smile and said, "That sounds like a book with a great message."

We talked for 20 minutes about our families, our childhoods and how we were raised. He said he was from Egypt and was brought up in a very strict Muslim home. I told him we were from Milwaukee, Wisconsin, and grew up in a large Irish-Catholic family. As he was leaving, Muhammad told us he had two little kids at home who he planned to "raise with praise." That amazed me to hear him say that! Tom and Muhammad Fayed were the first people I told about the book idea and their upbeat reaction meant a lot.

Not only did my parents raise me with praise and respect, but my brothers and sisters played a key role and were a positive influence on me as well. They still are today!

For the past 29 years, I have been blessed with the opportunity to work with both my parents in our family business and have listened to them tell many stories about their childhood, my grandparents, World War II, our ancestors, aunts and uncles. I thank God all the time that my parents are alive and healthy, because I know they won't be around forever!

Over the years of working with Mom and Dad in our mixing business, I have always been amazed at their uncanny memory, and I loved how together both tell stories with remarkable detail as you'll read and discover in the chapters to follow.

We have worked together and struggled together for the past three decades to build our business, Continental Products Corp., into a world leader in mixing and coating technology.

The fact that they come to work every day, at their age, and work tirelessly at their job is rare. We, my four brothers and I, rely on them each day to perform key functions in our company, and I believe that is one of the reasons they both are still going strong. They feel counted upon – which they are! Because of our close working relationship, my parents have become more like older brothers and sisters and key co-workers to me than parents.

My father was born in 1921 and my mother in 1925; they are now 88 and 84 years old, respectively. As I mentioned, they are both very active in the day-to-day operation, as my mom is the treasurer and works the books and my dad is the company president and also does the purchasing.

"Raised with Praise" highlights my parents' approach to raising children and captures my life as a child, teenager and parent. It includes stories from my family, parents, brothers and sisters, aunts, cousins and friends.

This book is for all the parents who were once children and ultimately the children who will one day become parents. My goal for writing this book is on a grand scale. I want to enhance the circle of life, in a positive way, for many generations to come. In the meantime, I hope you enjoy the book and it puts a smile on your face and happiness in your heart!

Chapter 1
The Making of Raised With Praise

Have you ever laughed so hard you fell off your chair? On March 5, 2000, my wife, Laurel, and I were invited to our friends' cabin in New Auburn, Wisconsin, to hang out in the north woods. Curt and Trisha are good friends and are raising a family of four children as well. We have watched each other's families grow for almost 20 years, from kindergarten class to graduation parties. Their oldest son, Nate, is our son Joe's age, and the two of them were probably the tallest kids from Eau Claire Memorial High School's graduating class of 2007. Their daughter, Lauren, is a close friend of our daughter Michelle's and those two have been laughing together since kindergarten.

That evening, we drove a short distance from their cabin on Chain Lake to the Pickled Trout Restaurant, had dinner, and shared some fun stories about how we first met our spouses. The four of us sat at an elevated wood table on rather tall stools and told stories about each other's grade school and high school adventures – the highlights and lowlights. I was telling a story about the time I was a freshman at Shorewood High School and asked a girl who was a junior to meet me after school on the bleachers by the baseball field. "I couldn't believe she showed up!"

I was explaining how she taught me to round first and go for second base! The details had everyone on the run, especially Curt. He was laughing so hard that he started drifting heavily to his left, holding his stomach with both hands and laughed his way off the stool and down to the floor. It had to be a good four feet to the ground, and he didn't go down from drinking too many Leinenkugel's either. He was just laughing so hard that he got swept off his chair by the humor. When he got back up and rejoined the group, he said it had been quite a while since he'd laughed that hard.

I know the feeling when your stomach muscles ache from laughing too hard. It's that feeling you have after going to Gold's Gym for an hour and exercising your abs to the point where it hurts to stand up straight – except genuine laughter is also exercise for your soul and can make you feel invigorated and young again – like a kid!

A genuine gut ache from laughing too hard is an exhilarating feeling that seems to occur less as we get older.

After dinner, we went back to their beautiful cabin and sat in the newly remodeled living room and continued sharing stories from our individual history books. The conversation went deep into the subject of raising children. For some reason I was moved and inspired that night like I hadn't been before. I began to preach about how I was raised by my parents in a positive light and how it's helped me raise our children in a similar way. The conversation went on for maybe 30 minutes and when I finally finished, Trisha said, "You should have been a priest." And Curt said, "I could sit in a boat in the middle of Chain Lake and listen to you for hours." After that special evening in New Auburn, I began to think more about the art of parenting and about how I was raised.

Rise above the situation

I had been gathering information, pictures and writings in a file for seven years with the hope to one day put it all into a book. It wasn't until my briefcase was stolen along with the file "Raised with Praise," that I became committed to finishing this autobiography.

In the dark of the night on May 26, 2007, some punk smashed the driver-side window of our company van and stole my briefcase. Business files and picture books were difficult to replace, but none of those losses compared to the irreplaceable missing "Raised with Praise" file. It contained personal, priceless, original data that was stolen from my locked car parked right in front of my house. For this kind of crime to happen in my town is rare. Eau Claire, Wisconsin, is nationally ranked as one of the safest cities in the country to live. I was stunned that the many years of accumulating writings and photos for this book - while on business trips, airplanes, vacations and at home - were gone. Vanished! Poof!

When I walked outside that Saturday morning and saw what had happened, I felt empty, disenchanted and infuriated all at the same time. I was sick to my stomach. Now what? Do I give up on this book idea or start all over?

From left to right: Bill Callaghan, Jimmy Pursell, Jim Nabors and Tom Callaghan at the Pursell Cup in June, 2003.

The following month, my brother, Tom, and I attended the Pursell Cup golf event in Alabama. I happened to be teamed up with a Southern Baptist minister for the David Pursell Invitational. They couldn't have put two opposite people together in the same cart. It was like pairing Bugs Bunny with Yosemite Sam.

The man was a gentleman. And although we discovered that our backgrounds weren't at all the same, we found that we had one thing in common, our faith in God. As we rode around playing the challenging Farmlinks golf course, I told him about this book I had been working on. He could tell I was still in a funk over the stolen file, so he said to me, *"Did y'all ever think that maybe God is trying to get y'alls attention? Ya'll been gatherin' info on this book for seven years and that's all y'all been doing. It's time to get beezy and feenish what y'all started."*

I realized that every time he said "y'all," he was just referring to me.

This Southern Baptist was a southern angel. I'm so glad he was in my golf cart on that day because his advice was exactly what I needed.

He sounded just like Gomer Pyle! And no wonder, Jim Nabors is from Sylacauga, Alabama, and was Jimmy Pursell's best man at his wedding. Tom and I got to meet 'Gome' at the Pursell Cup in 2003. Gomer Pyle was one of my favorite TV characters in the '60s, and to meet him in person was an awesome experience. For me, it was like meeting Batman or Jim West or Captain Kirk!

Then in August of 2007, Liam Marlaire wrote a story about our family's business in the Eau Claire <u>Leader-Telegram</u> titled, "Master Mixoligist." He interviewed my parents, brothers and myself for about three hours and wrote a nice article that captured the spirit of our family operation. At the time, I was looking for someone to help me craft this book into a finished product, so I asked Liam if he wanted to help.

In October of that year, Liam and I began recording stories with my parents on many Friday mornings at The Plaza Hotel & Suites. We met in Burgundy's Restaurant on ten separate occasions and collected around 20 hours of classic stories that spanned more than 80 years. I can't wait to share them with you!

This book covers my family's migration from Ireland to Chicago, then to Milwaukee and finally Eau Claire, Wisconsin.

Who would've thought I would write and publish a book? Especially someone like me who didn't read a lot as kid. I was the opposite of a book worm!

The making of "Raised with PRAISE" has been an amazing experience. I am so grateful for the input and encouragement I received from God, my wife, kids, parents, brothers and sisters, aunts and friends. Every time anyone offered a suggestion, idea or comment; I followed up – and acted on it. Thanks to all of you who took interest in my book and helped me finish what I started nine years ago!

There's nothing you can do that can't be done!

Chapter 2
Raising Eleven Children

From the very beginning stages of writing this book, I planned to record my parents together so you could hear them explain, in their words, their stories and how they adopted a different approach to raising children.

The following interview took place in the spring of 2008 with my parents at Burgundy's Restaurant in Eau Claire, Wisconsin:

Bill: Tell me about starting a new life together and raising a family.

Mom: We had just got married in June and attended the Notre Dame game in the fall of 1947.

Dad: My brother Tom was aiding the Secretary of the Navy and every time there was a Notre Dame game, the secretary would give Tom the tickets because he knew I went to Notre Dame. Martha's mom and dad would go to the game, too, it was perfect. And the fun part was on our way walking down we'd pass her mother and dad and Mimi would say 'eh, eh, eh' because they're in the very important rows.

Mom: They were seated about midway down to the field and we're walking along and I'm waving to them as I'm passing and we go down to the front. My mother sees us and she knows I'm doing well and she knows that if Coyne saw two empty seats he might go sit there. And so I turned around after I sat down, and I'm waving to them, and she yells, "Are you sure you're in the right seats?"

9

One time we drove Mimi and Daddy with us from Chicago to South Bend to see a Notre Dame game. The games were always crowded and tons of traffic to deal with. Coyne doesn't like being stopped behind a whole pile of cars, so he knew a back road into Notre Dame and decides to go the back way.

Notre Dame had put up some mobile homes on the grounds, a place they called Vetville, for people who came back from the Second World War and wanted to go to college. Most of them were married and had these places they could live in right on campus. So the back road into Notre Dame took you right through Vetville. There were some other people who knew about Vetville too, so when we pulled up to take the back road to avoid all the traffic, there was a line going into this area. There were police at the other end and a barricade across the roadway. They would let people in only if they lived in Vetville.

Coyne decides he doesn't want to wait in this line. He's got my father in the car too. So I'm in the back seat with my mother, and he's in the front with my father. All of the sudden, he pulls out of the line and into the lane where cars are supposed to come this way but there weren't any. And my father said, 'Coyne, do you know what you're doing?' And he says, 'Hang on, Ed, it'll be all right.'

We get up to the front and two policemen come over, you know, and they're like, 'I got this guy cold.' Coyne puts his head out the window and says, 'Get that barricade out of my way! Get rid of that thing!' The guy says, 'Who do you think you are driving in here?' Coyne says, 'I'm a vet!' With that, they pulled the barricades aside and let us go through.

We parked – we had a fabulous place to park - and went in to our seats. The next day, we're back in Chicago, we were at Mimi and Daddy's apartment. The phone rings, and I don't know why I answered it, and this voice says, "Do you know where I can find Coyne Callaghan?" He must have known that he had married me; the guy was probably at our wedding. I said, "Yes, he's right here." He said, "Tell me. Did he go to the Notre Dame game yesterday?"

I said, "Yes, as a matter of fact, we did go. We had a wonderful time." He said, "I knew it - he was screaming - I was in the lineup of cars to go in the back way and a car pulls out in the wrong lane going down the wrong way and they got through." I said at the time "there's only one guy in the world who could pull that off, and it's Coyne Callaghan."

Dad: He and I were engineering students at Notre Dame.

Mom: I graduated on June 2, 1947, from Trinity College in Washington D.C. and then came back to Chicago for my wedding.

Dad: That was a busy week!

Mom: My mother made all the arrangements; she was very thrilled with the fact that she was going to be putting on a wedding in Chicago. She looked forward to that all her life. So we were married June 28, 1947. The following April 29, our oldest son Marty was born.

Martha & Coyne Callaghan Married June, 28, 1947, at Holy Name Cathedral in Chicago, Illinois.

From left to right: Ro Martini, Louise Habenstreit, Anthy Martini, Coyne Callaghan, Martha Callaghan, Macie Knapp, Kathryn Hayes, Chuck Knapp, Mimi Hayes, Ed Hayes

In June of '49 we spoke with Mr. Boheim up in Milwaukee who asked Coyne to come and work with him in Milwaukee. So we drove to Milwaukee, and this real estate lady showed us around town. She was told by the wife of this man that hired Coyne that we should find a place on the west side near his work where the apartments and condos are available to rent - Industrial Mills was located on the west side.

Dad: Land-locked on 83rd and Center.

Mom: We're in this real estate gal's car and she drove us out to the west side. Of course, your father grew up by the lake in Chicago, and I didn't know Milwaukee from a hill of beans - except it was along the same lake. She said this is a very nice place over here. And he looked at her and said, "Could you please show us somewhere near the lake?" So we came down Santa Monica Boulevard in Whitefish Bay, which is a couple of blocks off the lake, and we noticed someone was building a brand new home. No driveway. No garage yet.
Dad: Across from Richard School.

Mom: We had the one baby-Marty, two months old. And Coyne calls the man in the front yard over to the car. It turns out he was the builder.

Dad: Carl Baur.

Mom: He was the builder!

Dad: And selling new homes. He built three or four at a time.

Mom: And Coyne asked him, "Is this house sold yet?" He said, "No!"

Dad: "I got these two here. Which one do you want?"

Mom: Coyne said, "I like this one" and we hadn't even been inside yet. Carl told us it had three bedrooms.

Dad: We came out of a one-bedroom flat in Chicago while I was working for an MBA at University of Loyola.

Mom: The bed pulled out of the wall – a Murphy type.

Dad: So this has lots of room, compared to where we started out.

Mom: Almost a mansion!

At any rate, we made all the arrangements, came back maybe a week later to the real estate agency, sat down with the people from whom we were purchasing the house and all the various people that had to be there. Carl told us it would cost $23,500 for this brand new brick house.

So I've got a tiny infant and all of a sudden we're living in Milwaukee and we've got a home without any furniture.
Dad: We had two twin beds, a card table and chairs and a stroller, and that was it.

13

Mom: We didn't even have a davenport. I got a piano from downtown on Water Street, and we furnished that house as we went along - it was absolutely marvelous. Then in July of 1949, we had our daughter Margaret Elizabeth, born July 3. Our house was filling up fast! And Dec. 30 of 1950, Coyne Jr. was born. So right within those three short years of being married, I had three little children.

It seemed not so long ago that I was enjoying a magnificent life in Washington D.C.- boyfriends, parties, places to go........

Dad: People to see!

Mom: ......and things to do. Now here I am a few minutes later and I have little adorable babies, lots of cloth diapers, and no sleep! But it was fun being with Coyne. And I just made up my mind if that's what happens because I like being with him, then so be it, accept it, and I did.

And then in March of 1952, Mary was born, and then Hayes was born 17 months later in August of '53. So now we have five kids and the oldest was five—and the house was too small. We only had three bedrooms and there just wasn't room for everybody. My cousin Annie Meara from Decatur was also living with us and going to Mount St. Mary's for four years of college. So we started to look around and found this house down in Shorewood.

Dad: You'd been there once but didn't like it.

Mom: I saw it with one of the real estate ladies that I knew and told her it's too big. I can't possibly handle that house. There were three floors. The third floor has three bedrooms and one, two, three, four closets. You know what I mean? That's a lot of whatever to think about.

Dad: Eight bedrooms, three baths. And a ballroom over the garage.

Mom: It was overwhelming to me when I saw that house. I thought, well I'll just put the babies on either side of me in bed if I have to and stay put, 'cause I can't handle that big house.

But then this real estate lady wanted to show us the house on Menlo and we had Coyne Jr with us, who was then two ½ or something like that. Coyne asked me to meet him there and I said, "What do I do with number three?"

Dad: I said, "Just bring him along."

Mom: So I grabbed Coyne Jr. and he climbed in the back seat. No baby seats in those days. Annie was at home with the other kids. I drove down to Shorewood and we met Coyne at 2724 East Menlo. He was already there, inside, and I parked in front. When he saw me pull up, he came out the front door. He was so excited and said, "Come on, come on, come on!" I turned around and looked and my two ½ year old has on one black patent leather shoe on.

Dad: Two different ones! One brown and one black. Left one going right. Right one going left.

Mom: He didn't have his shoes on when we left so he just grabbed the first shoes he could find.

Dad: One sock up, one sock down!

Mom: I can't take this child into this house, they'll think we're idiots. But Coyne said, "Come on, come on!"

So we go inside and we go through the whole house. And he's walking around the house—not with the owner, but with the real estate lady, and the owner and his wife were sitting in the sunroom.

Dad: They were in the living room Mart.

Mom: I thought they were in the sunroom.

15

*Dad: We didn't even know there was a sunroom when we bought it!
– It was full of green plants.*

*Mom: So we go through the whole house, and we're coming down
the stairs and Coyne walks into the living room saying to the man
who owns the house, "This house reminds me of the house I grew
up in Chicago."*

Dad: Mr. Lowie, I love your home but I can't afford it.

Mom: He said, "I just can't afford it."

*Dad: The owner already had a bid of $60,000 from a doctor from
Wauwatosa. This other buyer didn't talk to the home owner; he
only spoke to the real estate guy, the guy that was selling. He
completely ignored the people who owned the house, Louie Lowie
and his wife. They built the home, and raised four daughters there.*

*When I looked at the home on an earlier occasion, I happened to
run into this other potential buyer. He was an arrogant bastard. A
complete ass! This guy was walking through the house and trying
to find faults and trying to diminish the value of the home.*

*Mrs. Lowie was a Jaeger of Jaeger baking in Milwaukee; Louie
was the Vice President of Jaeger Baking Company. They were the
nicest people in the world.*

Mom: They had the house built in 1926.

*Dad: As a matter of fact, when he got to the point of finishing the
woodwork, he hired a couple of cabinet makers from Germany to
come over and finish the woodwork. The dining room was paneled
in Walnut. It was a magnificent home!*

Mom: And aren't the chandeliers from Spain or something?

Dad: All the wrought-iron stuff was imported from Spain: railings, *wall sconces, etc. He told us that he had $85,000 in it at the time, before he hired the cabinet makers—and I don't know what that added to it, but it was a great home. It had been on the market for maybe six months, and at that time a big home wasn't selling in that area - there were a lot of big homes available then.*

Mom: It was 1953.

Dad: I told him I couldn't afford it, but I wanted him to know I appreciated the tour. Then he said, "Why don't you make me an offer?" I said, "That would be ridiculous. I wouldn't want to insult you.

I figured I could get $24,000 for our house up on Santa Monica. I can probably get a $10,000 mortgage, maybe get 35. I said I think can handle $35,000. He said, "Gee, I don't know." Then he said he just put new overhead doors on the garage to replace the old swing out type. He said he still had $500 to pay on those doors, and he asked, "Could you make it $35,500?" I couldn't believe my ears!

Mom: Yes, we'll take it! And the real estate person's in the background and she just stood there listening. So we bought the house in November of '53 and Mr. Lowie asked if he could spend their last Christmas in the house.

Dad: Great people! The poor guy was embarrassed to ask for extended occupancy.

Mom: We said fine 'cause we had to sell our house.

Dad: And Hayes was the baby.

Mom: While all this was going on, Coyne was working different jobs, while I'm at home having baby, baby, baby. Then Tom was born in '55 and we suddenly have six children. And by 1957 I had Muffie, the character she still is. She's number six.

Dad: Number seven.

Mom: Oh, yeah, Number seven.

I remember my mother came up from Chicago to visit us in Milwaukee, around Easter time, just before Julie was born. Her birthday's the 20th of April. I hadn't seen Mimi since Christmas time, so this was some months later. I didn't tell her I was pregnant with the eighth child at that point.

Dad: In fact, just after Margaret was born, Mimi said, "Well, now that you've had your family – you're all done having kids." We had a boy and a girl!

Mom: Yeah, now that you've had your family!

Dad: We had a long way to go! We picked out 12 names on our honeymoon.

Mom: Anyhow, when my mother came to the house, I went to the front door to let her in, and I'm out to here with another baby. So I opened the door.

Dad: Mimi could barely get in!

Mom: And she looked at me and said, "Oh, Martha."

Dad: Where is that guy!
Mom: And I knew exactly what she meant. And she was just dumbfounded that I was pregnant once again, and I didn't tell her. I remember saying to her, for her sake, "It'll be all right!"

Dad: I was working for a real jerk at the time. He was always complaining and having me work ridiculous hours. One day while I was sitting at my desk, I got a nose bleed, which really woke me up. When my dad was only 51 years old, he traveled with my kid brother Marty to Colorado and he gets a nose bleed and in fifteen minutes he's dead - cerebral hemorrhage. I thought, I'm not going to have this happen to me; I've got all these kids, I can't do this."

So, I said to Martha, the first thing I'm going to do when we get back from vacation is quit. I'm going to quit my job. She said, "What'll we do?" I said, God will provide, don't worry, we're going to make it! Let's go on vacation and we'll figure it out.

The first trip we took to Florida was in December of '59 in that big blue Pontiac station wagon. Julie was the baby. You know the rear seat looked backward, the middle seat was forward and there was a little space in between - that's where we kept Julie! We took eight kids in one car.

Mom: And I was pregnant with Billy at the time.

Dad: While we were heading south on Highway 41(no interstates at the time) Margaret #2, was using the flash of our headlights on road signs to teach Hayes #5, how to read. Margaret is so special! Suddenly Hayes spotted a sign that read, "Demming Hotel – Children Free." When I heard that, I immediately pulled off the Highway.

It was dark, about nine or ten o'clock at night and I walked into the hotel lobby and said, "I saw a sign out there "Demming Hotel, Children Free," is that right?
He said, "Sure, bring 'em in!"
Wait a minute; you have no idea what you're saying.
How many you got?
Eight children - there's ten of us altogether.

With ten people in the car, we had to pack light, so before we left home, we bought big beach towels. Each one had a different color so there wasn't any confusion. We'd have each kid bring a couple pairs of play clothes along with nice clothes for Mass on Sunday. We also had our own little duffle bags from Japan Airlines. Each kid had a change of underwear and a tooth brush in his duffle bag.

19

Some of them had a comb, some of them didn't. And that was it. While I was talking with the night attendant, I asked the guy, "Are you sure - eight kids?
Oh yeah.
What are the accommodations?
Well, I've got these display rooms. I'll get the maintenance man and we'll put some beds in there for you.
It was $7.50 for the night for everyone. I went around with him collecting beds and when I figured I had enough beds, I said, okay, bring them in. Our rooms were so filled with kids and beds, that we put baby Julie in the bottom drawer and wrapped her in blankets. She had the best sleep of anyone! So each child walks in with their own little duffle bag. Breakfast the next morning was only $8.50 for all ten of us.

Mom: On the way down to Florida, we stopped in Columbus, Georgia, and went into a restaurant. All ten of us sat around an island at the counter. Everybody in the restaurant was very friendly and the kids are all behaving when all of a sudden this waitress comes up to the island, turns around, sees all these kids, turns around, walks back and says, "I quit."

Dad: She left. She really did. She threw her apron on the counter and walked out the door.

Mom: After that, everybody was real friendly to us, especially the other people that were running the place. And they said, "Where are you going?"
We are going near Daytona Beach, Ormond Beach.
"How long are you going to be there?"
We'll be coming back through here a week from today.
"Okay, we'll see you then."
So we came back as planned the following week.

Dad: When we arrived, the guy opens the door and says, "Good morning, Mr. Callaghan!"
Mom: And they had the mayor of the town there to meet us,

because they could not get over this large family traveling through town. To us it was no big deal.

Dad: Remember, that's when someone asked if we were transporting an orphanage.

Mom: Our trips to Florida during Christmastime were very special! By 1966, we loaded up two Volkswagon buses.

Dad: One was blue, one was green. You know the round VW emblem? I took that off, and replaced it with the Continental "C logo." Our trips to Florida were two trips in one. Half the fun was the trip down and back, the other half was being there. That's how our family looked at it!

On the way down, we would all walk into the lobby of the Holiday Inn and Martha would take the sitters, and I'd take the short horns. We'd go to the bathroom and wash our hands.

Mom: "I took the girls and he took the boys. We'd clean 'em up and get 'em ready.

Dad: You know, presentable. And I'd walk up to the gal in charge and I'd say, "Could I please have these two, three tables here. I've got a lot of children. Also please bring two or three high chairs to go with them. In the meantime, I want you to clear the table. I want you to take everything off the tables—all the glassware, all the sugars, salt and peppers, all off the table." She said, "Well how will you eat?" I'd just smile and say, "Don't worry about that, we'll manage." I'd tell her what we wanted and I'd say, "Please don't bring any liquids until the food is here." And it worked out fine; that's how we did it.

Mom: Remember the time we stopped in Macon, Georgia?

Dad: That was the worst food. We got there kind of late in the evening; it was about 7:30, 8:00. We said, "Is the dining room open?

21

"Oh, yes."

Fine, so we had the same deal, clear the table, sat down. So we ordered hamburgers all the way around, maybe something else - that was about it. So they brought 'em out, and even the kids were complaining how awful they were. These hamburgers were terrible; they were like shoe leather. So, I said to the maitre d', the man in charge, these hamburgers are lousy. Please collect them, take them out to the kitchen, throw them down the trash barrel, and get a new batch going. I want them fat, thick and juicy – fresh!

"We can't. The kitchen's closed."

"What? Kitchen's closed. All right, bring out some cold cereal. And jugs of milk, we'll improvise."

"I can't do that."

Okay, kids, let's go. I got up and the waitress said, "What about the bill?"

I said, "You eat it; I couldn't stand your food."

"I'm going to call the manager."

Give me his number, I'll call him. I'll report you guys for serving lousy food.

She said, "Get out of here, get out of here."

Mom: Well, it was in the '50s that we had that horrible Polio scare. That was very scary!

Dad: At the time, you weren't allowed to take your children out in public. They pretty much quarantined everyone. That was right at the time when Saulk was just coming out with his vaccination. They didn't allow children to go to movie theaters, community swimming pools – anywhere!

Mom: Oh yeah, you had to keep your kids in your own backyard. It was odd to see children traveling around in those days.

Dad: They didn't want anybody out because they didn't know what was causing polio. I remember some people thought we were transporting orphans.

Mom: "Someone asked us if we were transporting an orphanage."

Dad: Yeah, "Which one of your kid's is an orphan?"

Mom: We were never offended. It's going to be a joke wherever we go. All of our children were immunized the first time we made our trip. They'd all had their polio shots.

Dad: When we got back, I told my boss I was leaving and that I can hang for two weeks or so and he said, "You're fired." So, I came back up to Osseo in January of '60 and asked these guys if they still wanted to pursue efforts in sales. John Ward was my good friend and said, "Sure come on."

Mom: On June 20, 1960, after William J. was born, Dr. McDonald walked into my hospital room with a blond hair baby boy wrapped in a warm blue blanket. He laid Number nine on my lap and asked me, "Now that you have nine children Mrs. Callaghan, what do you think you'll be doing different with this one?" I said, "As a matter of fact, I've decided to raise him with praise." And that's what I did, too!
And you know what it did? It changed everything else I was doing. That attitude of, you're not wrong because you did something that was wrong—you're not wrong. You just need help in learning how to do it right!
By that I mean, for example, when your child comes in the back door with mud on their shoes, you want to stop them in their tracks. So, rather than raising my voice, "What do you mean bringing that mud in here? I just scrubbed the floor." Instead, look at them with a calm voice and say, "Looks like you've got some of the backyard on your shoes. Here, let me help you remove those muddy shoes!"

I thought, let's change it, let's show them how to do it right. And that's what I did. Not that I was totally wrong with the other children, but I had to do something different. It gave me more energy and I felt better. I couldn't be up in the morning, change *the diaper, and feed the baby. I had to have another boost back in the back pocket. A different approach! And I used to practice that whether I felt like it or not.*

Dad: You would pantomime and imagine you were in Washington, happily singing and dancing to Glenn Miller and the "Chattanooga Choo Choo.

Mom: (singing)

Pardon me, boy
Is that the Chattanooga Choo Choo?
Track Twenty nine
Boy, you can gimme a shine
I can afford
To board a Chattanooga Choo Choo
I've got fare
And just a trifle to spare

Mom: I love that song!

As a matter of fact, you know that clock we have on the wall in the kitchen?"

Dad: Yes, the Philco clock.

Mom: For years, I'd have an infant over in the wash bucket on the counter, another in a high chair, others just scrambling around and I'd expect three more to walk in from grade school for lunch, and maybe another one from high school. The Clock's going around telling me I have to have this many sandwiches and soup, and all this stuff ready. I remember looking at that clock and saying to myself, I'm really not here at all, I'm going to lunch at the LaSalle DuBois, which is a marvelous restaurant in Washington D.C. And dear me, what shoes shall I wear with my outfit today? Immediately, I was not there in the kitchen—I was somewhere else.

Dad: With red shoes on.

Mom: But I was able to go through with making the sandwiches because I knew that that would be over at some time. I knew it'd be over by the time they went back to school. So I did a lot of mental gymnastics while I was raising these kids, and it certainly helped me keep, you know, certain means of sanity. It worked, too!

Callaghan's Kitchen in Shorewood, Wisconsin

Dad: On May 12, 1963, I came back from Columbia Hospital at about eight o'clock in the morning. I took you to the hospital early that morning, Mart.

Mom: Yeah, that was Mother's Day; Jim was born on Mother's Day.

Dad: I was so excited that I had a new baby boy! I came back home to tell everybody, Mom's a mom again! I was yelling, "C'mon, everybody out of bed, everybody out, it's Mother's Day and James Michael Callaghan is here!"

Mom: Our kids thought maybe they had a relative visiting.

Dad: In 1970, we had some kids in college, and Martha had nine kids in a row. Three years later, Martha gave birth to number ten.

25

I was running out of gas. Then seven years went by and by that time we had older guys coming up. We discovered we were going to have John and decided we'd better let the family know what's happening here.
So I said, "Let's have a real celebration, put the fine linen on. Get out the Bone China, the Sterling silver, and goblets from Steuben. Muffie, I want you to pour the wine. Excitedly, Muffie goes around pouring the wine into the wine glasses." "What's going on?"
We'll tell you. Mom's in the kitchen cooking up a storm. So everyone sits down and they kept saying,
"What's going on? What's going on?"
I said, "Were celebrating." Everybody wondered why we were celebrating? I said, "I'll tell you, I'll tell you. All right, what's the celebration?

Father's Day!
What do you mean, this isn't Father's Day, Father's Day is in June, and this is March.
"Well it is father's day because I'm going to be a father again. So let's have a toast! There was a moment of silence in the room – literally a pregnant pause by the children. One by one, each of the kids turned to the other end of the table and asked Martha, "Did you know about this?"

Mom: I laughed out loud and said, "Did I know about this?"
Dad: That was the announcement - that John was coming. Welcome aboard!" We all lifted our glasses and toasted Mom.

Mom: "I recall being in the kitchen one afternoon, and there was a lot of commotion going on. I was standing at the sink, looking up out the window towards Keane's house.

Dad: Martha didn't know Muffie was there in the kitchen!

Mom: I was searching for something up above me, beyond me. I didn't think anybody else was nearby, and I said out loud, "Where am I?" And with that, this little four year-old is behind me

*playing with a yo-yo and said, "You're in the kitchen Mommy."
It just brings you back down to Earth. And helps you get back
in the saddle, and keep you going. The innocence of a child is a
wonderful thing!*

*"Things at home were very busy with eleven kids; I had kids in
college, high school, grade school, and kindergarten. When things
got hectic, there were times I would decide to run over to St.
Robert's Church. The doors were always open and I'd go in there
and pray, "Dear God, not my will, but yours be done. I can't figure
this out so you figure it out, and I know that you'll come up with
a good solution. But give me the strength to bear with it." Then
I'd leave and come back home, feeling so much better. Praying to
God, seemed to take a huge burden off my shoulders*

*When John would come home from school for lunch, many times
he would have his friend, Chris Dresselhuys with him. He would
walk home with John, and he knew that John's mom was home, and
he knew that lunch and a hot bowl of soup would be ready for him.
Chris knew that if he went on home, the chances were his mother
wasn't home and he'd have to make his own lunch. I didn't hear
that part of it 'til much later. But, he'd come in the back door with
John and I'd hear him saying, "No John, I shouldn't, I should go
on home." I said, "Is that you, Drell? Come on in, it's all set."
It was such a routine for me to be fixing lunch in a hurry according
to a clock, for the benefit of those who'd have to be going back to
school I'd been doing it since, let's see, Marty was born in '48. So
Six years later, in '54, he was going to grade school. Let's say it
started in '55. Now here's John born in '70. So maybe close to 30
years of having to have children coming in at lunchtime, and eat,
and be happy about it, then get back to school on time.*

Dad: For thirty years, we had somebody at St. Robert's school too.

*Mom: I had a child at St. Robert's school for 30 years without
cease. And one year I believe there were five or six Callaghan's
attending at the same time!*

27

Dad: Six.

Mom: Six kids in grade school. (Laughing) All the teachers knew my kids!

Dad: You know, Isabel (Murph) McBride was doing the same thing; she had a number of kids as well.

Mom: "Murph and Peter had 13 children. We developed a special friendship with the McBride's through all those child-rearing years! She was an angel and Peter was a saint.

Mr. Peter McBride sporting a bow-tie and jingling change.

Dad: Occasionally the phone would ring, and Murph would say, "Martha, it's time we had a meeting."
And Martha would say, "Your house or mine? I'll be right over."

Mom: No matter what time, I mean if it was 5:30, and I was cooking a roast for dinner or something, I'd ask one of the older kids to keep an eye on things. And I'd say, "I'll be gone for 15 minutes, and this is in the oven, no problem, nothing needs to be cooked on the stove." Then I'd go out the front door, up Keane's driveway next door, and into Murph's house behind them. And I'd go over there and sit down in the McBride's living room. She'd come in with drinks, and the two of us sat in the living room. Not one of her thirteen children would come near the room, or dare to say "mom, mom, mom!" none of that. They knew, this was Mom's time-out. Maybe we might hear someone carrying on out there, but we kept on our conversation. Then I'd say, "See you later, it's time to go back to work, good-bye" and I'd walk home.

Dad: They'd talk about Washington, a lot of things.

Mom: Murph went to college in Washington D.C. at Immaculata Junior College. And Peter went to Georgetown and graduated from there. She was from Montclair, New Jersey, and he was from Milwaukee. They met out East.

Dad: Can you believe we raised our children without requiring health insurance? In fact, Dr. Polachek came over to our house to administer vaccinations. Back when doctors made house calls!

Mom: The doctor used to come over to our house, rather than going one by one or two by two to the hospital. That was such a break for us! He lived a couple of blocks away over on Shepherd. He would come to the house. I remember we were passing out some vaccination or shots or something, and Coyne Jr. - I don't know how old he was - but he didn't want to get the shot. I said, "You're going in here and getting the shot 'cause it's good for you." As I was organizing kids in the living room, Coyne, Jr. climbed over the fence and went over to the McBride's house. I don't know if Coyne ever got immunized!

Dad: The girls were going to get their tonsils out. What was his name? That doctor came over the night before, so he could sell it to the kids because they didn't want to do it.

Mom: He was coming over to describe to the children what was going to happen when they have their tonsils removed.
Dad: When we were kids, tonsils and adenoids, it was automatic. When you were five years old, you had your tonsils out. Almost like circumcision.

Back in those days, you never went to the hospital unless you were about to die.

Mom: When I went in to have babies at Columbia Hospital, I stayed eight days in a private room. And the nurse gave me a bed bath for the first four days. After that, I was allowed to get up and take a shower. It was the greatest vacation I had, once a year. Going in once a year, having a baby.

Dad: Remember the girl doing the floors? She always said, "Haven't I seen you here before? Yes ma'am. I'm sure I've seen you before!" She had a mop in both hands and she'd stop us in the hallway and say, "What are you Catlick or something? She would say that all the time. Remember?

Mom: Vaguely

Dad: You were half asleep at the time!

Bill: What about our family trips to Florida. How did you manage to travel with so many kids?

Dad: On one family trip to Florida, we brought along our neighbors Mary and Kevin Keane and we took Mimi and Louise with us too.

Mom: No interstates, remember. They were building I-75 through Atlanta at the time.

Dad: The traffic was backed up as far as you could see. You could take the shoulder, which was my favorite lane, passing everybody. But there was a little slippery slope on the shoulder. It was mud; no, clay."

Mom: "It was wet, Georgia clay."

Dad: Marty was driving the green Volkswagon with Meem and Weez and the big zoo, (Margaret, Coyne, Mary and Hayes). And I was driving the blue bus with the little zoo, (Tom, Muffie, Julie, Bill and Jim). We're driving through Atlanta and suddenly we get to where everyone's stopped. We came upon a major traffic jam, so I decided to take the shoulder. Marty's right behind me and I leaned my head out the window and I said, "Follow me!" As we ploughed through the traffic jam, Mimi's in the backseat of the green bus going crazy and screaming — "Don't follow him, he's nuts! Marty get back on the road!" Mercy!"
The VW bus was at such an angle that I had to get all the kids to sit on the left side of the bus to act as a counter balance while we drove through the red clay.

From left to right: Jim, Bill, Julie, Muffie, Tom, Mary Keane, Hayes, Mary, Coyne, Jr., Kevin Keane, Margaret, Marty, Mom, Louise, and Mimi en route to Daytona Beach, Florida in 1966.

Mom: "Marty just did what his father told him to do and we got through it; thank God for that! Without meeting the Georgia State patrol!

31

Dad: We stopped at a gas station on the way and one of the snack dispensers was jammed, tilted or something. Louise put a nickel in the machine and candy bars started pumping out. More and more candy bars kept spitting out, without any more nickels inserted. Louise was laughing like a little kid. She was having a ball; she never saw anything like this. We all had a delicious snack. Everyone got back in the car and we took off. And I looked around and said, "Somebody's missing. Who's missing? Sound off!"

Mom: We were five or six miles down the road.

Dad: It's Julie! No Julie. We gotta go back and get Julie. Sure enough, Julie was sitting there at the gas station patiently waiting for us to return. And that wasn't the only time we lost Julie on that trip!

Mary, Jim, Bill and Margaret in Florida

Mom: When we finally arrived in Florida, we stayed at Ormond Beach, in a house we had rented in Eleanor Village.

Dad: They had A, B, C, D, & E type housing accommodations. We got an E—which had 4 bedrooms, two baths, a living room, dining room, and a kitchen. And we had them take all the sofas out; bring in five card tables and sixteen chairs. If it started to rain, the kids had a place to sit down and play cards. We always had to think ahead.

Mom: We played games.

Dad: We brought our own artificial Christmas tree from Sears in Atlanta. We didn't have any ornaments so Marty and Coyne said, "We'll get some." So they went down to the drugstore and bought a box of colored Dixie cups. Everyone helped decorate the tree as we placed the Dixie cups on the ends of the silver branches and created our own ornaments! We had a little rotating screen set in front of the Christmas flood light. The screen wheel was made of four pie shaped segments of different colors: gold, blue, red and green. The tree changed colors as the screen rotated slowly around. It was beautiful!

Martha, Louise, and Bill in the Atlantic Ocean

One afternoon we went to an inland harbor, a fishing village, and met Redwood Warden who gave deep sea fishing tours. I took my three oldest sons, Marty, Coyne and Hayes with me to go deep sea fishing. During the adventure, Marty snagged a Devil fish—a big ray. It was a big fish. Redwood said, "Hang with 'em." It got to the point where Marty brought him up to the boat, and Redwood didn't want him in the boat 'cause he was dangerous - so they cut the line. You know who was on that trip with us? The Smucker boys from Orrville, Ohio. Smucker Jams!

We came back with quite a haul as we caught 56 fish that day.

We took the fish we caught to the Publix meat department to have it cleaned. I had never seen anything like this store. They had the biggest meat department ever and the fish department alone had five butchers, so you can imagine the size of this place. One of the butchers named Jim was very friendly and he liked all our kids.

Mom: People didn't travel with their families in those days. He thought we were rare.

Dad: We all got in there and watched as Jim professionally scaled and prepped our catch. We caught so much fish, that we had fish for breakfast, fish for lunch, and fish for dinner, for the rest of the trip. Jim wrapped up the raw fish filets, we get in the car and went back to Eleanor Village.
We were serving a wonderful fish dinner that night and Martha put a plate of food together for everyone. This guy, this guy, and this guy, and all of a sudden we had a plate left over. Hey, who's missing? Julie. Someone yelled, "Oh no, not again!"

We immediately packed everyone into both busses and drove back to the Publix market. There's Julie sitting on a bench with some lady. This is an unusual story. She had seen Julie walking around. She said, "Is your family gone? Yes! Well, I'll wait with you because. I'm sure they'll get back." Julie said, "Oh they'll come back. They did before!

Mom: She's used to it!

Dad: The black lady was sitting there talking to Julie the whole time we were gone. Then all of a sudden, Julie said, "Here they come," as the two busses were racing into the store parking lot.

Mom: But you know what? When Julie came to get in the car, we turned around to thank that lady and she was gone!

Dad: We couldn't find her.

Mom: She wasn't there.

Dad: We're in the middle of the great big Publix mall parking lot. She couldn't have gotten away that fast. She vanished into thin air!

Mom: "It was a huge shopping mall and there were just a few cars in the lot; probably the people that worked there - but it was getting dark.

Dad: The amazing thing was that the woman was there, talking to Julie the whole time and then she vanished into thin air!

Mom: We drove in to the Publix and saw her sitting there on the bench. When we were driving toward her, all the kids screamed, there she is! It was the greatest feeling in the world.

Dad: We all give Julie a big hug and everyone was so glad to see her. When I turned around to thank the lady, she was gone – she disappeared! The kids all say it was her guardian angel. She just was not there; it was most unusual!

Mom: You know, I've been blessed over the years. How many people do you know our age that get to work with and see five of their eleven children every day? It just doesn't happen! We enjoyed our kids. And they knew we did! I think it all came to a point when we went into the raised with praise approach, and that change brought everything to another level. Treat them with kindness and respect! We were very, very blessed and we both knew it.

Dad: The kids all were fun, too.

Mom: Part of that is because they knew we liked them. And we enjoyed them. We didn't like some of the crap that went on, and they knew we didn't like it. They also knew it didn't mean we didn't like them.

Dad: We didn't have much of that, you know? We didn't have much of the crap. People loved to come to our house because it was fun and they felt welcome at our home.

Mom: I wouldn't trade raising 11 children for anything!

In 1964, when Marty was 16, he was a sophomore in high school and wanted to drive up to Brian McCormick's cottage. Marty said, "Dad, do you think I could take one of the Volkswagon busses and drive up to Manitowish Waters? Well, the day came when Marty was going to go with a few of his friends from the west side.

Dad: It was Max McGinne, Dennis, and Steve Kuehnmuench - the insurance man.
Mom: And these are punk kids in high school. And they didn't even come in the house, just kind of hanging out on the lawn next to the sun room.

Dad: Sitting there on the front lawn.

Mom: "They were sitting in the grass near the driveway with their backpacks, waiting to go up north for the weekend. When they all got in the car, I said, "goodbye and have a wonderful time."
Dad: Behave yourself.

Mom: "Behave yourself" was the last thing I told them. They said "goodbye" and they take off.

Marty tells us years later. "I was a big gun (he was 16). I had a car; I had my driver's license and a gas card. I was in charge. And when I got outside the city limits, I thought, Yeah! VROOOM, and I started to do that, and then I thought, I can't do this, my parents trust me."

Now, you can lecture kids, "Don't you ever," and so on, but if they use their own brain and figure, I can't do that, because they trust me! – that is the best!

Many years later, we're at a business meeting and I see Steve Kuehnmuench on the other side of the table from me while we're

36

talking business. All of a sudden I look over and see that same face and start to laugh. I could still picture that same punk kid in the backyard, when he was just 16 years old. I couldn't stop laughing. For some reason, I would look at him and we both just burst out laughing. He's a grown man, now 60 years old. He looks at me across the table and says, "It's okay, Mrs. Callaghan, I did grow up."

Chapter 3
Growing up #9

Milwaukee was a wonderful place to grow up. A port city comprised of many ethnic groups and cultures including, German, Polish, Jewish, Italian, Irish, Asian, Hispanic, and African American. And besides being once a heavy industrial manufacturing town, Milwaukee is known for beer, bowling, bratwurst, bubblers, the Bucks and Brewers.

My parents' house is located half a block from the great Lake Michigan in the village of Shorewood. Built in 1926, this classic Spanish Colonial design home includes stonearched windows and a red slate roof. I spent many hot summer nights lying in my third-floor bed with the windows open, listening to the fog horns from the Lakers and Salties (ships travelling to and from the Atlantic Ocean). They'd communicate with the lighthouse as they made their way closer to Milwaukee's harbor. It was the most relaxing way to fall asleep, especially because we didn't have air conditioning. The low, steady tones from the lighthouse and the even deeper groans from the ships were immensely soothing. I can close my eyes now and still hear the fog horns sounding off. What a cool childhood memory.

When I was six years old, I was in bed one night - when it dawned on me that one day my parents were going to die. I couldn't believe it. I was hoping it wasn't true. How could I get through life without them? I was so sad I cried myself to sleep. I don't know why I remember that moment so vividly, but it changed the way I looked at life *and* my parents.

At a young age, I realized that life on earth was only temporary and that we all eventually check out. So I made a decision to enjoy my parents and family as long as possible while we're all here together.

By the time I was born in 1960, both my grandfathers and one of my grandmothers had already died. The only grandparent I knew was my mom's mom – Mimi. She was a classy lady who lived to be 87. My brother Hayes would say to his friends, "Hey, do you want to see a picture of my grandmother?" Then he would pull a dollar bill out of his wallet and show them a picture of "her." Mimi forever held a stark resemblance to George Washington. Hayes is one of the funniest and most talented individuals I have ever met.

Marty, Mimi and Tom on Menlo

One of my favorite things to do was pick up my grandmother Mimi (Margaret Hayes) from the Milwaukee Train Station when she came up to visit with Louise from Chicago. It was so cool - Mimi set up a sewing repair shop in our living room and my Mom would ask us to gather our clothes that required buttons, mending and patching, and she'd fix our clothes. Mimi's father, Thomas Muleady, was a tailor from Decatur, Illinois, so stitching fabric was in her genes. It was also very helpful to my mom because it allowed hand-me-down clothes to survive another child. I enjoyed sitting by her and listening to her stories from the early 1900s. She was my only connection to that generation.

Out of the blue you'd hear, "Who ate the last one?" That was a question heard often in our home. Since we had 13 people sharing the same refrigerator, food was consumed in record time. But there was always one pickle or one piece of Kraft cheese left in the fridge because no one wanted to be the one who ate the "last one." It's kind of funny when I look back on it now. We had no problem pounding a jar of pickles or gobbling up the Kraft cheese slices every chance we could, but heaven forbid if you took the "last one." That seemed to get everyone's attention. We learned to share, even if it was the last one!

You can imagine with eleven kids, my parents had to have some simple rules in our house, including:

No sleepovers. I never went to a sleepover nor had a friend sleep over – my kids couldn't believe this. It was probably because my parents had so many kids that additional guests would have made it seem as though they were running a hotel instead of a home - always having to keep track of who's checking in and who's checking out. I didn't miss it growing up; after all, how can you miss what you don't know? I also don't think sleepovers were as popular in the '60s and '70s as they are today, either.

Kitchen is closed. After breakfast, lunch and dinner were served, Mom had a rule that the kitchen was no longer open for service. Once the meal was over, the dishes were cleaned and the counters were wiped down, the cafeteria/kitchen was closed. That meant we needed to eat the meals that were prepared for us because we knew that was our chance to eat; no afternoon snacks or people coming in whenever they felt like it, making their own meals and their own mess.

Don't say "shut-up." This rule was heavily enforced. Telling someone to shut-up was like telling someone to f-off. It was considered rude, demeaning and way out of line. If you were heard telling someone to shut-up in our house, which rarely occurred, you caught the wrath of my parents and even my older brothers and sisters. It was considered a swear word in our home that simply wasn't tolerated. "Please be quiet" was the phrase I heard often growing up. If you said shut-up, you might get your mouth washed out with soap. The "S" word and "F" word didn't exist in our home either; those were words we never heard.

No one allowed above the Big Room level. Some people would call it a great room; at our house it was called the big room. Thanks to my brother Marty, when he was six years old, who coined the phrase when he first walked in, "Wow, look at this Big Room!" It was located above the garage between the first and second floors and housed many parties and neighborhood sporting events. If anyone other than a Callaghan went beyond that point and wandered up the second-floor stairs, they were considered *way* out of bounds. The four girls and my parents slept on the second floor and the boys slept on three. It was set up like a college dorm with split-level living arrangements; everyone had a roommate. Bedrooms were not a public place to hang out with your buds. Bedrooms were private in our home. If you wanted to sit around with your friends, it was in the living room or sunroom, but never in your bedroom. The rule helped maintain order and was strictly enforced. It probably prevented a lot of nonsense and who-knows-what-else from taking place.

Even today, when I see my kids' friends in their bedrooms, it just doesn't look right. Maybe because it's just foreign to me or maybe it's because their rooms often have the previous day's clothes on the floor, including dirty socks and underwear, so who would want to hang out in there anyway?

No tattling. My parents said if you tattle on your brothers or sisters, you'll get spanked. Not the person you're telling on – you, the tattler. To some people this probably makes no sense, but it was effective. Your kids are going to have differences of opinion, arguments, fights – the standard stuff siblings who live together go through. If you react every time your child runs up to you and

41

says, "Tom just snapped my leg with a towel and it really hurts" or "Muffie took my favorite shirt and won't give it back," as a parent you are immediately put in the judge's chamber and have to make a ruling – not knowing the circumstances that led to the confrontation. If you react to the tattler and punish the accused, you set yourself up for future tales. Nobody likes a tattle tale!

Kids, however, love it when parents react to their "problem" and take action. Unaware of what transpired, how can you know what the right decision is? A problem usually involves at least two people. What if you make the wrong call?

With eleven kids, my parents couldn't be everywhere to see who is doing what to whom.

On the other hand, if you tell your kids that tattling will not be tolerated, you create a different atmosphere altogether. You allow the kids to settle their problems on their own. If your kids know that tattling has no impact, they have no choice but to figure it out and get along. This rule was very effective. When I would tattle on someone to Mom, she would say, "You're not tattling, are you?" The no-tattling statute actually solved a lot of problems and taught us how to work out our differences.

Go to church on Sunday. Not only is it the day of worship, but from the time I can remember, our family started every Sunday with mass at St. Roberts Church in Shorewood. And in keeping with the Catholic tradition, we weren't allowed to eat anything before church. Everyone in the house hustled to get ready, then piled into our two Volkswagon buses to get to 10 a.m. mass. Sometimes we actually made it on time and, needless to say, we would fill the entire pew. Every Sunday after mass, we had brunch. It was a Callaghan ritual that included ham and buns, fruit salad, brown beans with cottage cheese and Geiser's potato chips.

Another rule my parents had, was simply that when they had a disagreement or needed to sort out an issue involving their kids, they went into their bedroom and closed the door. It was a private discussion between the two of them. Growing up, I don't recall seeing my parents argue. When they resolved their differences, they would come out of their room and continue on with a cohesive plan they agreed upon. We always got a consistent message from both of them.

Every house seems to have its own guidelines or rules. As I look back, it seems that these rules were unique to our family. When I tell someone today about the rules of our house, they look at me with a somewhat baffled expression. What? No sleepovers, no friends allowed in your bedroom, a closed kitchen, can't say shut-up, no tattling, have to go to church on Sunday – sounds really strict.

The rules we lived by as a family actually created harmony in our home. At the time, I never looked at them as a set of laws, but rather guidelines to live by. Now that I'm older and have my own family, I realize how smart my parents were for establishing specific rules of the house.

Growing up in Milwaukee

When I was eleven years old, my father helped me create my own business. I was an entrepreneur at age eleven and started Bill's Bike Shop. I repaired bikes in the neighborhood, because there were so many kids on our block, and there were always bicycles in need of repair. I set up shop in my parents' garage, and my neighbors brought me their Schwinn bicycles with blown tires and broken chains. After assessing the repair work, I'd ride my bike to Claude's bike shop on Oakland Avenue and pick up the parts and fix them. It was a fun experience and a happening business in the summer of 1971.

My dad taught me at a young age that I could run my own business and that the sense of accomplishment is one of the best feelings there is. He is an engineer and an accountant, so he made a ledger book to help me document my activity. I learned how to account for each transaction and turn a profit by charging for materials and labor.

Shopping block

As I was growing up, most of my clothes were hand-me-downs from Tom, which most likely originated from Marty or Coyne. They made their way past Hayes thanks to Mimi, and then found a home in one of my drawers. I didn't mind because I was always just glad to have some clean clothes to throw on.

I'll never forget the time I went with Dad to the Sears store at the Bayshore Mall in Whitefish Bay. Seventh grade was only a few weeks away and we were shopping for clothes – for *me*. I was pumped. I couldn't believe I was going to get my own shirts, pants, socks, a new pair of shoes and, last but not least, my very own underwear.

When we walked into the store, my dad spotted this tall, skinny kid in the lawn and garden department sporting a red, spiked Mohawk hairdo. He looked like the Statue of Liberty's younger brother, but his crown was heading north and south in true Mohawk fashion, a rare sight in 1972. My Dad, who doesn't mince words, looked across the aisle and shouted, "You look like an ass!"

I must say, I was even surprised at my dad's reaction. This dude's physical appearance was shocking, as was intended, and it didn't sit well with Dad. Most people would have kept on walking by without a comment. But not Dad, he couldn't resist. It was one of the first times I remember seeing him really angry.

The kid actually took exception to my father's comment and confronted him. My dad moved in closer and said, "You look like an ass – what's a matter with you?" The teenager started backing up and flashed his middle finger at Dad and said, "F- off old man." I was shocked. I had never heard the "F" word until that day, and it was directed at Dad. This wasn't looking good, so I told my "old man" he should give the kid a break and let him be. I told him, "You never know, maybe he's on his way to the barbershop." I took my father's hand and headed past the riding lawn mowers toward the boys clothing section as I didn't want anything else to disrupt our shopping plans. I couldn't believe the kid told my dad to "log off."

Learning experience

While I was waiting once at the airport in Charleston, South Carolina, to catch a flight home, I noticed a woman reading a Time magazine. The Oct. 29, 2007, issue featured a cover with four brothers and sisters holding hands and the title, "The Secrets of Birth Order – New research shows how your family's pecking order really does shape your destiny." I went to the gift shop and purchased a copy. Here is an excerpt from the story:

Of all the things that shape who we are, few seem more arbitrary than the sequence in which we and our siblings pop out of the womb. Maybe it's your genes that make you a gifted athlete, your training that makes you an accomplished actress, an accident of brain chemistry that makes you a drunk instead of a President. But in family after family, case study after case study, the simple roll of the birth-date dice has an odd and arbitrary power all its own.

So, Do You Fit Your Birth-Order Profile?

- *Oldest Siblings:*

May be better educated than younger siblings

Likelier to hold a professional position

More concerned with meeting parents' expectations

Likelier to serve as family historian and guardian of aged parents

Higher IQ than younger siblings

- *Middle Siblings:*

May take longer to choose a career than other siblings

Less connected to family, more to friends

May de-identify from firstborn, making opposite life choices

Lacks the parental recognition first-and last-borns enjoy

May develop self esteem issues

45

- *Younger Siblings:*

More tolerant of risk

Likelier to be artist, adventurer, entrepreneur

Often physically smaller than firstborns

Less likely to be vaccinated than firstborns

Frequently funnier than other siblings

Let me add,

Less photographed than older siblings!

As I applied these categories to my siblings, I found some of them were right on and others weren't even close. After all, what writer can research or examine a family with 11 siblings born over a span of four decades.

I am the 9th of 11 kids in our Irish Catholic family.

Callaghan family on Mother's Day in 1975. Back row from left to right: Jim, Julie, Dad, Marty, and Hayes. Front row: Coyne Jr., Tom, John, Mom, Margaret, Mary, Bill and Muffie.

My parents had children born in four different decades: the 1940s (2), '50s (6), '60s (2) and '70s (1). Given those numbers, we could be considered a classic post-World War II baby boomer family. As I grew up, I never thought our family was any different from the norm. I assumed everyone came from a large family. It wasn't until I was older that I realized 11 kids was a huge family. Maybe that was because there were many large families in our neighborhood. In the early 1970s, someone counted 88 kids living on our immediate block. The McBrides had 13 "McChildren" and lived behind us on Newton Avenue.

My cousin Rich Martini from Los Angeles, California recently sent me this note:

I think it's unique that you guys grew up behind the McBrides. Truth be told, Bill, for years when I was a kid, since you had blond hair and everyone else had black hair, I thought you were a McBride. Of course I was young at the time, but I thought to myself, "Who is this kid and how did he get in here?"

This is fascinating. While my parents were in a row boat on their honeymoon in Three Lakes, Wisconsin, they planned their family of 12 kids (seven boys and five girls) and picked out their names. They ended up with seven boys and four girls. Amazing! Anna Louise would have been the 12th Callaghan. When Social Security numbers were assigned to every U.S. citizen in the '60s, my parents picked up ten in a row. Consequently, we all know our Social Security numbers by heart, and each other's!

Those 11 Callaghans have more than tripled into 35 grandchildren for my parents to enjoy. I think that has contributed to my parents' thankfully slow aging process. If you are constantly surrounded by family, young children and new life, it's difficult to get old. My folks are living proof that age only exists between your ears.

What a force!

The phrase "there is power in numbers" has never been more evident than at our family reunions. Most of our family reunions have 45 to 60 people. With the exception of 1997 - the year we celebrated our parents' 50th wedding anniversary on Menlo Boulevard - our reunions have been held at The Plaza Hotel in Eau Claire since 1986, the year Laurel and I were married. We have been known to occupy the entire top floor of the hotel's tower and fill up the rooms with family members from out of town. We celebrated my parents' 60th wedding anniversary *and* the reunion at the same time in 2007. Summertime reunions work best because most Callaghans are able to attend. It allows each of the 11 kids to establish their own family traditions during Thanksgiving, Christmas, Easter and other holidays. The reunions are filled with laughter throughout the weekend and the closeness pulls everyone together. Because of the yearly get-together, cousins, nephews, and nieces know each other like brothers and sisters.

Four generations of Callaghans at Mom & Dad's
60th Wedding Anniversary

Reflections of the Callaghan Family, Rebecca (Becky) Welke, The Plaza Hotel & Suites:

The year was 1963: The initiation of the Apollo space program, civil rights movement and the assassination of President Kennedy. In the midst of turmoil, a grand hotel was built in Eau Claire, Wisconsin – a hotel that in recent years would host President Kennedy's daughter Caroline, brother Ted, and President George W. Bush!

Little did they realize it at the time, but this grand hotel now known as The Plaza Hotel & Suites, would become the second home for the Callaghan family. Planning for the annual reunion has become one of my best times of the year. I also have the pleasure of seeing Coyne Sr. and Martha quite often as they dine in Burgundy's Restaurant. Martha has shared many family stories with me, and I can't think of a more generous mother. I really feel like I am a part of this noble family.

A real treat for our staff and me is the annual reunion when the Callaghan children venture to The Plaza from all over the country. It is amazing they all seem like best friends united. Our banquet manager, Sharon Utegaard, has been with the hotel for 40 years and has had the pleasure of serving the family banquet annually. Sharon and her staff also feel very much part of the Callaghan family. Treated with warmth and kindness, this is a special time of year for all of us.

Thank you, Coyne and Martha, for sharing your family with us. Your kindness, thoughtfulness and love will remain in our hearts a lifetime.

Becky Welke

General Manager

Remember the days when families would meet on Sunday afternoons at Grandma's house to share a meal and spend time together? We all live in a fast paced, hectic world that at times seems like your front door is a turn style and you're running the amazing race. Some families, like ours, make a point of meeting once a year, so we can continually build strong relationships. Nothing is more important to me than my family – both extended and immediate.

49

Television time

Does this sound familiar to any of you? On Saturday morning, I'd wake up my brother Jim, and we would run downstairs to watch cartoons together. Our generation was fortunate to have classic cartoon characters to watch, including Speedy Gonzales (my Los Favorites), Bugs, Daffy, Porky Pig and Yosemite Sam. Those were just some of the characters Mel Blanc created.

After school, instead of doing my homework like most kids do today, I would race home to watch "Batman," "Gilligan's Island," "Wild Wild West," "Mission Impossible" and "Star Trek." I loved watching all those shows, especially the sci-fi stuff. Gene Rodenberry's vision of a world with personal communicators, tri-corders and voice-recognition computers was not far off. Shows like "Lost in Space" and "Voyage to the Bottom of the Sea" sparked my imagination. After getting my dose of television, I would finish my homework. I know the schedule sound backwards, but there was no such thing as a DVR or a VCR, and I didn't want to miss an episode.

On Sunday evenings we would gather in the sunroom to watch "The Ed Sullivan Show," "Laugh-In" and best of all, the ABC Sunday night movie from Disney. Oh, my brothers and sisters couldn't wait for Sunday evening to come around so we could watch Disney! On special occasions, we'd eat chocolate cupcakes with cream filling in front of the tube as we watched these classic TV shows in black and white. What a treat! Even when the kitchen was closed, we got some treats once in awhile.

I'll never forget when I was seven years old, in 1967; my father brought home a Sony Trinitron color television. That night we watched the movie "Fantastic Voyage" with Raquel Welch and Donald Pleasance (1966). The ship and crew of scientists were shrunk to the size of a blood cell and traveled through a person's body to remove a life-threatening blood clot. Not only was it a fascinating education on human anatomy, but seeing that movie in color was remarkable. The change from black-and-white to color television was astonishing.

Organized Chaos

I met with my sisters Mary and Muffie in the dining room at our parents' house on Menlo to rehash the past.

Mary: Of course, the first story that comes to mind is making chocolate chip cookies. Fortunately there were enough ingredients to feed the number of kids I used to take care of. Even now when I make cookies, I feel like Hayes, Tom, Muff, Julie, Bill, Jim and John are right there with me. And I make them with pure joy every time. I remember after the dough was made, I would walk away and pretend to look for a cookie sheet and keep my back turned, while you all knew it was time to pound the cookie dough as fast as you could while my back was turned. Everyone enjoyed making cookies with me. The kitchen was full of little stools pulled around the cutting board with every size kid from one to 12. I loved that!

Muffie explains: In early 1960, my parents moved Julie out of the crib in the file room because Billy was coming, so she upgraded to a baby bed in my room. I was only three or four years old at the time; Julie was a year old. We were in our room one night, couldn't sleep, and there was a cool basket-shaped chandelier hanging from the ceiling. Everyone in the house was getting ready for bed but we weren't tired, so I thought of something to do. I climbed onto the top of Julie's bed and somehow got my hand out far enough to pull the light fixture toward the baby bed. Julie crawled in. She looked like a monkey in a cage, with her legs dangling over the side. I said, "Okay, you ready?" and I would jump up from my bed and grab onto the monkey cage and swing back and forth. Julie would yell "wee, wee" each time we went from side to side. I would jump off and onto my bed while Julie was still swinging from the ceiling. She got more of a ride than me. We did it as many times as we could until the whole thing came crashing down. Luckily no one was hurt. I knew it wasn't a good thing, so I hid the broken swing in a closet. It's still there today. I was sure no one would notice it was missing, much less the hole in the ceiling.

I don't recall getting in any trouble for breaking the light, and Julie wasn't old enough to explain what happened. I think my parents figured it just fell from the ceiling one day. I'm sure they would have been shocked if they walked in and saw their two youngest monkeys hanging from the ceiling. Our house was like a zoo and a circus, all operating smoothly under one roof.

Julie, Jim and I were in the second-floor file room one day. My parents called it the "file" room because it's where they kept the company files. I was 11, Julie was 9 and Jim was only 5 (though he'd been able to read since he was 2). Julie and I were looking at our report cards from St. Roberts and my grades were all Ds, Fs and a few Cs. Jimmy looked at my report card with a disgusting look on his cute face and said, "You are so stupid, you even got an F in sex." Julie and I knew that was off, so we started laughing real hard, and Jim didn't even get it.

Weekend warriors

Saturdays were always big work days involving around eight people and whatever McBride stopped by. Frank would often ring the doorbell hoping there was something he could do to help. Everyone would be busy cleaning the garage or washing the windows, and I would look around and notice Jim wasn't anywhere to be found. I would call out, but he wouldn't answer. I went inside to hunt him down and sure enough I found him hiding in the bathroom, waiting for the work to be over. I would say, "Jimmy, what the hell, get going." Jim was the smartest kid in the family but he did some dumb stuff. I could never tell if he was the smartest dumbest kid or the dumbest smartest kid I have ever met.

Team effort

One of my favorite stories is one Julie told me about Muffie. When they were both teenagers, Muff said to Jules, "I can't believe Margaret's my sister," and Julie replied, "What makes you say that?" "Because she is so nice!"

Marty and Margaret are my godparents and in a sense my second set of parents because they are the two oldest in the family. Coyne and Mary were my third set of parents and when they weren't around, Hayes and Tom were my fourth set. And if they happened to be gone from the house, then Muffie and Julie filled in as my fifth set of parents. I had plenty of care when my parents were out of the house.

Margaret is the second oldest and my parents' first daughter and unknowingly helped train my parents how to be parents. When Marg was in the sixth grade, my dad wanted her to wear her hair like Grace Kelly, pulled way back from her face because he was a big fan of Miss Kelly. Poor Margaret wore her hair like that for about a year before she was able to switch off the 1940s hairstyle.

Dad had an account at the barber shop on Capital Drive and had us boys in for haircuts every chance he could; I think it was a holdover from his days in the Navy. I came home once from the Shorewood Barber Shop with a new haircut and Dad told me to go back and have more taken off the sides and top. I hated having to ride my bike back 15 minutes later and tell the barber that my haircut was not done yet.

Sired help

Margaret was always a big help around the house. Although Mom had hired outside help from time to time, including Laura Cooper and her daughters - Quincella, Paralee and Buehla Mae - Margaret and Mary were always doing things around the house for my parents and us younger kids, usually with a warm smile and calm disposition.

"Mary and I would iron piles of shirts in the basement; our record was thirteen shirts per hour," Margaret explained. "When Coke came into the house the older children would each take a bottle and hide it. Marty would find my bottle and leave me a note explaining how he found it - signed by Sherlock Holmes."

My parents held family prayers at night. We would kneel on the second-floor landing while viewing the statue of the Virgin Mary across the banister ...

"God bless Marty, Margaret, Coyne, Mary, Hayes, and Tom. ...

God bless Marty, Margaret, Coyne, Mary, Hayes, Tom, and Muffie.

God bless Marty, Margaret, Coyne, Mary, Hayes, Tom, Muffie, and Julie. ...

God bless Marty, Margaret, Coyne, Mary, Hayes, Tom, Muffie, Julie, and Bill."

It took a few weeks each year to get used to it when new names were added to the list.

Numbers game

Margaret continues: Bebe Collopy lived down the block on Menlo and was my best friend growing up. I wanted to go to her house after school because there was always soda pop and we could play a board game without babies crawling all over the board. She wanted to come to my house after school because there was always something going on.

Around our block between Menlo Blvd. and Newton Blvd. lived more than 80 children: Lings (6), Maas (2), Mestiers (3), Cannons (7), Sensenbrenners (2), Keanes (4), Callaghans (11), Meisners (4), Keysers (7), McNeils (2), Foxes (4), Reichs (3), McBrides (13), Levinsons (2), Dentons (6), Shields (4), Ross (3) and Millens (7).

The grade-school nuns at St. Roberts gave piano lessons to our family's four oldest children. Nuns told my parents to give it up because no one practiced. As it turned out, it was Hayes, No. 5, who had the talent and taught himself how to play the piano by ear.

Margaret married Paul Wittig in 1973 and the wedding reception was held at my parents' house on Menlo. It was great party. I was in eighth grade at the time and my brother John was celebrating his third birthday on that special day in August.

Sound of music

The Beatles were my favorite band growing up and still are four decades later. My favorite Beatle is Paul McCartney, a gifted musician, brilliant songwriter and ballad master - an amazing entertainer and pioneer. I can't say enough about his music's influence in my life, especially the positive outlook he magically embraces through his music. He and I are a lot alike in that regard.

My brother John gave me a book titled <u>Each One Believing: Paul McCartney – On Stage, Off Stage, and Backstage</u>. Here is an excerpt:

This book tells the tale of the 2002-03 Paul McCartney World Tour. The tour was the most successful of Paul McCartney's post-Beatle career, during which the man, who has successfully changed the sound of music since the sixties, performed to two million people.

McCartney writes: When we started Wings, we had to overcome the shadow of the Beatles. So we couldn't do any Beatles songs. And that was difficult, that was more difficult than now. Now, well, I don't care, I'll just look at my whole career and just choose anything I fancy doing…..

And there I was in this amazingly special place in time and space. And imagine then if I had been able to say to my dad, "Hey Dad, you know, I just had this premonition. I'm going to be in Red Square in front of the president, the ex-president, and by Lenin's tomb, and I'm going to have all these people listening to me. And I'm going to be singing to them all. And they're all going to dig it." He would have thought I was mad. But, you know, it has happened and I love to think of how proud he would have been. My mom and dad are no longer here. Just think how proud they'd be that something like that could happen in our family.

Interview in Las Vegas: You have three dozen songs in the set, only five of them from the new album. So there are a lot of songs going back a number of years. Do you remember all the words?

Paul: I remember most of it, especially when you have a few gigs in. But I need to rehearse them and I need to relearn them. I don't just carry them in my head all the time – there's too many. I've written something like 300 songs on my own and with John and other people, and that's a lot to carry in your head..... That's one of the nice things about doing the show, you know, I get to see these lines again that I've written in the past, and I think, "Oh, I'm glad I wrote that ..... 'Let it be, there will be an answer' ... that's good, that's positive. You know, 'Take a sad song, and make it better' ... that's good." I'm proud of it, actually, because there is a lot of that in my stuff. And in music I've always loved that, when I've heard, like a really cool statement in a song and it's made me choke and think, "Thank God for that song." So I love to be a part of that, I'm proud of it.

One of my favorite songs McCartney and Lennon wrote is "Can't Buy Me Love." My older sister Julie and I would put the 45 on a record player in the big room, grab a broom guitar and sing that song over and over at the top of our lungs. In 1967, we were seven and six years old at the time and knew every word to the song and – at least in our minds - hit every chord on our brooms. Julie and I are only 13 months apart.

Travelin' clan

Florida trips have been a part of my life since I was a newborn. Our Christmas present was a family trip to Florida in December. My parents loaded the family into two Volkswagen buses, and Jim and I had the honor of riding in the back above the engine compartment and exhaust fumes. There were no child seats or child-restraint safety laws at that time.

I'll never forget the time we were backing down the driveway en route to Florida after a big lake-effect snowfall. Snow banks framed the sidewalks in front of the house. I looked out the back window of the bus and spotted a kid riding his red wagon down the block with a brown paper bag over his head. I realized he wasn't going to stop so I yelled to Dad, "STOP!" The VW bus stopped just in time to let my friend Dave Cannon roll past our driveway in his Radio Flyer. It was close. We nearly ran over him. Dave never saw us coming and, even if he did, he didn't have brakes. He did have two holes cut out of the bag to see but his peripheral vision failed him. Thank God we missed him.

Wintertime in Shorewood, Wisconsin on Menlo Blvd.

The first trip to Florida was in December 1959 when Julie was a baby.

We were supposed to leave at 6:30 in the morning, so all eight of us had breakfast and then got in the car and waited way too long," Mary explained. "We got out of the car to have lunch, got back in the car, got out of the car for dinner, and then we finally shoved off at 8:30 at night. Dad would say, "I'll be right there," but an engineer's work is never done. Once we got rolling, the ride was a lot of fun. Dad would have us all singing, 'Merrily we roll along' and 'I've got six pence, jolly, jolly six pence. '

Coyne would take his stuffed lion named Gilbert and hold it on his lap. As we drove by other cars, Coyne would pretend Gilbert was looking at the people in the other cars, slowly turning its head as we would pass them. It was so entertaining.

Before interstates were built, we took 41 South through Indiana and ended up staying at the Deming Hotel in Terre Haute.

*We had so many kids in the room that the addition of rollaway
beds and baby cribs couldn't accommodate everyone, so Julie, who
was only 8 months old, slept in a bottom dresser drawer. The next
morning we had races up and down the elevators, with many of us
getting lost throughout the hotel. We played a game where you try
to get around the hotel room without touching the floor. We jumped
from bed to bed and walked across the dresser to complete the
oval track. Muffie would stand on the bed and get launched as kids
bounced by.*

*The first place we stayed in Florida was a rented home in Ormond
Beach in Eleanor Village. We would go to Black's Pharmacy to
have a Cherry Coke, which was the newest, coolest thing. We were
all little so we would sit up on stools and look across highway A1A
at the Atlantic Ocean to watch the waves roll in.*

*"We walked back to our house after we had been pool hopping at
the Makai," Mary said. "I recall feeling right at home in Florida
and very safe. The Makai is an oceanside motel that had a heated
pool. It was lit up at night with a twisting water slide and couldn't
have been more beautiful. The palm trees along with sound of the
waves coming ashore and the smell of the warm ocean breeze was
heavenly."*

During our Florida vacation in 1966, my parents announced we
were all going to the outdoor drive-in movie theater. Marty drove
the older zoo members in one bus to see the new James Bond
movie "Goldfinger," while my parents drove the younger animals
in the other bus to see "That Darn Cat."

Our parents weren't big on presents at Christmas, so the family
trips served as a memorable time together that allowed us to get
to know each other better. It was a lasting gift because I know
all my brothers and sisters well and have a deep respect for all of
them. Family vacations were valuable to me as a youngster and are
equally as important to me as a parent. They are one of the most
effective ways to bring a family closer together because you create
and share memories that last a lifetime.

Mom at the VW Bus stop in Daytona Beach, Florida

In fact, I'm always reminded of Florida every time I have McDonald's food. Most of our family was sitting around the pool at the Quality Motel, when Marty, Margaret, and Coyne walked in with white grocery sized bags filled with hamburgers, cheeseburgers and French fries to feed the masses. I'll never forget the moment. It was hard to believe I was eating a warm hamburger with mustard, ketchup, and pickles, and hot French fries and a cold Coke by the pool along the Atlantic. It was too easy! One moment I'm swimming in the pool and the next I'm sitting poolside eating cheeseburgers and fries – without going anywhere! Talk about fast food. When I have a McDonald's hamburger today, the scent of the food will trigger my memory banks and replay that day in Florida. I'm suddenly back at the pool having lunch along the beach.

When Disney World opened in Orlando in 1971, we happened to be staying at the Quality Motel in Daytona Beach. So our family packed into the VW busses and caravanned to the Magic Kingdom for a day. We rode in on the monorail and saw Cinderella's castle sitting in the center of the park. I remember thinking at the time; this place is much bigger than FunTown on Capital Drive in Milwaukee. I was 11 at the time, a perfect age to take in Disney World.

Oh, brother

My brother Tom is the sixth of eleven, which puts him right in the middle and means he grew up living with all the family members. I asked all my brothers and sisters to add something to the book and Tom came up with the following family recap titled "Raised with Hayes." Tom not only shared a third-floor bedroom with Hayes on Menlo, they also shared a dorm room at UW-Eau Claire and later lived off campus together.

Tom coming up with the "Raised with Hayes" title is indicative of his clever wit, which I have listened to for years. For example, while we were putting the finishing touches on the world's largest rotary drum mixer for a customer in Belgium, I remember Tom telling someone on the phone, "The mixer is so big, it takes two people just to look at it." Tom graduated from UW-Eau Claire with a degree in communicative disorders.

Raised with Hayes
By: Thomas Andrew Callaghan III

I would like to share a little tidbit about my brothers and sisters and lessons I've learned from each.

Marty (MTMC3):

The eldest. It's the summer of '68; I'm only 12 and hitchhiking north on Lake Drive to go caddying. Marty drives by in Dad's '65 Riviera going south on Lake Drive. He says "get in, where ya going?"
"I'm going to Milwaukee Country Club, but I sure don't want to."
"Why not?"
"All my friends are at the youth center at Shorewood High — that's where I want to go."
"Tom, you're doing the right thing, going caddying," Marty says.
"It's easy to do the fun thing, but it's better to do the hard thing first and then the rest will be easier, even though it doesn't seem that way right now."

So, instead of seeing all the girls at the YC, I went caddying and at the end of that summer, I made honor caddy and retained that title the next four years. Honor caddies got more dough, more work and away tournaments like the Greater Milwaukee Open.

*The cool thing I learned from Marty was: **Do what you have to, then what you need to, and then—and only then—what you want to. In that order!***

Margaret (Schmelgrit, Blurge):

In Margaret, I always picture positive, kind, giving, pretty—did I say kind?

*I turned 16 on the 1st of October, 1971. It's maybe August. I'm driving the VW bus with a bunch of idiots in it, and I'm stopped at a red light at State and Wells. Who is in the passenger seat of the vehicle that pulls up on my left? Oh no, it's my sister. I'm done! Margaret looks over (I'm thinking it's over) and says, "Hi Tom," just like she always does. And I'm thinking, Wow, she probably thinks I have my license and everything's fine. That's how sharp Margaret is. I don't see her very much, but if Margaret is your friend, and I don't know whose she isn't, you'll always win. She taught me to **always be kind!***

Coyne (La Boyne):

*Coyne is five years older than me. He is the only one of us that is part Ojibwa. He worked at Pundl's and Gollar Stein (had a fabulous wardrobe) and then went west to Portland and then to North Carolina to work at AMC. I was working at Schlitz; it was probably the spring of '78. Having arranged a football game with a bunch of guys from work, who shows up in a pretty dapper looking suit and overcoat? Coyne! I hadn't been playing well, but all of a sudden I was tremendous (if I do say so myself). I could do anything and our team went up by three touchdowns. He didn't stay too long, and after he left my game went back to normal. But holy cow, what a burst of confidence. Thanks, Boynie. **The good things take time!***

Mary (HiLarious):

Mary worked in Palm Beach, Florida, as a registered nurse. At the prompting of Bob Green of Green's Pharmacy, she began modeling on the side. Mary entered a modeling show in New York, and my cousin Dickie Martini wrote the script she performed at the show. She won that part of the competition and was overall runner-up to none other than Christie Brinkley. Mary can make chocolate chip cookies with the best of them and always with a smile! In the summer of '64, Mary and I went with our dad and Larry Ludeman in the VW bus to Omaha, Nebraska, to demonstrate the Rollo-Mixer. The demo and presentation seemed like it took an excessively long time, so I asked Dad, "Are they buying?" And with that, Dad asked the no longer potential customer the same question, who responded with, "No!" Then Larry Ludeman looked at me sideways like I had just ruined the sale. I was sure glad Mary was with me that day. Thanks, pretty Mary. **There is always hope!**

Hayes (Hoseme Mobarhae, Cheese Scrost, Hazey Daze):

Need anyone but Hayes say anymore? Hayes was my roommate almost all the way through college graduation. Hayes was my biggest influence in music and that started before we went to Daytona Beach, Florida, in 1970. In the fall of '69, we were trying out for football at Shorewood High. I'm a freshman and Hoze is a junior — he is going to be the kicker. He suggested to the coach that there was no need to go through the calisthenics or contact parts of practice because all he was going to do was kick. The coach suggested he take up another sport—so much for his football career. **Stay cool under pressure!**

Tom (Bigger than life Ed):

The first thing I remember as a kid was lying in the back of Dad's TR3, listening to "High Hopes" on the radio. We were at the Costin's in Eagle River and about to head home to Milwaukee. I'm a very fortunate kid. I'm right in the middle so I know all of my brothers and sisters. In raising five kids with my fabulous wife, I can appreciate a little bit of what my parents went through. **Life is short. Rejoice and be glad!**

Muffie *(Fluff, Boobliosi):*

Luckily, I got to spend a lot of time with Muffie. She is only two years younger — same schools, similar friends, large amounts of fun and a member of "The Shart Blossom Gang" - an exclusive neighborhood club. Muff came to UW-Eau Claire in '75, and in the fall of the following year we drove over to the Twin Cities to see Earth, Wind, & Fire in concert. Then, at the concert, some guy says to me, "Is she fo sale?" Muffie looked over at him and said, "Hell no." Now I get to play golf with her when I get to Milwaukee. Thanks, Muff. **Take your work seriously, but not yourself!**

Julie *(Jewels, Mom Jr):*

Capable of throwing eight things in the air, sewing up a dress, and still catching everything before it hits the ground: Julie is what "able" is all about. Julie is and always was a doer. When Jewels went to college in Madison, I was working at Schlitz and she called to ask if I wanted to get paid for going to a Jimmy Cliff concert in Badtown (Madison). One of her roommates staffed people to help with seating. That was about as cool as it got — until she called me a month later and asked if I wanted to "help" at a Bob Marley concert. Wow! Julie married Bob Nelson the same year Kathleen and I married—1984. She had four boys and a girl and we had four girls and a boy. Nowadays, going to Julie's place in Chicago is like going to a playland for kids and a resort for adults: unbelievable meals, clean and comfortable rooms, lots to do — a lot like heaven on earth. Did I mention an 18-hole champion golf course next door? Thanks, Jewels! **Do as much as you can—every chance you get!**

Bill *(Taco Beeo, Billy Boy):*

The Golden Child – he was the only one born with blond hair. Billy was born in 1960, my next younger brother. He was always good at stuff—a funny and happy kid—who, when nervous, would bite his right index finger. I remember towel-snapping him in the bathroom on Menlo and then trying to cover his mouth so Mom and Dad wouldn't hear. Nice guy I was. Billy and I were up the block at a vacant lot overlooking Lake Michigan with my friend Knotts. We were swinging on a rope — Bill was on the rope, Knotts jumped on, and they both fell off. Bill was on the ground and in pain (he had broken his left elbow). He stopped crying, looked up, and said, "Oh the pain, the pain" in his best Dr. Smith (Lost in Space) impression and then started crying again. I couldn't believe it.

I was a senior at Shorewood High in 1973. It was Saturday morning basketball and the first round of the playoffs. My team (The Boys) had four players and I was one of them. Not good. I went home, woke Billy and he came back to SHS with me. My team was in last place all year, so we were playing a top seed. We took them into overtime, losing at the last second. Bill was only an eighth grader and was scoring huge points for The Boys.

*We had a croquet tournament at our house on Menomonie Street in 1985. I thought it was a tough course, but there was Bill, resting on the couch, with his match about to begin. I told Kathy, "Wake up Bill, the match is about to start." Bill got up, came out, and trounced his next two opponents to win the trophy! Typical Bill. He hits a golf ball like he's playing a Mario golf video game, with what appears to be very little effort. He can even sink a three-pointer with the best of them. Fortunately for me, I've been working with Bill for the last 29 years and it's always good! **Blue sky and sunshine, regardless of the weather, that's Billy.***

Jim (Jimbobway, James Michael):

Born on Mother's Day in 1963. It was a Sunday morning. I was asleep when Dad yelled up the stairs, "James Michael Callaghan is here" and "Get up in time for church." I had no idea who James Michael Callaghan was. An uncle, a cousin — who was this guy? I was only seven and didn't know biology. I had heard some birds had been stung by bees, but never put the two together. It turned out that James Michael Callaghan was the new baby at our house — another younger brother.

Jim was always a good-looking kid. He was the mascot on my eighth-grade basketball team.

One of my early buddies, Tom Foran, had a younger brother Patrick whom they called Packy. Tom and I made a go-cart out of junk, but it was too small for us so we let Jim and Packy ride in it and called it the Jim-Pack mobile.

In the summer of 1978, Jim was washing my car in the backyard. I saw my car looking like a million, but where was Jim? There he was hiding behind the sponge, his voice was quivering.

"What's wrong?" I asked.

"I had an accident with your car."

"What? What did you do?"

"I tried to put it in the garage and got stuck."

I walked to the other side of the car to discover the carnage. Doggone it, I wish I had said. But instead of hauling off and clocking him - I know he didn't try to do it - we looked up a few auto body champs in Milwaukee. We found these guys that would do it for $800 and SLICK (Replaced the BU with SL) was born. Jim is still paying me off in car washes, but how cool was Slick? Thanks, Jim! **Have fun in life!**

John (Park Avenue, JP, Johnny):

John was born when I was 15. As a matter of fact, the day John was born - Monday, August 24, 1970 - I was competing in a caddy golf tournament at Milwaukee Country Club. Mom was about 10 months pregnant at the time, yet I still got her to come with me. I could drive with a licensed adult since I had my "temps." I drove out there. Mom slowly moved over into the driver's seat and drove off. I shot an 88 to win the event. When I got home, everybody was in the big room. Mom had John that afternoon.

I took John to a Brewers game — he might have been six — when the guy next to him offered him some peanuts. "Give some to your dad," he said. John looked at me and said, "This guy thinks you're my dad." We laughed together and ate some peanuts. If you want to laugh hard, get a hold of Johnny. Thanks, John! **Life is great!**

Family photo taken in Jim's backyard in 2005. Sitting-Dad and Mom.
Standing- left to right: Marty, Margaret, Coyne Jr., Mary, Hayes, Tom,
Muffie, Julie, Bill, Jim, and John

Mom and Dad are amazing people. Look at what they've accomplished. Eleven kids, seven boys and four girls that honestly look forward to each others' company.

My parents are kind, generous and were always there for us.

I was playing high school football in my usual position (on the bench) at Brookfield West, the middle of nowhere, when who shows up but Dad. He knew there was a better chance to fly without wings than there was for me to get in the game, yet he was there. I felt *great, even though I never got in.*

*When Marty smashed our green bus and Coyne smashed the blue
one, Dad's response was, "Are you okay? Is everyone else okay?"
Not, "You dumb #@$$%. Why didn't you #@$%*."*

*For the past 29 years, I've gotten to work with my folks. How
fortunate for me. I get to work with Dad, who can still correct an
erroneous entry, without disdain, and Mom, whom I get to travel
with all over this beautiful area we call west-central Wisconsin.
Thank God!*

*Our parents taught us to be thrilled for what you have, not sorry
for what you don't! Get a haircut! Go to church on Sunday! Don't
listen to that crap!*

My sister Julie sent me the following letter:

*Before I was born in 1959, my Mom made a special Novena
(prayer) to Blessed Julie in hopes that I would be a normal,
healthy baby. A number of women she knew had children with
Down's syndrome as a result of their eighth pregnancy. My sister,
Muffie, with whom I shared a room, bed, clothes, bathroom and
pretty much every aspect of my childhood, caught wind of this
extraordinary deed and reminded me of it at many opportune
times. If she wanted me to do something for her (like bring her the
bathroom toilet, which I'd try to do and she'd sneak around the
corner and laugh while I tried to lift it) or maybe was just bored - I
was told, "It's starting to happen, Mom didn't pray hard enough,
you look a little different" and so on. After I'd finish the task, she'd
tell me I looked much better.*

*Muffie told me that Mom did some kind of Novena so I wouldn't
be Mongoloid and if I didn't believe her to ask Mom. It took me
quite a while - maybe because I didn't want to know the truth - to
build up the courage to ask Mom the fateful question: Was there
a special Novena for me before I was born so that I wouldn't
Mongoloid? Yes! I was Muff's slave for years.*

In the second grade, 1966, we made our annual trip to Daytona Beach, Florida, for Christmas. I looked forward to it from the minute we got out of the car the year before! One late afternoon, we all went to the Publix Market to load up on groceries. We were on the buddy system, and naturally, Muff was my buddy. We were looking for Oreos when I told her I had to go to the bathroom. At home, Shore Vu's bathroom was in the back, so I wandered off in search of the bathroom. Publix is much bigger than Shore Vu, and I was in the back area of the store for a long time before I found the bathroom. When I came out, I couldn't find my family. I asked the checkout lady if she had seen a woman with many carts and children and she said they had left.

Being December, it was getting dark when I headed out to where the Volkswagen bus had been parked. It wasn't there. For some reason, I felt no fear. I took a seat on a bench at the bus stop and waited. An African-American woman sat next to me. Having grown up with Beulah Mae - who ironed in the basement listening to a transistor radio, dancing and singing, and whom I adored and credited my love for black music and best dance moves - and of course, not being shy, I felt right at home asking my new friend what she was up to. She said she was waiting for the bus and offered me a piece of Juicy Fruit gum. Out of habit, I thanked her, split it in two and gave the other half back.

Many busses came and went but none of them were hers. We talked about everything: school, family, Florida and what kind of car we drove. I told her it was a blue Volkswagen bus - not a van as hippies drove vans - and that it had a sunroof that we could see out of if we stood on the seat. "Like that?" she said. Entering the Publix parking lot was the best sight I'd ever seen. The blue Volkswagen bus was peeling toward us with nine heads poking out the top. They pulled up screaming my name and everyone jumped out to get me. (Muffie asked where I got the gum!) I told them about the nice lady at the bus stop who was with me and gave me Juicy Fruit gum (my favorite). When I turned around to point her out, she wasn't there - she had disappeared! I've been a true believer in guardian angels since 1966.

*In the fourth grade, 1968, I went up to the office to ask Dad if I
could have a bike. He was on the phone so he smiled, offered me
his lap and gave me a pencil and pad of paper. I wrote, "Dad, can
I have a new bike?" He wrote back, "Sure, as soon as I get off the
phone." I was ecstatic. I went out in the backyard and told Bill
and Jim and whoever else I could find that Dad was going to take
me to Claud's and get me a new Schwinn. After a couple games
of Around the World, Horse and whatever else I could do to kill
time, I went next door to my friend Emily's. When I returned home
I couldn't believe my eyes. Tom, Muffie, Bill and Jim were riding
four shiny-blue Schwinns around the backyard. I ran into the yard
shouting, "Wow, are those cool. Which one is mine?" When no one
answered, I realized I had missed the boat. Bill rode up to me and
said, "Here, you can have mine." I don't know if he was just the
nicest person in the world or if he wasn't going to be caught dead
on a girl's bike. My Dad refused to buy a bike with a bar across the
top because he was convinced that you would break your "tail."*

*Life on Menlo was never dull. There was always something to do
and someone to do it with. If I ever mentioned to Dad I was bored
he'd say, "Go fly a kite, walk around the block, read a book."
Every night Mom would cook a great dinner and we'd all sit
around the breakfast room table and talk about our days. The boys
in the house all had to have short haircuts, in spite of the long-hair
trend of the '60s and '70s. Dad would never allow hair over your
ears or anything pierced. The girls were told if they pierced their
ears, he'd pierce their noses (a fate worse than death back then).
If someone was having a bad day, it was soon forgotten by being
surrounded by eleven wonderful people - later twelve - who loved
you no matter what stupid thing you did.*

*The stories that were told by young and by old were hilarious.
The story of Dad's new neighbors, the Dahmshitz, was my
favorite. No one ever swore at our house and this story brought
the house down!*

When I was in high school, Mom would go to the plant or on a business trip with Dad from time to time. As was the custom, when the cat's away the mice do play. Well, we'd have parties at our house - all the time. We'd rope off the living room and dining room as well as entrance to the second floor.

During one of the parties, Emily Meisner and I were collecting money for "a-buck-a-cup" beer at the front door when all hell broke loose. At the top of the red-carpeted staircase stood a three-foot tall statue of The Blessed Mary - gilded, blessed by the Pope (we thought) and protected in a little alcove in the wall. In what seemed like slow motion, someone bumped into Mary. She teetered, forward and backward. Everyone on the stairs backed away, much like the parting of the Red Sea, and down she came. Everyone froze. The music even stopped. As she rolled down the stairs, everyone's mouths were hanging open. This was not only bad; it had to be blasphemous.

When she got to the Spanish tile floor at the bottom, miraculously she was unscathed. But, as we lifted her up, her foot broke. Billy and I put her back and later glued her foot back on. We forgot to get our stories straight and later both confessed to knocking the statue over to my very upset Mom. She told us to quit having parties when she was gone. We did … for a week.

My childhood is one I cherish. The main ingredients were faith, love and laughter. I was loved and praised every day of my life. We were raised believing that we didn't need anything as long as we had each other and would simply "be nice."

Thanks Mom, Dad, Marty, Margaret, Coyne, Mary, Hayes, Tom, Muff, Bill, Jim and John.

Love – Jules, #8.

Marquette University Priests

Mary explains, "Mom and Dad were surrounded by priests and nuns all their lives. Dad was raised by nuns at St. Joe's; Mom went to Barret College, an all-girls school run by nuns. Mother Burke came to our house for a luncheon one summer and apparently it was the first time she was allowed to enter a person's home. She otherwise lived in a nunnery. Mom used to drive the nuns at St. Roberts around town when they had appointments or wanted to visit friends.

Celebrating Fr. Murphy's Birthday in the kitchen on Menlo Blvd.

When Marty started going to Marquette High School, two priests, John Casim and Patrick Murphy, showed up at our home one day looking for donations. They were studying to be Jesuits and their mission was to go door to door, seeking monetary support in their quest to become priests. Mom and Dad invited them in and they instantly became part of the family. My parents welcomed them like they had known them all their lives. Fr. Casim and Fr. Murphy loved all the energy and nonsense that went on in our house. They wouldn't stop laughing.

I don't think the two them went to another house after that visit because it seemed they were at our house all the time. They were educated, very funny and they spoke the same language, which was laced with plenty of Irish humor. They couldn't believe all the stuff that would go on around our house. All the commotion and noise

71

must have been a refreshing change from Marquette University.

Muffie: Mom loved having Casim and Murph around because they were always entertaining. Father Murphy would act like a gorilla, complete with the face and sound effects, and chase us around the house. He looked a lot like Sampson the gorilla from the Milwaukee Zoo.

During one of his visits, Father Casim, with his funny Irish voice, said, "So where do you sleep?" I said in the crack, and he fell apart with laughter, but it was actually true. I slept in the crack of the bed between Margaret and Mary.

On one hot summer day, Casim came into the house with hair that looked a little frizzy from the humidity. He stood in the living room by the piano and I said, "What's with your hair, Curly?" Father Murphy started laughing, and from that point on Casim's nickname was Curly. He got such a kick out of some little kid giving him crap about his hairdo.

Fr. Casim and Fr. Murphy saying mass in the Big Room on Menlo.

These young Jedis became close friends of our family. The group included Herman Powers, John Daly, M.L. Countryman, Murphy, Casim and Father Callan. When they completed their training in the priesthood at MU, they invited our entire family to attend their ordination at Jesu Church in downtown Milwaukee.

Country Life

In July of 1968, we went to Philo, Illinois, to attend John Daly's first mass and stayed on Bundt Daly's family farm. I was in the country for the first time. Daly's farm had tractors to ride, chickens nervously running around the yard and lots of pigs and piglets. It looked like Dorothy Gail's farm on the Wizard of Oz. We woke to the sound of a rooster at sunrise. I distinctly remember going outside while the sun was still rising and for the first time taking in the smell of the morning earth. The country fresh air was something I had never smelled before while growing up in Milwaukee. It was an aroma I was downloading for the first time.

The sense of smell and your memory banks are directly wired. To this day, when I'm traveling around the country and take in that heavenly fragrance, I immediately go back to being eight years old on Daly's farm in Philo.

Muffie: I remember the Dalys had pigs and one of the sows was about to give birth, so Bunt Daly had all of us kids inside the barn and explained that as soon as the piglets were born, he had to get them away from the mother or she might eat them. All of a sudden the sow gave birth to 12 little piglets and we got to hold and play with them – they were like Beanie Babies. It was so different in the country.

Mugs Collopy worked in Mequon, which back then was mostly rural, and had a farm with lots of kittens. Mugs, younger sister, Bibi, was Margaret's close friend and picked up a cat for Marg because she had rheumatic fever, and Bibi thought a cat would help. Even though Dad was allergic to cat dander, they let the kitty stay in a crib in the living room. Margaret also got a few other perks - like Aunt Audrey's TV.

Mary: Dad and I took that Delco TV to Kensington TV near Riegelman's Pharmacy. While we were in the repair shop waiting for the guy to fix the TV for Margaret, he got an electrical burn. Dad looked at me very calmly and said, "OK, Mary, I want you to go over to Rigelman's and get some ointment and bandages – they are on the right as you walk in the store."

He was so calm and composed as he gave me specific instructions. I ran over and got the supplies and ran back as fast as I could. Dad, like a doctor, helped the man wrap his burnt hand. Dad taught me how to be in control when an emergency arises and that has helped me in my nursing profession. Anyway, Margaret was only in third grade at the time and she had to stay off her feet and take penicillin the whole summer. She got a TV and a cat. I was only in first grade at the time and thought it was called "romantic" fever.

Muffie: Oh well, it probably seemed romantic because Bibi used to come over every day with two trays of food that her mother would make for each of them. Bibi was even allowed to go up to the second floor, which was hard to believe, but Margaret was getting the royal treatment that summer. The two of them would have lunch in Margaret's room, watch TV and hang out every day. When I see Bibi to this day, she still knows everybody's birthdays, she knows everyone's middle name; she knows everything about our family.

In the late 1960s our entire family was invited to Campion, a Catholic seminary located on the opposite side of Wisconsin in Prairie Du Chein. It was a campus of brown, brick buildings overlooking the banks of the Mississippi River.

The barge traffic was constant as we picnicked on the beach with about a dozen priests from Marquette University. Seeing these young Jesuits hanging out in their swimsuits, drinking beers, burnin' smokes and partying with our family was a rare sight. One of the resident priests made an announcement to all the kids to stay out of the water when the barges go by. The undertow created by the massive engines on the tug boats is very dangerous and can draw you away from shore and into danger.

Even though I had big ears, I wasn't paying attention as a large barge was creeping by. I was swimming only 15 feet from the shore when I suddenly found myself silently drifting away in the strong undertow. When I realized I was quickly disappearing and in over my head, I begin to yell for help. It all happened so fast.

74

At the age of nine, I was not strong enough to overcome the tracking beam that was pulling me toward the ship's propellers. I swam as hard as I could but was being sucked closer to the huge barge.

Left to right: Hayes, Linda Reich, Jim, Bill, Julie, Gretchen Reich, and Muffie playing on the Mississippi River.

We looked out when we heard Billy yell for help and I remember seeing him and his blue-and-white striped swimsuit closing in on the barge as it slowly floated past, Mary adds. Father Murphy saw what was happening and immediately ran into the water and swam as fast as he could to snatch him from the deadly current. He somehow caught up to him as he was drifting into the ship's wake and carried him on his back as he fought the magnetic suction of the barge and brought him back safely. He got to Bill just in time and saved his life,"

Games People Play

The following Interview took place in January 2009 in Los Angeles, California, with my close friend and childhood neighbor, Frank McBride:

Bill: Tell me what it was like growing up on our block.

Frank: When I would come over on a Saturday, we wanted to go out and play but there was always something you had to get done first, whether it was emptying the garbage cans or bringing up the laundry from the basement or washing the windows. Until the work was done, we weren't going anywhere - so I would always pitch in so you could finish the task quicker. I remember seeing your dad upstairs on the landing and calling out the work to be done and then he would spot me in the front hallway and say, "Oh, there's a McBride, start by grabbing the garbage cans and start at the bottom and work your way up."

One thing I remember about Marty was playing the game "Rebound," which meant he got to shoot and I got to rebound. He sold it so well: "Okay, Frank, we're going to play this game called Rebound and I'm going to shoot and you get every rebound." I was still pretty young and I'm like all right, all right. Then Hayes caught on and he would run out the back door and have me feed him the ball over and over again at the exact same point so he could turn and shoot the "automatic." Hayes was a pretty good shot – so was Marty!

Playing Capture the Flag or night games like chase always involved many neighborhood kids. Someone once counted something like 102 kids on our immediate block. My brother Mathew would climb up into a tree or up the telephone poles and no one could ever find him. It's sort of ironic that Matt would grow up and work for a company in California supervising crews that hang cable lines from pole to pole.

Your mom told me, after my mom had died, that the two of them would get together, it might have been a while since they last had a "meeting" - and she said they would usually hang out in the back yard of Keane's house (the halfway point between our houses) and they would both show up with their cocktails and smokes. She said they would always pick up where they left off and the conversations a lot of times weren't about the family or the kids but just whatever was going on in the world that day or that time of year. But they never missed a beat and I really thought that was amazing, because they knew exactly what was going on in their busy lives with all the kids yet they would make a point of stealing 20 minutes or half an hour to be together, until someone would find them when they would both return to their posts.

The McBride home on Newton Avenue was really designed for sleeping and feeding a large number of people. The kitchen was set up like a service kitchen in a restaurant; we had the breakfast room between the dining room and the kitchen, where the family would sit and there was a sliding door on the countertop for the cook to deliver prepared meals to the masses. The refrigerator had access from the kitchen and the pantry so when Frenzies Foods would deliver boxes of food each week, the fridge could be stocked without disturbing the progress in the galley. My mom would call in the grocery order! With four big compartments in the kitchen and two on the pantry side, the refrigerator was so large that it had a separate compressor located in the basement.

**Meeting on Menlo with Mrs. Callaghan and
Mrs. McBride and brother John in 1973**

77

Although I don't recall ever using it, the house had a clothes dryer in the laundry room that was about eight-feet tall, 10-feet wide and 12-feet long with a series of tall, narrow drawers side by side. To dry many clothes at once, you pulled them out one at a time and hung the wet clothes on rods and closed the drawers into the stationary dryer. It was unique. It's remarkable that my parents found a home that would ultimately house 15 people.

It's funny because when I tell people that I was raised in a family with 12 brothers and sisters, they always acted startled. "Hey, it was great," I tell them. "We had a great time and the Callaghans lived behind us and they had 11 kids." I would always joke and say if I didn't like what we were having for breakfast, I would just buzz over to the Callaghans and join them. Their parents were always like, "Oh Frank, come on in and pull up a chair, we're having bacon and scrambled eggs."

Photo taken at John's wedding reception on September 20, 2003, at the MAC in downtown Milwaukee. From left to right: Dan McBride, Paul McBride, Peter McBride, Mark McBride, Marty, Jim, Tom, Margaret, Bill, and Bill's guardian angel. Middle row: Mary, Coyne Jr., Julie, Matt McBride, Maureen McBride, Frank McBride, Susan McBride, Vince McBride, and Margaret McBride. Front row: Hayes, Madeline McBride, John, Marianne (Anselment), Dad, Mom, Ellen McBride, Muffie, and Joe McBride.

One summer the Yankees were in town to play the Brewers and my dad knew the umpire, who escorted my father and my brother Vincent into the visitors' clubhouse after the game. Vince was given a Northern ash Major League Baseball bat from Reggie Jackson that he used in the game that day. And didn't Vince let you, Bill, use it the next day at one of the Catholic Little League games and you cracked it in half while fouling off a pitch?

Bill: Yeah, I was playing for the Monks and when it broke I felt terrible and I remember the look on Vincent's face when I brought the bat back to him in two pieces. He looked at me and said, 'You have got to be kidding me!' "Oh No – Not my Reggie Jackson bat!"

Cannonized

Our neighborhood was filled with things to do, especially when I got to go to the Cannon's house. I logged many hours playing at the Cannon house during my childhood summers on Menlo. Their toys had all the pieces to play with. The batteries in the Hot Wheels speed booster always worked, and all the army men were accounted for when Dave and I would do battle. I had so much fun playing with Dave as a kid. We played Rock 'em, Sock 'em Robots until we both got our blocks knocked off. We took the time to set up the Mousetrap game and then played until we finally dropped the cage on the mouse. Designing and engineering elaborate Hot Wheels tracks in Dave's basement was one of my favorite things to do.

One afternoon I was invited to stay for lunch and Mrs. Cannon made up two plates of food, each fitted with a Braunschweiger sandwich, three carrots, two Oreo cookies and a glass of milk. I hadn't seen or smelled a sandwich like that before and wasn't interested in finding out if it tasted any good. Peanut butter and jelly sandwiches were really all I knew. So I asked Dave if he would trade his two cookies and three carrots for my sandwich – straight up - and he refused.

Top row from left to right: Bill and Dave Cannon.
Bottom row: Paul McBride and Jim.

I thought it was a fair trade. So when Mrs. Cannon left the kitchen, I got up and helped myself to as many Oreos as I could fit between my thumb and forefinger, stacked like poker chips, and proceeded to fill up on cookies before going back down to the basement to play. When Mrs. Cannon walked back into the kitchen and noticed the depleted package of Oreos, she was furious and stormed down the basement stairs and kicked me out of the Cannon house for a week. What a harsh punishment! Everything was accounted for at Dave's house and when she realized the next two day's allotment of cookies disappeared in one meal, she had enough and sent me home.

The following interview took place in January 2009, with my close friend and childhood next-door neighbor, Emily Meisner Kaplan, who now lives in Los Angeles, California.

Bill: Tell me about your memories of growing up on Menlo.

Emily: Julie and I spent every moment of every day together. There was a time - I think it was during a Catholic holiday, maybe Good Friday - when Julie and I couldn't hang together for three hours. She couldn't go outside or talk on the phone during that time of the day; I think it was between noon and 3:00 pm. Having to separate for reasons that we didn't quite understand led us to our desperation to connect, so we set up a pulley on a string from my mom's bedroom window by her sewing machine to Julie's bedroom window, which was probably 40 feet away. We attached baggies to the string with clothes pins and Julie would send over three Oreos because we never had good snack food, and I would send back three pickles because we only had healthy food. We would write notes to each other just to stay connected during the three-hour timeout.

Our family moved in next door in 1963, just before my fourth birthday. Julie and I became very close friends, and some of that had to do with the fact that we both loved to sew. We built our friendship around doing something productive and fun and creative for both of us. I learned a lot from her because she was a perfectionist and I was not. I loved to sew with her, admired her and looked up to her like an older sister.

We had go-cart races from the top of Menlo Boulevard all the way down to Hackett Avenue. During one race, I accidently fell off the back of the go-cart and scraped my knee along a rusty nail. We would take apart old strollers, roller skates, skateboards and, with the help of one of your older brothers, attached the wheels to plywood, nailed sides around the cart and tied a rope to the front axle so you could almost steer. For three days I was in bed with a swollen, infected knee and I had to go to the doctor and get a Tetanus shot. I still have that scar on my knee and I think about that memory all the time – even that was fun.

There was a time in the mid-1970s when your dad's business was having a difficult year - I think it was Julie's senior year in high school - and it looked like there wouldn't be any Christmas presents for the kids. Julie told me, "Gosh darn it, I'm going to make sure that there is at least one thing under the Christmas tree for every person in the family." So she made 13 stockings with everybody's name on it and sewed together a gift for everyone in the house - whether it was a tie, a skirt, a shirt – she made it

*possible that everyone had something to open Christmas morning
and it was all homemade. Although she was only 17 years old at the
time, she was taking full responsibility for the whole family to make
sure everyone was accounted for that Christmas. She is amazing!*

*Something I remember witnessing at your house that I hadn't
heard before, and haven't observed since, was your parents' desire
to have you guys answer to them with, "What is it?" and not
"What?" when your name was called. It was definitely unique
to your family and yet makes so much sense to me – it's just so
respectful! They would keep calling out your name until they heard,
"What is it?" Your parents had something important to tell you and
it was almost like it wouldn't be reverent or very considerate if you
just answered, "What?" I thought it was beautiful!*

**Emily Meisner Kaplan, Julie, Martha, Bill and Coyne Callaghan
at the Whitefish Bay Inn - 1998**

*We had plans to go to the beach once. One of your parents' friends
had a house on Lake Drive next to Atwater Beach. But before we
could go, we had to wash the Volkswagon buses – inside and out.
We spent all day thinking of what it was going to be like going
swimming at the beach, but we had to make the cars immaculate
first. I'm not sure if it was because your dad was engaged in his
work up in his office, so he was just giving us something to do, or
if he was teaching us a lesson that before you are rewarded – you*

need to do some work. We cleaned all the cars inside and out and still had to wait. I felt like it was so much about the waiting and we couldn't wait to get there. When we finally got to the beach, the clouds start rolling in. I thought we could have been there all day and it would have been fun playing in the sun and water – but we had to work hard first. Your dad was always so involved in his work – it's like he was never finished.

We would have parties in the big room and it seemed that the whole neighborhood was there. Your mom would be in her bathroom coloring her hair and getting ready. When she would walk into the party, I remember thinking – Wow, Mrs. Callaghan looks fabulous! After all those years of raising kids, it was great to see her enjoying herself with her kids and their friends. She loved to party with us, and I don't remember any other parents doing that.

I have great memories of growing up on Menlo. When you think about our neighborhood and how much fun we had, we didn't have to have other friends – we had our family and our block. I have so much gratitude for my childhood, and if I were to tell anybody what it was like and how great it was – they probably wouldn't believe me.

Piddle Bill

When I was growing up, I shared a bed with my brother Jim and had a problem wetting the bed. Sometimes, I would wet my side of the bed in the middle of the night, wake up in a puddle of wiz and then slide over to Jim's side of the bed (where it was always dry) and try to fall back asleep. Jim would quickly wake up and say, "Get away from me, you're going to wiz on me." Mom had plastic mattress protectors on our bed in an attempt to keep the mattress dry.

My older brothers would come home late at night from work or the bars, and Dad would come to the foot of the third-floor stairs and yell, "Marty, Coyne, Hayes, Tom, piddle Bill for me, will ya?" Dad was trying to catch me before I could dream of whizzing in my sleep. He used to say in jest, "Maybe I should tie your tail in knot." Nobody would answer him at first and then Tom, being the youngest of my older brothers, would finally answer, "All right, I will." He'd walk into my room and wake me out of a deep sleep, escort me to the bathroom, turn on the faucet and the showers and wait and wait and wait.

One time Tom was getting impatient waiting for me to go and rolled up a towel into a rat tail and snapped my leg with his homemade whip. Needless to say, that woke me up! Apparently he figured he would jump-start the process but it did just the opposite. I screamed as a strawberry-sized welt grew on my thigh. Tom scrambled for ways to quiet me down, but I was beyond pissed, and the last thing I could do was wiz.

My youngest brother John sent me the following letter titled, "Best Seat in the House."

Being the youngest of all the Callaghans is an amazing place to grow up. I often refer to it as "the best seat in the house." As I get older, I realize my position as the youngest of 10 others built just like me provides a dynamic that is both helpful and powerful at every age.

Being raised by our mom and dad was an incredibly happy and meaningful part of my life that I still peer into daily. Everything they taught us had a theme of humility, strength in your faith, yourself and being thoughtful of others. My dad would say, "take your job seriously, not yourself."

From there, everything made sense. Treating others the same way you would want to be treated was a great idea. Somehow, trying to justify going against my mom and dad was never a thought. They were only accommodating, thoughtful and helpful all the time. The respect they gave us made it more important to respect them.

I was born in August 1970. The day I came home from the hospital I had brothers and sisters in college, high school and grade school. I was an uncle when I was one, a great uncle at 28. And now with 33 nieces and nephews, the road was paved a bit for me to become a father of two.

From left to right: Mom, Margaret, John, and Julie.
Photo taken outside our home on Menlo in 1971.

Many people have given me the typical youngest child comment,
"You must have been spoiled," which is a great opportunity to
explain what it was like to always have someone to play catch
with, watch you do something, ride a bike with or give a ride
somewhere. Yes, I was spoiled in the way that my mom always had
kind words as I walked in the house. She was no pushover, but was
a consistently perfect mom, the best in the business. Certainly,
I was spoiled with people to play with, people encouraging me,
positive reinforcement from every direction, at every age. I was the
only kid in little league who had 12 to 16 people in the crowd – just
to see me. My brothers, sisters and their friends were usually at my
sporting events growing up. That is spoiled, no question. It's also
rare, fantastic and as motivating as anything you can imagine.

One obvious example of my Mom's steady, understanding and
praising approach was when I came home with C's on my report
card. Her comment was, "Well, now you know where you can do
better." Now that I am older, it is obvious that my mom and dad's
positive philosophy in raising kids has been coming my way from
everyone before me.

My brother Bill has always been a main source of encouragement.
I have always looked up to everyone in my family, but Bill always

85

seemed to be very aware of me and was always patient and kind. The picture is very telling of my life growing up – being held up and praised by my brothers and sisters, with Secret Service-like protection.

Bill, Jim (background) and John in 1971

Whether I was two or 32, Bill had a keen and important impact into my life. He always seemed to have time to hit me fly balls, show me something that many wouldn't stop to do or just tell me how great he thought I did. It's incredible how important subtle encouragement is. Bill offers truckloads of it. I fill my kids with it to this day as well.

Bill taught me something one Christmas that I hope everyone can put in their mental pocket. For an 18-year-old, you would think that philosophizing about the meaning of Christmas to a kid ten years younger would be an incredibly difficult thing to accomplish in five minutes.

It was a wintry night in Shorewood, and I was looking out my mom and dad's bedroom window. I was watching the neighbor's living room, which was filled with lights, toys and action - just what my young mind was locked in on. The year 1978 was not a good one for Rollo-Mixers and Christmas presents were not in the plans.

I was feeling like there wouldn't be anything under the tree with my name on it. Certainly there wouldn't be an Atari or the sports equipment I really wanted. But I still have what Bill gave me that Christmas, and it is still one of the most valuable things I have.

He told me that us Callaghans had the gift of each other, filled with mutual respect, humor and the intelligence to think of others who are less fortunate or may need a friend. He said, "God gave you brothers and sisters, a warm house, the ability to throw a ball like no one else your age." Bill explained that no toy, present or amount of money could compare to the gifts we had in each other. I was sold for life. Presents have never had the same meaning.

These days, Bill and I go into meetings with Fortune 500 companies together and we carry all those gifts into those meetings. The praise we were raised with is evident to strangers. Often our meeting is sidetracked with, "so you two are brothers – wow, you get along so well." That causes my mom and dad's widest smiles. Bill has been teaching those subtle yet powerful things to many people for a long time. That is what I think he wants the effect of his book to be.

I am really proud to be their son, their brother, their uncle, great uncle and employee. As Walt Disney once said, "Sometimes when you live right, things just happen right." It seems as though that holds true for our family. We are all blessed to have each other – and in good health. Mom and Dad have done it right.

Grade school

With all the demands on my parents at home and running the family business, it was rare to see them attend my baseball, basketball or football games. It was a thrill when they did come to see me play. I never expected them to attend every game, because I knew they were busy with many other responsibilities and would make it if they could.

During my eight years at St. Robert's grade school, I excelled during gym class, and got straight A's in recess and lunch hour.

It was on that playground where I honed my interpersonal communication skills. I loved mingling with the other kids, playing four-square, dodgeball and kickball. I know some kids dreaded recess because interacting with others was not comfortable or enjoyable. Those kids would rather be back in the classroom taking a math quiz or just be left alone. I would make a point of including the kids who felt like they didn't have any friends to play with. I felt sorry for them. I think having so many older brothers and sisters helped me develop valuable people and recess skills.

Five of the eight teachers I had during grade school at St. Bob's were Dominican nuns: Sister Marie David, Sister Valentine, Sister Michaela, Sister Margaret Mary and Sister Alice (she was my eighth-grade teacher and the first nun I knew who wore pants and skirts as opposed to the typical black gown with white head dress.) My favorite teacher was Miss Miley. She lived alone in the Cudahy Apartments overlooking the bluffs of Lake Michigan and rode the city bus to and from school. I'm not sure how many years she taught third grade - I know it covered many decades - but her teaching style was legendary and her command of the classroom was unique.

Miss Miley had the Tie & Shine Club. To be a member you had to come to school wearing a tie with shined shoes and neatly combed hair. If you were part of the club that day, you had special privileges like being the first in line to go to recess and the multi-purpose room, as well as end-of-the-day duties such as cleaning the green chalkboard and taking the black erasers outside and clapping them together until the chalk dust was all over your light blue shirt.

Miss Miley was a very strict teacher with an imposing build, a huge head and she usually meant what she said. One day as we were leaving the classroom for recess, in single file, she stood up and pointed her finger at me with her jowls wobbling and her aged arm-fat sagging from her body and yelled in her deep voice, "Callaghan, stay where you are and get out." I was only nine years old and terribly confused. I didn't know what to do. The last thing I heard her say was "get out" so I did just that as fast as I could, in single file.

Bill in Miss Miley's 3rd Grade Class

When I was in Mrs. Mulligan's fourth-grade English class, she asked the class to make a complete sentence with two rhyming words that were spelled differently. Within two seconds I had structured a rhyming sentence and was the first one in the class to raise my hand, which didn't happen very often.

"Mr. Callaghan, what do you have to share with the rest of the class?" she asked. "I took a glance at her underpants," I replied.

My classmates thought it was pretty good. But Mrs. Mulligan seemed caught off guard, and taken aback, and told me to get out of my chair and leave the room. I thought it was a clever use of two different words that rhymed perfectly, but she didn't like my sense of humor or my answer and immediately sent me to the principal's office. When I arrived, I told Sister Mary that I didn't know what I did wrong. She told me I was a smart ass. Being an optimist, I took it as a compliment. It sounded to me like constructive criticism.

While attending one of Sister DeShantel's spelling classes, Chris T. was causing trouble and sassing Sister when all of a sudden the elderly nun, who looked like the wicked witch of the east *and* the west, grabbed Chris by the ear and dragged her to the front of the class. DeShantel swung her chair out from behind her desk, sat down, bent Chris over her draped black gown and lifted her green dress, pulled down her panties and spanked her bare bottom in front of the entire class. It was crazy – I felt so sorry for my friend Chris and couldn't imagine how humiliated she must have felt. After the spanking, Chris stood up red-faced and red-bottomed and ran out of the classroom crying in embarrassment. I think that was her last day at school, and I don't recall seeing Sister DeShantel around St. Robert's much after that deplorable event.

My fondest memory of grade school was during the fifth grade in Sister Michaela's class. John Honzik, who is a dear friend and shares the same birthday as me (June 20, 1960), was tormenting Bob Niemczyk to no end, which Honzik loved to do. Sister Michaela was a large nun whose face overflowed out of her black habit. She was also one of the kindest Sisters at St. Roberts. As I sat at my little desk, Bob was losing patience and began chasing John around the room so he could give him a grundy or a nuggie or something. Sister was in the middle of the room trying to conduct class with eleven-year-olds running around everywhere. Honzik was a little guy and apparently ran out of places to hide so, in a desperate attempt to avoid getting caught, he sought shelter under Sister Michaela's wide black dress that draped to the floor. The funny thing was that neither Niemczyk nor Sister knew where Honzik was. I watched him disappear!

My memories of St. Robert's grade school were very positive. There were only a few mean nuns that might have spoiled it for some, but I met many wonderful priests and sisters who dedicated their lives to the service of others. And I met so many people during those eight years that are still close friends and will be for life.

In 1972, Johnny Nash came out with a hit song that spoke of hope and courage as well as a bright outlook on life. I was 12 at the time and I always felt this song encapsulated the way I look at life. It applies now more than ever. Bob Marley's Whalers were the backup band to "I Can See Clearly Now," which according to songfacts. com was No.1 on the music charts for four weeks straight.

I can see clearly now, the rain is gone,
I can see all obstacles in my way
Gone are the dark clouds that had me blind
It's gonna be a bright (bright), bright (bright)
Sun-Shiny day.

I think I can make it now, the pain is gone
All of the bad feelings have disappeared
Here is the rainbow I've been prayin' for

It's gonna be a bright (bright), bright (bright)
Sun-Shiny day.
Look all around, there's nothin' but blue skies
Look straight ahead, nothin' but blue skies......

My younger brother Jim sent me the following story from our days at St. Bob's:

Bill and I watched many episodes of Star Trek together in the late 1960s. My favorite, though, was the one Bill produced for the St. Robert's variety show in 1974. I was in fifth grade at the time and sat with my class in the middle of a blacked out gymnasium/ auditorium filled with first through eighth graders and the teaching staff, which included priests, nuns and a few lay teachers.

Of course, Bill played James Tiberius Kirk. Jim Johnson was Spock, Jim Kortebien played Scotty and Rick Whittman was Bones. The curtain opened with the timeless "Star Trek" soundtrack playing in the background and a model of the Enterprise hovering high above the planet. "Space, the final frontier – these are the voyages of the Starship Enterprise ..."

The landing party was marooned on City Alpha 6 dying of thirst and in need of fluids. Once Captain Kirk realized the severity of the situation, he quickly summoned Scotty on his communicator and ordered him to beam down something to drink. Commander Scott didn't think the transporter would be operational in time and warned Kirk. "We're running low on supplies, Captain, and I don't think the transporter can handle it – but here goes."

Then the sound of the ship's transporter came on and the next thing we see is a case of Pabst Blue Ribbon beer floating down out of nowhere, while a spotlight followed its decent. Bill and his stage crew had strung two fishing lines from the top of the gym wall all the way down to the stage floor. With the lights out, nobody could see the transporter's transparent track and, sure enough, the case of beer landed smoothly on the planet surface. It was perfect. The props, the sound effects and the special effects were ahead of their time for a St. Bob's variety show.

The place erupted in laughter and everyone stood in applause. The ship's captain and crew walked away with the competition. With the mission accomplished, Bill had boldly gone where no eighth-grader had gone before ... to the principal's office for beaming down a case of beer in front of the whole school.

The Mighty Bobcats

My friend Mike Ewens was a grade school and high school classmate of mine, and the two of us have stayed in touch over the last 30 years. Every time we talk on the phone, it seems that time has stood still and we laugh hard as we both take each other back to our memorable childhood at St. Roberts. Mike and I both played on St. Robert's record-setting basketball team in 1974. He recently sent me the following email:

Hey Bill,

As always, it was great talking to you today.

I still find it remarkable that when we went to grade school at St. Bob's, we were 41-1 in league play, during 6th, 7th and 8th grade. Our only loss was to St. Peter & Paul (our 10th game), during the

8th grade season. It was the only loss in three years in league play! Think about that. I realize we were elementary, but I have lots of nieces and nephews and have been to a lot of games. And I don't remember seeing anything close to what we accomplished.

Obviously, Coach Callan had a lot to do with that. I remember how he ran us with sprints and physical endurance tests. He then split us into guards, forwards and centers. Do you remember all the layup, tip, dribbling, jumping and defense drills? The guy knew what he was doing. And the reason why Malloy, Brill, and Johnson were so good, game after game was because of guys like you, Carter, and Weir, who battled those guys every day after school during those intense practices in the school gym. Our practices were so tough that when it came to the games, we just dominated our opponents. We were an exceptional basketball team and always maintained a humble attitude. Success never spoiled our team spirit!

Top Row from left to right- David Carter, John Malloy, Jim Johnson, Steve Brill, and Bill Weir. Second Row: Jim Kortebien, Tom Gallen, Jeff Pink, Kevin Moriarty, and Bill Callaghan. First Row: John Honzik, Chris Byers, Rick Wittman, Steve Jennings, Mike Ewens, Dave Christenson, and Coach Callan. (Photo courtesy of John Malloy)

Anyways, the record will show that I was kicked off the team, prior to the St. Peter & Paul game (10th game of the season), for smoking cigarettes. Mind you, my parents had just split up and this was a difficult time. Now, that does not make it okay that I was

93

smoking at a young age, but you get the picture. We lost that game at their gym on Murray Avenue and when we rode home in the van after the game, Coach mentioned that we lost the game because I ruined the morale of the team. When we pulled into St. Robert's, many on the team were ready to give me a Grundy and hang me up in the locker room by my underwear, but somehow I managed to escape.

After that game, I got my revenge. Honzik and I became team managers and we bought soda and chips at Shore drugs (across from Atwater school) prior to practices and consumed mass quantities while you guys ran sprints.

Those were the days, my friend!

Mike

Shorewood High School

In August of 1974, I attended my first day of football practice at Shorewood High School. The team was made up of three-quarters Shorewood Middle School students and the rest from St. Roberts, so I was getting a chance to meet many new classmates as well as teammates.

While we were unpacking our school-issued football gear and suiting up for practice, I looked over at this tall, thin lanky kid who appeared to be wearing girls underwear. I looked at him and said, "What's with the fancy undies?" He responded in a very monotone, curt manner, "What? It looks like you're wearing your dad's underwear," as I stood in my white boxers. From that day on, Jesper Dinesen and I were great friends. He was pure Dane and I was pure Irish – our differences went well beyond our tastes in underwear.

Jesper will always remind me of Spock from Star Trek. He was from another country and continent and was the oldest of three Danes with two younger sisters. Being the older sibling, Jesper tought his parents how to be parents. They came to the U.S. from

Denmark when the kids were young, and the family spoke in its native tongue in their Shorewood home. It sounded so different to me when I visited – almost Vulcan.

Unlike me, Jesper always did things "by the book." Logic dictated his actions and decisions. Jetstar, as he was often called, was also one of the smartest and well-read individuals I have ever known. Other than my wife, I have never met anyone who worked harder every day. It must be in their Danish blood.

In the movie "Star Trek II the Wrath of Kahn," Admiral Kirk asks Captain Spock, "These cadets of yours – how good are they? How will they respond under pressure?"
"As with all living things, each according to his gifts," Spock logically responds. Jesper was a man of many gifts but also possessed a fragile heart. He believed the needs of the many outweigh the needs of the few – or the one. He was constantly giving. As it turned out, however, the needs of one outweighed the needs of the few or the many as Jesper died in 2003 alone in Denmark. He was a special one-of-a-kind friend who taught me much about life.

Jesper once told me that women dance like they make love. "Some women just dance around uninterested and some women are all over the dance floor," he said. Jesper must have done enough research to draw that remarkable conclusion. He was exceptionally bright, and I wasn't about to refute his unique perspective.

To Jesper: I have been and always shall be your friend. I miss you so much!

Family Support

I'll never forget the time my brother Coyne showed up at Shorewood High to watch me play in a junior-varsity football game. I was on the field waiting to punt the ball when I noticed Coyne standing in the first row of the bleachers wearing Dad's dark-blue coat. I was so excited that Coyne was in the audience that I kicked the ball as hard as I could and it sailed over the punt returners head and bounced end over end to the other end zone. Seeing my older brother in the stands cheering for me was worth millions.

My brother-in-law, Paul Carleton Weise, had his own business called Carleton Tree Service, which included an old Dodge dump truck, a beat up pick-up, several Stihl chainsaws, ropes and slings, and a hard-working crew of four. Matt McBride and I worked the grounds as Paul and Jimmy Cataldi climbed high in the trees and strategically cutting down large branches. Our job was to clean up under the trees, cutting limbs into smaller pieces and separating the larger logs from the smaller branches that had fallen to the ground.

We were on location once in Elkhart Lake, Wisconsin, taking down some dead oak trees for one of Mrs. Conklin's real estate clients. The day was overcast and dreary and it looked as though a storm was brewing in the western sky. Paul was topping a tree on another part of the property, while Matt and I were cleaning up under a tree Jimmy was thinning. All of the sudden, I noticed the branches had stopped falling.

I looked up to see Jimmy shaking uncontrollably while his chainsaw dangled from the rope tied to his belt. His body had shifted in the tree and his right leg had lodged between two limbs and prevented him from falling more than 60 feet to the ground. His twitching body was hanging there, short-circuiting upside down. I yelled to Matt above the ringing of our chainsaws to find Paul and get him over here right away. I helplessly stayed with our crewman who was somehow miraculously still pinned in the tree. I was sure he was going to fall out of the tree and to his death at any moment. What do I do? Try and catch him? Jimmy forgot to take his bull rope with him and tie himself down in case he lost his footing – a standard safety procedure he overlooked.

When Paul and Matt arrived on the scene, the three of us looked up and realized Jimmy's body was going to shake free from the security of those two tree limbs and ultimately fall to the ground. Paul strapped his tree spikes to his boots, threw a bull rope over his shoulder and, like a human cat, ran up the tree as though he was running up a ladder. Paul knew he was running out of time. He managed to make his way to the top and out to the limb where Jimmy was still shaking violently. Paul tied a rope around his waist and slowly lowered him down to Matt and me, who were on the receiving end to catch him.

Someone had called an ambulance, which fortunately arrived shortly after Jimmy was safe on the ground. We later learned that he was having an epileptic seizure. I was amazed at Paul's ability to scale that tree in seconds and his strength to gently lower Jimmy down from the top of the tree. I had witnessed true grit and pure adrenaline working overtime. Paul wasn't concerned about his own life as he ran up that tree and heroically and instinctively saved his friend's life. I learned a lot that day about the man who would eventually marry my sister Muffie.

Part-time Politics

Toward the end of my junior year in high school, I ran for senior class president. My goal was to unseat the incumbent who had been our class president for three years. She was a friend of mine I had known since grade school, but I didn't feel she was bringing the group together and decided to do something about it. I felt it was time for a change. Shorewood High School had the typical cliques, such as the band geeks, the jocks, the nerds and the druggies. During my time spent in high school, I got along with all of my classmates and made many friends.

The field of presidential candidates was ripe with ambitious student council members, honor students, 4.0 champs and the sitting class president, but I really wasn't fazed by their credentials. Trying to look the part, I dressed for my campaign speech with a three-piece corduroy suit. My opponents wore regular school clothes.

Before the election, I went out to the "Calavan" in the school parking lot and listened to one of my favorite tunes to get me in the groove for my speech. From their hit album in 1975, Parliament and George Clinton landed the "Mothership Connection" with brilliant funk music that sounds more like a funky jam than a studio recording. I love their music – their horns take me out!

"P.Funk (Wants To Get Funked Up)" {G Clinton, W Collins, B Worrell}

Vocals: George Clinton, Calvin Simon, Fuzzy Haskins, Raymond Davis, Grady Thomas, Garry Shider, Glen Goins, Bootsy Collins. Horns: Fred Wesley, Maceo Parker, Michael Brecker, Randy Brecker, Boom, Joe Farr.

Good evening.

Do not attempt to adjust your radio, there is nothing wrong.

We have taken control as to bring you this special show.

We will return it to you as soon as you are grooving.

Welcome to station WEFUNK, better known as We-Funk,

Or deeper still, the Mothership Connection.

Home of the extraterrestrial brothers,

Dealers of funky music.

P.Funk, uncut funk, The Bomb.

Coming to you directly from the Mothership

Top of the Chocolate Milky Way, 500,000 kilowatts of P.Funk-power.

So kick back, dig, while we do it to you in your eardrums.

And me? I'm known as Lollipop Man, alias the Long-Haired Sucker.

My motto is:

Make my funk the P.Funk

I want my funk uncut (make mine the P)

Make my funk the P. Funk

I wants to get funked up. (wants to get funked up)

I want the bomb, I want the P funk,

I want my funk uncut!

When it was my time to speak to the future class of 1978, I took a different approach with an entirely different message than most. I told my classmates that I was running on the party ticket and that when my parents went out of town we could have parties at my house. The place erupted with laughter. Most of those in attendance had been to parties in the big room on Menlo and could relate.

I further explained that although we'd been through three years of high school together, we didn't know each other as well as we should and that I wanted to break down the barriers (the typical clicques) that divided us - and unite our class. My message came through loud and clear; I won the election with 80 percent of the vote.

The summer of 1977 was so much fun. The music in our generation was some of the best ever written. I was listening to classic rock from Supertramp, Led Zeppelin, The Who and Paul McCartney, as well as rhythm and blues and funk from the Ohio Players, Earth, Wind & Fire, and Parliament.

I looked forward to becoming the leader of our class in the fall and putting my mandate into action. Then in October, only one month into my senior year, my parents announced that Marty, my oldest brother, and his family were moving into Menlo and living with us for six to nine months while his new home was being built in Brookfield.

"Oh, no!" I thought. With Marty's family living in our house, how could I have parties when my parents leave town? Now I had two sets of parents. This would have an immediate impact on my campaign promises and was a devastating setback to my presidency. In fact, to make matters worse, the three-term president, who wasn't expecting to lose the nomination in May, sent a petition around the senior class to try and impeach me. She was trying to shake my confidence, but I held my ground, played high school politics and had a lot of fun my senior year with many classmates.

Bill, Senior Year at Shorewood High School, in 1978

I actually enjoyed having Marty, Barb and their five little kids around our house. They were the first of my parents' 35 grandchildren, and it was fun to get to know them at a young age. One day I was on the third floor listening to Strawberry Letter 23 by The Brothers Johnson, when I heard someone shouting downstairs. I ran down to the living room to see what all the commotion was about and learned that my nephew's Star Wars cards were missing. Michael was upset that he couldn't find his R2D2 and C3P0 rookie cards and was frantically searching the house for his prized collection. Out of nowhere, his sister Mary yells from the second floor landing, "The Staw Waw Cawds awe in Bawb's caw."

I couldn't believe my ears. It made me laugh every time I would repeat it. That phrase will stick with me all my life. I love it when kids roll their R's into W's. It is a brief phase in their speech development that can turn up some "weal winnews." Maybe that's why I enjoyed Elmer Fudd so much!

Growing up on Menlo

Billy Fox, the oldest of four Fox kids, lived behind us in Shorewood and we became very close friends. I am a big fan of Bill's brother Tim, and his sister Jennifer as well. Bill possesses one of those genuine happy-sounding laughs that is highly contagious - kind of a Ga, Gak, Gak, Gak, Gak, Ga - that makes anyone within earshot automatically smile and laugh.

He and I were different in a lot of ways, and yet we are very similar characters. He was the oldest of four in his family and I was at the tail end of 11. If you've ever had a close friend with whom you know each other's thoughts and impulses – you know what I mean. That kind of friendship is special and such chemistry comes along only once or twice in a lifetime.

I don't get to see Bill much anymore as he has lived in Philadelphia for more than twenty years and has worked hard to become a successful banker. I miss his laugh and look forward to seeing him again. We certainly had fun growing up together.

Fox came over to my house one summer day in 1977, and we drove up Summit Avenue to pick up our friend Mark Wolff. When we pulled up to Wolff's house, the front door opened and Mark flew out the door. He was on the receiving end of his dad's right foot as Mr. Wolff literally kicked his son out of the house and yelled, "Don't come back home unless you find a job!" Bill and I looked at each other and shook our heads in disbelief. I thought to myself, why is Mr. Wolff so tough on Mark? Ironically, of the five Wolff brothers, Mark was the spitting image of his dad.

I didn't get it - how humiliating! I really felt sorry for Mark as he walked sheepishly toward the car. When he got in the VW bus he

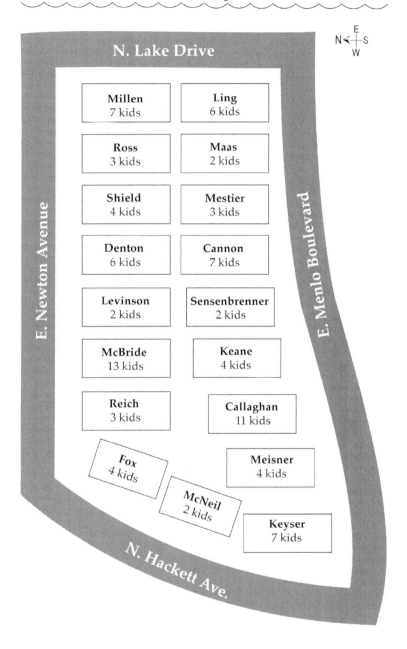

Map of our neighborhood block in Shorewood, Wisconsin in circa 1970's.

said, "I have to get a job today, guys, or I won't have a place to sleep tonight. For some reason my old man is really pissed at me."

The three of us took off on a mission to find employment – especially for Mark. We drove to the northwest side of Milwaukee and applied at various factory jobs, but it seemed no one was hiring. The goal of finding a job wasn't looking good, but we didn't give up. We headed down Good Hope Road near 76th Street and stopped at the Regis Paper Co. I walked into the reception area with my two animal friends. It was just before noon and the receptionist, who worked inside a glass-enclosed work area, slid three job applications under the glass and through the 10-inch wide cutout in front of her desk. She said they may be hiring soon to fill one or two openings in the plant, which raised Mark's spirits and gave him hope that he might find a job and consequently a way back into his home.

Before the lady went off to lunch, she instructed us to fill out the apps and slide them under the glass. She would forward them onto the personnel department when she returned at 1:00 p.m. Foxy and I finished our forms in about ten minutes, slid them onto the desk and waited and waited for Mark to complete his detailed application. He wanted to add every bit of information he could to help him secure a job. You could imagine his incentive!

Finally at around 12:25 p.m., Mark finished his resume, looked it over closely, walked over to the glass window and pushed his application through the slot with finality. The three of us watched as it slid off the desk and floated directly into a waste basket. Bill and I died laughing! Poor Mark looked like Eeyore from Winnie the Pooh and watched as his hopes for employment landed in the trash. The receptionist wouldn't be back for half an hour, so I suggested he write her a note telling her where she could find his well-written request for employment. But Mark was so down and distraught, he said "Forget it – I don't care if I get a job or not," and we walked out. Fox and I were holding our guts and bent over in pain from laughing so hard. That evening Mark stayed at Fox's den and slept on the couch in the living room.

I have always admired Mark. He is a kind and compassionate person who is very intelligent and, despite his less-than-pleasant childhood, grew up and went on to be the general manager of Cargill's meat storage facility outside of St. Louis. He married a sweet gal from Missouri, and they live in a beautiful home with three children. Mark's dad was a successful businessman in Milwaukee as president of a tannery company that processed animal hides for the leather and upholstery industry. Both father and son had similar careers in the animal processing industry – reselling hides and meat.

Milwaukee was a wonderful place to grow up; there was always something to do. During one hot July evening in 1977, Matt McBride, Bill Fox and I decided to do something really stupid and drove down to the Pabst Brewery terminal and helped ourselves to cases of Blue Ribbon from the loaded refrigerated trucks parked in the lot. When you're 17 and 18, you have the potential to do some really foolish things!

The three of us left the east side and headed downtown to the warehouse, which was not far from the Milwaukee Arena – between Juneau and Knapp Street. I was driving my brother Tom's '65 Buick Special convertible and because the two front bolts on the front seat were missing, every time you accelerated from a stop, the seat would raise up off the floor board so far that your right foot would leave the gas pedal. Since my job was to drive the get-away car, I dropped off Bill and Matt at the fenced lot and drove off. The plan was to come back in ten minutes and pick up the guys and the cold beer and head back to the vacant lot.

As I drove down Water Street and arrived back at the rendezvous spot, I saw Matt and Bill leaning up against the chain-linked fence with their arms and legs spread wide and three unmarked cop cars on the scene. For some reason, when I saw Matt being frisked, it didn't look too bad and he didn't look too concerned, but the expression on Billy Fox's face was one of total fear and frustration. He looked way out of his league as he was being arrested. I had seen enough and decided to high-tail it out of there when suddenly one of the officers looked over at my car, figured I was part of the caper, and ran as fast as he could to get into his cop car and chase me down. At that moment I had two options: pull over and wait to be arrested or take off and try to get away.

I remembered seeing the look on Fox's face and decided to avoid jail time and attempt the great escape. I stepped on the pedal and nearly landed in the back seat as I sped away from the crime scene. Tom's "drop-top" as he called it was not easy to drive but was very fast out of the blocks. I headed up Knapp Street and looked behind me and saw a single red light flashing on the roof of the cop car about four blocks behind. My adrenalin was racing so fast, I felt like Steve McQueen in the movie "Bullet," only I wasn't driving a souped up Shelby Mustang. I took a quick right at the next block and flew down Milwaukee Street for about three city blocks as I saw him gaining on me in the rearview mirror. I took another hard right and was flying down State Street and noticed a warehouse building coming up on the left with semi-trailers sporadically docked in a row. Before the cop could see me, I turned off my lights, slammed on the brakes and ducked in between two long trailers and came to an abrupt stop. My heart was still going 100 miles an hour. I looked over my right shoulder and watched as the cop went screaming by the parked trucks. I laid there in the front seat and waited for more than five hours before coming out of my hiding place. The ride home was nerve wracking – I was sure some Milwaukee cop would spot me and arrest me so I could join Matt and Bill in jail.

As the sun was beginning to come up over Lake Michigan, I drove into our driveway and went to bed. Later that day, I called over to Fox's house to find out what happened. His sister Jennifer told me that Bill wasn't home and that her dad was on his way downtown to get Bill out of jail. Good friends don't rat on each other as neither Matt nor Bill tattled on me.

Supercalafragalistic

Will Stevens is another good friend I've known since I can remember. He recently sent me the following email:

Super-Cala,

I was thinking about your Dad the other day when he caught me smoking freshman year and hit me with the classic" What, do you think you're the Fonz? I still get a kick out of that. Hope all is well and try to make it to the big city soon.

Will is one of those few close friends who can make me laugh hard. He and I see things in a similar light. Mom once told me that humor is a high form of intelligence, which would make Will a genius in some respects. With Will, there's no limit to the height of hilarity that we can reach or the depth of serious, meaningful discussions we have shared since our childhood. I told Will that he is in my book and he responded with, "Cala, I don't need to be in your book, I'm comfortable being in your head!" Will is too much fun.

Once in the early 1980s I had come home for the weekend from working in Osseo, and Will and I went for a ride in the Calavan. As we drove down Capital Drive, just past Oakland Avenue, Will noticed that I would wave to every oncoming car or at the people walking down the street, a habit I had acquired while living and driving around Osseo. Will thought it was strange that I would acknowledge and greet everyone in my path and began mocking me by waving at everyone in sight. I knew he was pimping me out, so I suggested we make a bet and have a contest to see who could collect the most waves in return. Will is a good athlete and well coordinated, so beating Will at any sport is always fun, especially the wave game.

Pre-Collegiate Program

I graduated from Shorewood High School in 1978 and decided to attend college at the University of Wisconsin-Eau Claire. Some of my older brothers and sisters had attended UW-EC and it was close to Dad's business in Osseo. To be accepted into the fall semester, I had to attend summer school at UW-EC and pass the pre-collegiate courses. Just two weeks after I graduated from high school, I was on my way to college.

Along with attending summer school, I was part of a new experimental pilot initiative called the Pre-Collegiate Program, which consisted of 30 select students. I got settled in my dorm room in Towers North and went down to a welcome banquet in the Blue Gold room. When I looked around at the other students, I took a head count and realized I was in a class with ten Native Americans, ten African-Americans and ten Caucasian Americans. I'm not sure, but I think the university was trying to blend diversity with education and see how well we would get along.

It was an excellent experience meeting and living with these fellow students from different backgrounds. While growing up in Milwaukee, I was exposed to many diverse ethnic backgrounds, especially while caddying and with the many different factory jobs I had. But Eau Claire was and still is your typical Scandinavian-settled Caucasian community with little cultural diversity. It must have been challenging for some of the African- and Native Americans to attend school in a city that is 96 percent white.

I had the Calavan (Volkswagen Bus) with me at UW-EC and every other weekend I drove home to Milwaukee and brought some black kids with me who were going home to Kenosha and Racine. We spent a lot of time together and got to know each other on our trips back and forth from summer school.

One of the black girls named Lynne was particularly friendly; she looked exactly like a junior Oprah Winfrey. She was always talking and smiling and had beautiful eyes. One day in English class I was walking up to talk to a professor and I caught her staring at my butt. It was kind of awkward and I called her on it. She always wanted to sit next to me at the lunch table and her friends followed along. I enjoyed her happy disposition. I think she liked me. In fact, I know she liked me because she wrote me a letter saying as much and sealed the envelope with a big lipstick kiss. It was the first letter I ever received that was sealed with a kiss.

One day we packed into four university vans and the Mod Squad headed out to the Lions Club Game Park, an animal park in Menomonie, to check out the rare critters in captivity. I'll never forget this Native American student named Johnny Whitecloud. As we walked around the park, I noticed he was standing alongside a huge buffalo with a fence between them, and the two appeared to be engaged in a serious conversation. I know it sounds odd, because it was, but after 20 minutes of hand motions by John and what seemed like head nods of acknowledgement by the ageless buffalo, Whitecloud walked back and joined the group. I asked him what was up with that, and he said the buffalo was telling him how sad he was for what the white man has done and that he doesn't like being fenced in this place. I was amazed at what I was hearing and the remarkable thing about his story is that it seemed like that is exactly what was going on.

I passed the summer program with flying colors and was accepted into college in the fall of 1978. I went home to Milwaukee for the last two weeks in August only to turn around and return to UW-EC for the fall semester.

Eau Claire was always one of my favorite cities to visit as I would travel up north with Dad when he worked at the plant in Osseo. We would stay at the Holiday Inn on Clairmont Avenue (now The Plaza Hotel & Suites). I loved the big sky sunrises and sunsets, the music playing as you walk along the streets downtown and the city busses had exhaust pipes pointing up to the sky – not in your face as was the case in Milwaukee. But most of all, I noticed the people were most kind and friendly. Little did I know at the time that I would one day get married and raise a family of four in Eau Claire.

The fall semester began with high hopes of continuing the good study habits that I had honed while in summer school. I was ready to get off on the right foot. Then when I arrived back on campus, I found myself squished into an overflow suite dorm with other incoming freshman. It was the opposite of the living conditions I had experienced during my summer school sentence.

I lived in a community dorm room with five other students. Sleeping conditions were less than ideal as I slept on a cot, squished between two bunk beds. For some reason I felt out of sorts. When an opening came up to move out of the shared barracks, I jumped on it and moved into a dorm room with this odd character named Dave from Pennsylvania. Now I know why there was an opening in his room. This guy was 4-foot-10, had hair down to his butt and had a thing for dropping acid. I wonder if he is still alive. He and I were extreme opposites. I felt like we shared a jail cell together, not a dorm room.

One day we were both looking out the window of our dorm on the eighth floor of Towers Hall and down at the students coming and going to school.

Suddenly Dave shouts, "Look, there's my girlfriend," "Which one," I asked, since many girls were walking around below.

"She's the one standing next to the oak tree," he said.

"Do you mean the one talking to the squirrel?" I replied.

"YES – that's her – Ruth – wait till you meet her!" he said.

I felt like I was on Mars. Fortunately, the time in hell didn't last very long and after a short-lived stint at UW-EC, I left school and went back home to work in Milwaukee.

In the fall of 1979, while employed at Allis-Chalmers in West Allis, Wisconsin, I was pushing a pallet jack around a corner stacked three tubs high with tractor parts. This Polish guy who I think had worked at the factory too long saw me negotiating the turn with this top-heavy load of cast iron and said in a frantic tone, *"Raise 'er down, raise 'er down! Some-of-a-bitch, raise 'er down."*

"Raise 'er down? Some-of-a-bitch? This guy is killing me," I thought. The last time I had heard something that confusing was in the third grade when Miss Miley said, "Callaghan, stay where you are and get out."

As you can see, my childhood was filled with family, commotion, close neighborhood friends and many lessons learned.

Chapter 4
Golf - The Game of Life

One of my favorite jobs was caddying at Milwaukee Country Club (MCC) during the summers of 1972 – '74. I learned so much about people during that time.

Golf is a sport that can bring out the best and worst in people; the game is a true test of character. It is also a great way to meet new friends because anytime you can spend four uninterrupted hours with someone on a course, you're bound to get to know each other better. It's one of the few sports you can play effectively throughout your life. I also enjoy golf because it's played outdoors, allowing you to download the smell of fresh-cut grass and blossoming flowers, the sound of birds singing and the warmth of the sun on your face. All the senses are in play. In my experience working on and playing the game, I have come across some magnificent wildlife on golf courses, including owls, alligators, snapping turtles, fox, deer and a naked woman walking out of the Atlantic Ocean.

My brother Tom was an honor caddie at MCC a few years before me and inspired me to tote bags at the club. Mom drove Mike Ewens, Frank McBride and me out to River Hills each summer morning. As we turned onto the private country club drive, off to the side you could see Judge Jennings perched atop a beautiful horse getting ready for a fox hunt. He was dressed up in his traditional derby, vest, baggy knickers and tall, shiny-black riding boots. To your left was the pristine green of the par-3 fourth hole. Further up the tree-lined road, Manual de la Torre was giving golf lessons at the driving range. Every morning started like the opening scene from the hit movie Caddie Shack. Sprinklers keeping time with the morning sun as it peers through the trees like ultra-violate rays from heaven. And just past the upper parking lot on the left was the cart shed connected to the white caddie shack.

When Harold Ramis and Brian Doyle-Murray wrote the screenplay to "Caddie Shack", it was as though they had written about my life as a caddie. In the movie - I'm Danny Noonan! In fact, back then I was the same size and stature, and had the same bushy blond hairdo as the Irish actor, Michael O'Keefe. Bushwood CC was exactly like Milwaukee CC in so many scenes, as I had lived those moments and caddied for the same cast of characters that included the Al Czervik's, the Judge Smails, the Ty Webb's, the Lacey Underall's and the Dr. Beeper's of MCC. Even the clothes Danny Noonan wore matched my 1974 wardrobe to a tee. One of the funniest comedies of all time opens with a portentous gopher dancing to Kenny Loggins hit song, "I'm Alright."

I'm alright

Nobody worry 'bout me,

Why you got to give me a fight,

Can't you just let me be?

MCC's magnificent golf course, with the Milwaukee River meandering through the back nine, was always in prime condition. It was and still is one of the top-rated courses in the state. The members at MCC were all very successful people and included the Uihleins, who owned Schlitz Brewery, Hal Koss of Koss Headphones, the presidents of First Wisconsin Bank and Wisconsin Gas Company, and some of the wealthiest lawyers, doctors and businessmen from the southeast corner of the state.

We caddied six days a week, Tuesday thru Sunday - 18 holes in the morning and, if it worked out, we would catch a second loop for 18 more in the afternoon. The going rate for caddies in 1972 was $4.25 per round and hopefully a 75-cent tip if you did a good job (today MCC caddies are paid $38.00 / round including tip). At the end of the day, I would come home with $10, exhausted after walking six miles with 35 pounds of golf gear slung across my back. Of course, my father made up a ledger book for me to track my wages and tips after each day, and the education was priceless. When you are a caddy, you're in the people business, and coming from the tail end of a large family, I found it easy to communicate with members and staff of all ages.

Some of the members took themselves a bit too seriously. On one occasion, I was walking to the second tee with a foursome and stopped at the ball washer to shine my golfer's ball. The group behind us was putting on the first green. Whenever you're caddying, you always say and do things quietly. While I was giving the ball a gentle scrub, a member on Hole No.1 missed a simple putt, and immediately looked up at me and screamed at the top of his lungs, "Would you shut the f--- up!" Apparently the thunderous sound of the bristles in a ball washer some 50 yards away set him off. His foul mouth and unwarranted reaction shocked me. At first I felt bad, like I did something wrong. Then I realized the guy was trying to blame me for his missed putt and thought, "what a horse's ass." His true colors came shining through. Golf will expose one's character - or lack thereof! I lost all respect for that guy and promised myself I would never be his caddy.

On Mondays, the club was closed to members for routine club maintenance. As a fringe benefit, MCC allowed the caddies to play 18 holes on a deluxe course and get free lessons from the club professional and swim in the prestigious country club pool. My brother, Tommy Callaghan, won the caddie tournament on Aug. 24, 1970, the day my brother John was born.

Manual de la Torre, the club pro, was originally from Spain and spoke with a smart, confident Spanish accent. He was a class act and very cordial to the members and caddies. What he enjoyed most was teaching people, especially young kids, about the game of golf. He has written instructional books - "Understanding the Golf Swing" is one title - and in 1986 was named PGA instructor of the year. De la Torre is considered one of the best in his profession. In 2007 he was listed as the No. 11 teacher in the nation by the editors of Golf Digest magazine. I once was hanging around the caddie shack and saw Carol Mann, a professional golfer, receiving lessons from Manual. She was the tallest woman I had ever set my eyes on. Ms. Mann must have been 6'-5" tall and when she wore a skirt, her legs were longer than I thought was possible. But oh man, could she hit a golf ball!

Young teenage kids from the Milwaukee area showed up at MCC for summer employment. I'll never forget Calvin, Malvin and Alvin, three black brothers who were always having fun with the white caddies. Their parents must have had a great sense of humor in coming up with those names. The three chipmunks and their friend Paul Henry, who looked like a young Lamont Sanford, were always joking around and saying stuff like, "*Callaghane, oz wich yo Mama lass night.*" As a young white boy trying to stick up for my mom, I would respond with, "No, you weren't, she was at home all night." They would fall apart laughing. Henry would often ask me, "*Hey, Callaghane, you got's fitty cent for a bag of chip?*"

This went on throughout the summer. I must admit, up to that point I hadn't been exposed to many other ethnic groups. The first time was in the summer of 1968. I was eight years old and Mr. Cannon took Dave and I swimming at the Gordon Park Pool, which was in a predominantly black Milwaukee neighborhood. At that time in Milwaukee, racial tensions were at an all time high. After Martin Luther King Jr. was assassinated, race riots broke out in the city and Fr. James Groppi was marching with a sea of black people into the Milwaukee suburbs. Watching them march directly towards our home from my living room window was unbelievable!

Dave and I logged a lot of time together growing up. He was my buddy and one of the red-headed Cannons who lived three houses up the block. And when Dave and Mr. Cannon and I walked into the Gordon Park pool area, all of the black people sitting around the pool were glaring at us and talking amongst themselves. All eyes were upon us! You could feel the racial tension in the air. I felt really white! We entered the boy's locker room and, as we were changing out of our briefs and into our Speedos, four young black kids were over in the corner and staring at Dave in amazement. One of them pointed to Dave and said with a big smile, *"Hey man, look – he gots a brass one."*

Dave realized they were talking about his amber-hued dunkler and quickly pulled up his suit. Mr. Cannon, a quiet man, just stood there … expressionless. I fell apart inside, but in all fairness to Dave, I couldn't really laugh outloud. It was one of the funniest things I had heard in my young life. But I didn't really understand why they were laughing so hard; their charcoal-colored wieners looked like they were left on the grill too long. We were all learning that day.

The black kids I got to know during my summers caddying were a lot of fun and became good friends. They were full of life and made the most of each day. I loved that they were always entertaining and enjoying themselves. And I'm proud of the fact that our generation (for the most part) learned to see past the color of someone's skin.

The caddie shack was a place where you could hang around and play basketball and pinball until the caddie master, Phil Kepke, called your name. Then you and three other caddies were sent down to the golf bag storage area for assignment. The honor caddies (the ones with seniority) were the first to get out each morning and the rest of the order was determined by when you arrived and signed in. The sooner you came in, the sooner you went out, and the more money you made. My goal was to caddie two rounds before sundown.

On July 2, 1974, I was sent over to Tuckaway Country Club in Franklin to work the GMO (Greater Milwaukee Open) Golf Tournament. Today it's known as the US Bank Championship and is played at Brown Deer Park. It was my third tour at MCC and I had made the honor caddie list. Each year the private golf clubs from around Milwaukee sent their most experienced caddies to work the tourney. The GMO was exciting because you were paid $10 for 18 holes plus a possible great tip.

While I was hanging around the caddie shack, waiting forever to hear my name called, I noticed Sam Snead walking into the club with a tournament marshall. It was easy to spot Mr. Snead with his trademark brimmed straw hat. Sam Snead was a hero – a champion! The GMO was a major golf event in Milwaukee but never seemed to draw the big names like Watson, Miller, Palmer, Snead or Nicholas. Most of the marquee golfers would skip the GMO and play in the British Open.

Snead was a golf icon. According to ESPN and the PGA, he still holds the record for the most career PGA tour victories with 82, followed by Nicholas (73), Woods (68), Hogan (64) and Palmer with (62).

Most of the caddies were inside the shack at the time, and I could tell the marshall was looking for someone to caddie for Mr. Snead. When the caddie master asked who wanted to go 18 holes with Sam Snead, the place went nuts. Everyone filed out of the shack like bees from a shaken hive to see if what they heard was true. Caddying for a golf legend like "Slammin' Sammy" had to be every caddy's dream, and each one wanted the job. Some of the older caddies shouted out their resumes, *"I'm a 10-year caddie," "I am the most experienced"* and *"I'm a professional tour caddie."* The competition grew and started to get out of hand while everyone was pleading their case.

I figured, I'm 14 years old and just a three-year honor caddie from MCC. With those credentials, my chances of being picked for the job were slim at best. So while everyone was arguing over who was the best, most experienced caddie, I walked over to Sam Snead's red-and-white Wilson bag and put it on my shoulder. It was the largest and heaviest golf bag I had ever picked up, but it felt great. The marshall and caddie master seemed glad that a caddie had been assigned, or self-appointed, and said, "You got the job." The other caddies were shocked and shouted, "He doesn't have enough experience," "He's just a kid" and "What does he know about caddying for a pro golfer?" I was thrilled – I was going to be Sam Snead's caddy.

They gave me a tan, short-sleeved jumpsuit to wear with "SNEAD" on the back. We walked to the practice range and people were snapping pictures all around us. It was a moment I'll never forget. I felt so honored to be Mr. Snead's caddy. Sam was all business on the course and, wow, could he play golf. His unique side-saddle putting style (facing the hole and putting from the right side of his body with a split grip) was very effective. On the par 4s and 5s, he would hit soaring 300-yard drives. I often lost sight of the ball in flight and had no idea where it went. I had never seen anyone hit a tee shot that far. If the ball went in the rough, I didn't have a clue where it was and it was my job to keep track of it. Fortunately, with the help of the forecaddies - tournament volunteers who spot tee shots - I was able to track down his ball throughout the round. Acting like I knew where it was all the time.

As we were walking up the 18th fairway, the crowd was cheering and people were taking pictures of us. The gallery in Milwaukee wasn't used to having such a big-name player attend the GMO. During the walk up to the green, Sam Snead acknowledged the crowd and tipped his straw hat to the excitement of the fans lined along the fairway. I was caught up in the moment, waving to the crowd, posing for pictures and soaking in the cheers while we walked down the home stretch. All of the sudden, I stepped on something round and hard. I looked down in disbelief. It was Sam Snead's golf ball, squashed into the ground. I was in shock! Sam Snead was amazed. I felt terrible and said, "I'm sorry; Mr. Snead, I didn't notice your ball (though it was right in the middle of the fairway)." He looked at me and didn't say a word, but his intense stare said everything: *"How could you step on my golf ball - in the middle of the fairway?"* Sam called over a tournament official to make a ruling on his ball and, based on his limited options, took a penalty stroke and lifted and dropped the ball from the imbedded lie.

I don't know why, but despite the setback I was still thinking I would get a big tip. It must be the optimist in me. I remember thinking, "This guy has golf clubs named after him and is in the encyclopedia." When we finished the round, he stared me in the eye, gave me a ten-dollar bill and said "Son, you have to be one of the worst caddies I have ever had." That was it! No Tip!

What could I say? I had stepped on his ball, which is the first thing you never do when caddying for someone, much less Sam Snead. I learned two really important lessons that day.

1. Sometimes in life you have to take a chance and grab hold of an opportunity when it presents itself.

2. Most times in life things don't turn out the way you planned.

Par for the course

I have always gotten a kick out of golfers who talk to their ball after they hit it; as if their last-second commands will have an impact on the outcome of the shot. Come back! Fade right! Draw left! Don't go in there! My theory is that if you want to talk to your ball, the time to do it is before you hit it – when it can hear what you're saying!

When I was playing golf in an Eau Claire YMCA fundraiser with Ed Kassing, Todd Johnson, Dan Donnellan and my brother Tom, I decided to test my theory. We were backed up on the eighth tee at the Eau Claire Golf & Country Club. When it was finally our time to hit, I was the first one up. I put my Titleist golf ball on the tee and, while checking down my grip, aim, stance and posture, I addressed the ball in my best Richard Pryor voice. *"I'm going to hit your white, Titleist-dimpled ass 280 yards down the fairway; and when I catch up with you, I'm going to hit your #4 ass on the green."* After I finished the instructions, I wound up and hit the ball hard - and it did exactly as instructed. It went down the center of the fairway – 280 yards from the launching pad. Everyone around me was surprised at what I was saying and marveled at the result. It was a tough act to follow but Ed and Dan decided to give it a go.

*From Left to Right: Tom Callaghan, Ed Kassing,
Dan Donnellan, Bill Callaghan*

Kassing was the second man up and he felt compelled to address the ball in a similar way. It was fun to listen to Ed's improv skills, as he scolded his Maxfli. Unfortunately, his ball barely made it past the ladies tee, almost bringing the Beaumont Rule into play. The next guy to hit was Dan Donnellan, who addressed his ball up close, holding it six inches from his face. Dan laid into his ball with, "Okay you white, two-bit buckaroo, do exactly what I tell you to do." Dan wailed into the shot and the ball immediately headed for the out-of-bounds/lost ball department. Obviously, Dan's ball was not motivated by his harsh pep talk.

I've found that talking to the ball in that manner gets your adrenaline going and builds an enormous amount of focus and energy into the shot.

The Pursell Cup

One of our customers and good friends in Alabama holds a fundraiser every two years to generate money for junior diabetes research. David Pursell and three of his six children have diabetes, so you can imagine his desire to find a cure. David and his beautiful wife, Ellen, have done a wonderful job creating awareness about the disease and have raised hundreds of thousands of dollars through the Pursell Cup golf tournament. As a mixing and coating equipment-supplier for David's company, my brother Tom and I have been fortunate to be included in the annual event since 1995.

David Pursell is a great dad, gifted artist and visionary who, along with Dr. Mike Hurdzan and Dana Fry of Hurdzan/Fry Golf Course Design in Columbus, Ohio, created the Farmlinks Golf Course in 2003 as a research-and-development golf course. It's the only one of its kind! The public course is located in Fayetteville, Alabama; just west of Sylacauga and is carved out of a beautiful piece of property owned by David's daddy, Jimmy Pursell.

When David developed his creative plan, he sent out the following newsletter:

Phase Three of this project is the most ambitious. "It includes building an 18-hole championship golf course called FarmLinks and constructing a First Tee facility for kids. FarmLinks will be adjacent to the corporate office and the lodge. We will use the course to showcase our fertilizer technology, entertain guests, and offer area golfers and corporations an opportunity to experience the game of golf in a truly pastoral setting," Pursell explained.

Hurdzan/Fry of Columbus, Ohio, which designed FarmLinks, is considered one of the top golf course design firms in the country. Michael Hurdzan was named Designer of the Year in 1997 by Golf World Magazine and 1999 Golf Course Architect of the Year by The Board Room magazine. Dana Fry, a partner in the firm, worked with Tom Fazio for five years before teaming up with Hurdzan. They have designed hundreds of courses in the U.S., Canada, Europe and Asia. The firm is best known for designs that preserve natural environments.

Pursell noted that the First Tee facility at Pursell Farms would help introduce kids to the game of golf. "I have six children who are all golfers, but I recognize that many kids do not have access to the game. We'd like to provide an opportunity for others to enjoy a game that we really love," he related. "Who knows, the next Tiger Woods may come from Talladega County, Alabama! Our overall vision for Pursell Farms is to provide a first-class facility to promote research and education," Pursell concluded. "By combining our corporate headquarters, research sites, training facilities, a golf course and recreation areas into one very unique complex, we are demonstrating our strong commitment to the green industry and to the game of golf. As far as I know, this has never been attempted by anyone else."

Hole #5 at Farmlinks

In June of 2007, my brothers Tom, and John, and sisters Muffie, and Julie, and I attended the Pursell Cup and met so many wonderful people from the south. One of our favorite friends that sell's for Pursell Technologies (now Agrium AT) is Tim Orton. He is a master story teller and one of the most entertaining people I have come across on a golf course. He's also an excellent golfer.

E-mail from Tim Orton:

Dear Bill,

I told David Pursell that I enjoyed playing golf with you guys as much as anyone I've ever played with anywhere.

I wish the Callaghan clan would share their family secret with the rest of the world! All the Callaghan's I have ever had the pleasure to be around are the happiest, most upbeat people I know. Y'alls joy is infectious.

It was my pleasure to play golf with you and Tom.

Best regards,

Tim

Fred Carney is another special friend from Sylacauga. He was one of the first people I met in 1987 when we started selling Rollo-Mixers to the Pursell family. He is an extremely bright individual and has a clever sense of humor.

E-mail exchange between myself and Fred Carney:

Fred,

It was great to golf with you again at Farmlinks. The best part of the trip was when you called out that bird on the 5th hole. What kind of bird was it again?

It was a prairie warbler. Do you keep a list of bird sightings?

The 1998 Pursell Cup was held at Greystone Country Club in Birmingham, Alabama. One item available for bid at a silent auction during the event was a weekend golf package for four at the Greenbrier Resort in White Sulfur Springs, West Virginia. The prize included lunch and lessons with Sam Snead! It would be so cool to take my son Joseph, my brother Tom and his son Shea to meet the golf legend, and have lunch and lessons with one of the game's best. I was also curious if he remembered the kid who stepped on his ball at the GMO in 1974. I was determined to outbid everyone in the room for the chance to hook up with Snead at the Greenbrier. I couldn't understand what the southern auctioneer was saying half the time, but I knew that if I kept raising my hand I would stay in the bidding. It came down to me and one other contestant, who eventually gave up. I figured it's difficult to put a dollar value to a once-in-a-lifetime opportunity like that.

The next day we played in the Pursell Cup and Tom's team won the coveted silver chalice. After the round, I was in the clubhouse having a soda pop with Tom and our friend Jack, reviewing the day's festivities. Tom was mapping out each of his shots in pencil on the scorecard's course layout. Jack was shocked that Tom could remember every one of his strokes on each of the 18 holes.

"Well, Tom, what'd you shoot out there today?" Jack asked.

"I shot a 106," Tom replied.

Jack's eyes grew wide as he exclaimed, "Tom, if I had 106 shots, I wouldn't have remembered a one of 'em."

In April 1999, the four of us (Tom, Shea, Joe and I) arrived at The Greenbrier, a five-diamond luxury resort tucked away in the majestic Allegheny Mountains of West Virginia. Built in 1778 and remodeled in 2007, the historic playground offers more than 50 activities on three championship golf courses, clay tennis courts, a professional croquet course, horse-riding trails, a movie theater, a bowling alley and a recently opened secret underground bunker. The covert hideaway was built to house members of the executive and legislative branches of government in the event of a nuclear attack.

And then there are the healing powers of the White Sulphur Springs. For many years, the natural resource has drawn people from around the world to bathe in waters that are said to miraculously cure most illnesses.

We met Sam Snead in the clubhouse before heading to the restaurant for lunch. When you shook Snead's hand, his fingers were somewhat curled toward the palm of his hand as if he was forever holding a 5-iron. I imagine if I held a club in my hand everyday for 70 years, my hands would eventually do the same.

The clubhouse offered a "Sam Snead Cheeseburger," "Sam Snead Club Sandwich" and other similarly named menu items. The man himself was wearing his trademark straw hat and a navy blue sweater. He told us stories of golfing against Byron Nelson and Ben Hogan. My brother Tom asked him what it was like golfing with Ben Hogan. "Hogan never said a word on the golf course," Snead said as he gestured locking his lips and throwing away an imaginary key.

Samuel Jackson Snead was born on May 27, 1912. He and two of the other greatest golfers of all time, Ben Hogan and Byron Nelson, were born within six months of each other in 1912. Sam Snead was one of the top players in the world for most of four decades. He won seven majors: three Masters, three PGA Championships and one British Open. Snead was inducted into the World Golf Hall of Fame in 1974, the year I caddied for him.

Sam was a southern gentleman; he was most cordial and couldn't be friendlier. The lunch meeting was going so well that I didn't want to spoil the atmosphere by bringing up our past meeting in Milwaukee. After lunch, we each received a 15-minute golf lesson at the practice range. When it was my turn for instruction, I told Sam I had trouble hitting long irons straight and that I tended to pull those shots to the left. He asked me to grab a 4-iron out of my bag and show him my setup and swing. After I hit the ball down the range – and to the left - he looked at me kind of tickled and said, "Son, this is not the ballet" as he imitated my swing with an exaggerated motion.

"Hold still when you swing the club; you are all over the place," Snead said.

It was surreal listening to Mr. Snead for a full hour instructing the four of us about properly swinging a golf club. My son Joe was only 10 years old at the time and listened intently as Mr. Snead swung the club and hit the ball effortlessly.

Joe Callaghan and Sam Snead at The Greenbrier

When the lesson was over, Sam returned to the golf shop and we went out to play the Old White course. We met up with Sam after the round as he was signing autographs in the pro shop. I bought a portrait of Mr. Snead after he won the Masters in 1938 and got in line to have it signed. I was like a kid waiting in line to see Santa Claus. When I finally reached the front of the line, I told Snead the story of caddying for him at the GMO. He looked up at me with that same intense stare he gave me when I was 14 and then wrote on the picture, "To Bill, my young caddy – Sam Snead." It was priceless! Sam lived for only three more years and died on May 23, 2002.

Life is like golf – It's not how you start, it's how you finish!

I love the game of golf. Until 2004, I was a frustrated 18-handicap golfer who would par some holes, bogey a few and blow up on the rest while shooting at least a 90. In February 2004, my friend Paul asked me to join him and his brother Jim, and a few of his high school buddies on a trip to Arizona to attend golf school. I wasn't sure what to expect, but I thought any insight and instruction could only help my game.

We arrived in Mesa, where the John Jacob's Golf Academy held a three-day swing school at Gold Canyon. The golf professionals split us up into smaller groups and ran us through all aspects of the game – paying particular attention to the proper way to swing a golf club. I must have hit more than 500 golf balls that first day. We learned how to consistently hit a ball out of the sand trap and other aspects of the short game - pitching, chipping and putting. It was like getting the answers before a test. After a full day of "class," we teamed up and played 18 holes before the sun went down. I was fortunate to be in Scott's cart after each day of instruction. Scott is a longtime friend of Paul's and is a student of the game. He has attended golf school in the past and has a 4 handicap to show for it.

As we applied the techniques learned in school earlier that day, I benefitted immensely from having Scott in my cart as he continued to teach me how to play golf the way it should be played. I learned so many subtle intricacies about the game that I graduated from golf school with a whole new perspective, a new friend in Scott, and an appreciation for the game I'm so passionate about. Even though Scott and I both lived in Eau Claire, we never knew each other before that point. Thanks to Paul, we became good friends during our trip to Gold Canyon.

For those who enjoy playing golf as much as I do, I highly recommend golf school if you want to lower your handicap, eliminate those 7s, 8s and 9s on your scorecard, boost your confidence and raise your expectations. It's the difference between knowing how to play the game and wishing you played a good game.

As I was saying earlier, when you're playing golf, you are bound to come across some beautiful sights. In 1994, my wife earned a trip for two to the Atlantis Resort in the Bahamas with the Longaberger Company. The tropical resort and hotel features a casino, deluxe spa, and is located on the shores of Paradise Island. The Atlantis is also home to one of the most elaborate underground aquariums I have ever seen. As you walk through the glass tunnels, you are encapsulated by beautiful fish floating above and around you. I felt like Don Knotts in the movie "The Incredible Mr. Limpet." The gigantic fish tank was swimming with every sea creature you could imagine, 10-foot sand tiger sharks, stingrays, barracudas, huge sea turtles, puffer fish, Jew fish, grouper and an array of colorful tropical fish I had never seen before.

Every time I have been blessed with the opportunity to travel on a Longaberger trip, I am exposed to wonderful places and new scenery that I otherwise may never have seen in my lifetime.

Watching the schools of fish at the Atlantis swimming in the water as one, reminded me of flocks of birds flying through the air or herds of Elk running across a field. Although these creatures move about in different worlds, their similarities made sense to me as they all come from the same designer – Almighty God.

During our vacation, we decided to play the Ocean Club Golf Course with Tim and Kim of California, another Longaberger couple. The course was in perfect condition, with palm trees lining the fairways and beautiful aqua-blue ocean water coming into play on the back nine.

We had played the front nine, when Laurel and Kim decided they had enough golf for the day and walked back to the beach to lie in the warm Bahamian sun. Tim and I played on. As we hit our approach shots into the 13th green, I noticed a woman swimming near the shore just yards from the green. I looked closer and closer and realized it wasn't my imagination!

"I think that woman in the ocean is swimming around topless," I said to Tim.

We parked our cart to the side of the green and marked our shots. If you happen to hit your approach shot too far, it would end up over the green and in the Atlantic. When I looked to see what the mermaid was doing, I froze and lost all concentration. She rose out of the shallow water and began walking directly toward me. This woman was maybe 40 years old, very attractive and by no means bashful or shy. She was topless and bottomless; I mean she was completely naked. She had long brunette hair, beautiful firm breasts and, to my surprise, her deal was shaved to the nines! I think she was from Brazil.

127

I realize that I was in International waters and not in Wisconsin, and that women from other countries often go topless on beaches in those parts. But seeing this woman totally naked on the golf course and walking in my direction was over the top. Tim looked at me in disbelief, with an expression of wonderment, as she slowly approached us. We tried to maintain our composure, stay the course and act like this was a routine occurrence - but it wasn't. I had always felt that women were God's greatest work of creation, and this just reinforced that belief. I couldn't talk!

After we both four-putted the hole, the suit-less, drop-dead gorgeous woman walked up to me holding two golf balls in her hand and said in broken English, "Do golf balls belong to golfer or to golf course?" Apparently she found the balls while swimming and wanted to return them to their rightful owner. I didn't know what to say. For probably the first time in my life, I was speechless. The question baffled me. Her beauty and nakedness mesmerized both sides of my brain. As she stood only a foot from me, I tried to maintain eye contact so she wouldn't think I was checking out her dripping, wet body. It was difficult. Then she handed me the balls, turned around, walked off the green and returned to the sea to search for more stray golf balls. Still in awe and shock, we both stared at her bare ass bottom until it slowly disappeared into the ocean.

Hole No. 14 was a short par-3 along the coast. Tim and I tried to refocus and play the hole while the alluring ladyfish was still scavenging around in the water. We both had trouble regaining our concentration from that point on. For some reason, Tim didn't want the moment to end and suggested we play the 14th over and over again so he could keep her in his sights. But it was getting late and I told him we had to get back to the Atlantis for a dinner reception with the gals.

We found our wives relaxing by the pool with other Longaberger women and told them the unbelievable news. Nobody believed us, which made the experience that much better. They thought we were nuts and making the whole thing up.

What happened on the golf course that day was a once-in-a-lifetime experience. It was like getting a hole-in-one, a feat that's escaped me. I'm glad I had a witness and the balls as evidence.

A good friend of mine, who recently retired after 30 years as a Research & Development inventor in Minnesota, once told me that golf got its name from a sign above the front door of a clubhouse at one of the first golf courses built in Scotland.

The sign read: Gentleman Only, Ladies Forbidden = GOLF.

There are so many golf stories to tell. Twenty years ago, Ron Jones flew in from Ennis, Texas, to run some trials on the Rollo-Mixer. We took him to Osseo Golf Club for nine holes with clubs borrowed from my brother that included a Patty Berg 9-iron from my mom's old set. When Ron got close to the first green, he reached into the bag and was shocked to find what he referred to as a Patty Do-Berg. "I can't believe it! I have never played with a woman's club in my life!" he said. He was taken aback. I probably would have left a better impression if I had just rented him a set of clubs!

On the next hole, his tee shot landed 20 yards behind a tree. So in an effort to cheer him up, I told him, "You know, Ron, you could probably hit the ball right through the tree. I heard a tree is really 90 percent air."

Without hesitation, he replied, "So is a screen door!"

Chapter 5
Moms - 25/8

When I was looking for a special woman to spend the rest of my life with, I naturally was looking for someone with qualities like my Mom: someone who is sincere, intelligent, and someone who would be kind and dedicated to her husband and children. She would be someone who would fill my life with love, laughter, joy and polish my star.

I am so thankful I married such a wonderful woman, who is energetic and a positive influence on me. What I love about my Laurel is that she is forever young, and I can't see her getting old on me. She has a refreshing disposition and is giving of her time and talents. Our marriage has been, and always will be, an exciting adventure because we both know we are in this together until the end. Time only seems to strengthen our love for each other.

After going out with different women and not finding what I was looking for, I sought guidance from above. In August 1983, I was attending Sunday mass at St. Patrick's in Eau Claire. As I knelt in the pew, I prayed to God and asked him to help me find the ideal woman.

"Dear God, when you get some time, could you please find that special woman for me to love and be with for the rest of my life."

The following Saturday - September 3, 1983 - I walked into Trader and Trapper on Clairemont Avenue in Eau Claire with my friend from Milwaukee, Mike Pierce. T&T was a fun place to drink beer, shoot pool and dance to classic music from the '70s and early '80s.

When we entered, I noticed a pretty girl in the distance sitting at the bar. When she looked at me and our eyes met, I waved at her. I don't know why I waved. I usually don't walk into a place and start waving at people, especially people I don't know. But there was something about her.

She was having a drink with a friend from North Dakota. After about 20 minutes, I walked up and asked if she would like to dance. She said … no. I must have scared her with that friendly wave during my entrance, I thought. After a few songs, I returned and asked her one more time, "Would you like to dance?"

If she had said no again, I probably would have let it be. "Well, Okay, I suppose," she said. I figured two "no"s and you're out. But there was something special about her.

She was understandably skeptical, but we made it to the dance floor. The DJ was spinning Michael Jackson's "Wanna be Startin' Something", a great song for dancing. I was showing off all of my best moves, which I learned at Papagio's and Park Avenue, two hot discos in Milwaukee. When the song "That's What I Like About You" by the Romantics came on, we were high-stepping and moving as one. We had so much fun dancing together; we danced for 30 minutes before finally running out of gas. She seemed to really enjoy dancing with me, and I loved her pretty eyes and warm and sincere smile. As I looked in her eyes, I wondered if this was the woman I asked God to find for me. Had God answered my prayer that fast? We dated for 2½ years and married in June 1986.

The song "Miracles" came to mind when God sent Laurel into my life. It was written by Roger Cook and sung by Don Williams and made it to No. 4 on the country music charts in 1981.

Miracles, miracles that's what life's about,

Most of you must agree, if you've thought it out,

I can see and I can hear – I can tell you why,

I can think and I can feel – I can even cry,

I can walk, I can run, I can swim the sea,

We have made a baby son and he looks like me

*Miracles, miracles that's what life's about, Most of you must agree,
if you've thought it out,*

Who is rich and who is poor – who has more than me,

Why I have quite enough to eat – and my mind is free

Miracles, miracles that's what life's about

I found you and you found me – we are not without

We are not without and I'm happy – we are not without

I think the job that moms do is amazing. If God had made eight days a week, I believe the eighth would have been Mothersday - right between Saturday and Sunday. That would be a fitting tribute for all that moms do and a way to recognize their hard work and dedication more than once a year. Moms are more minute by minute, moment by moment when it comes to caring for kids. Dads are more day to day. Moms are like home air traffic controllers – they know who's taking off and when, and they keep track of every scheduled appointment. And they know when everyone is landing.

Our house is busy all the time, especially during the school year, with homework, dance class, school sports, religion class and music practice, not to mention cooking meals, keeping food in the house, doing laundry and going to work. With so many activities, it's surprising how parents make it through the week, much less the day. I feel for single moms or single dads; I don't know how they do it.

My wife shared a quote with me I thought was fitting. "A woman is like a tea bag; you don't know how strong she is until you put her in hot water."

I was fortunate to have a mom who ran an organized house and was always there when I came home. You could always hear my mom before you saw her because the charm bracelet on her left wrist forever jingled with the names of her 11 children hanging from the chain. Something about that sound was very comforting. She was a stabilizing force in our home, while my father traveled the country building his mixer business. Mom dedicated every day of her parenting life for more than 40 years to caring for her children. When she wasn't doing something for one of us, you could find her upstairs in the office, doing the weekly payroll, filling out ledger books or figuring out a way to pay the bills with Dad. I took it for granted that my Mom would always be home – because she always was.

Mom taught me that if you are troubled and your mind is cluttered with stupid thoughts, make the sign of the cross, and it will help you clear your mind and chase away negative thoughts. You know what? It works!

While Laurel and I were on a Longaberger trip in Hawaii, in 1994, we drove to the north side of Oahu and stopped at the Dole Plantation's visitor center. I bought a gold chain with a pineapple pendent that sparkles like a shiny diamond as a Mother's Day gift for Mom and my wife. For the past 15 years, Mom has worn that Hawaiian pineapple around her neck everyday!

My wife, Laurel, is an amazing mom as well. Superman got his power from the sun; I get my power from Laurel! She is one of the most accomplished individuals I have ever met. Marrying a wife who is also a Registered Nurse is like winning the lottery. It's like having an Emergency Room (open 24/7) right in your home!

Laurel is the youngest of three girls and doesn't fit the typical "baby of the family" birth-order profile. As my father says, "Laurel is a doer!" I was so impressed with all that she does for our family that for Mother's Day in 1999, I bought her an engraved trophy that reads "1999 Mother of the Year." Our kids were 11, 10, 8 and 4 at the time.

Laurel (pregnant with Meghan) and Bill in Hawaii in December 1994

The Led Zeppelin II album (I mean CD) contains many classic hits, but there is one track that sums up my admiration for my wife and the job she does as a mom. It's simply titled:

"Thank You"

If the sun refused to shine, I would still be loving you

When mountains crumble to the sea, there will still be you and me

Kind woman, I give you all

Kind woman, nothing more,

Little drops of rain whisper of the pain

Tears of love lost in the days gone by

My love is strong, with you there is no wrong

Together we shall go until we die, my, my, my

An inspiration is what you are to me

Inspiration, look .... see

And so today, my world – it smiles

Your hand in mine – we walk the miles

Thanks to you, it will be done

For you to me – are the only one

Happiness, no more sad, Happiness .... I'm glad.

Likewise, every time I hear the song "Maybe I'm Amazed" by
Paul McCartney, I think of my wife. *"Baby I'm amazed at the way
you love me all the time."* And nobody I know gets more done
in a single day. She takes care of all of us and successfully runs
her business out of our home. I think the drive she possesses has
a lot to do with her ancestral bloodline: a father who is Danish
and German, a mother who is French and Polish. Laurel is an
industrious mix of determination and creativity. She exudes hard-
working traits that add up to a very skillful, proficient person.

Laurel's great grandfather came through Ellis Island with a
boatload of Jensen's from Denmark. As he embarked, and went
through the processing line, the immigration official told him
they had too many Jensen's. Then the official said, "What town
in Denmark are you from?" Apparently her great grandfather
originated from Astrup, a town in central Denmark – and that
became his surname.

When I met Laurel Astrup in 1983, she was a four-year RN
working as a pediatric nurse at Sacred Heart Hospital. Her nursing
skills were exceptional and well-regarded by doctors and nurses. In
1990, we went to her sister Elaine's house in Johnston, Iowa, for an
Astrup family Thanksgiving. Her home was filled with many hand-
woven baskets, apparently produced by the Longaberger Company

in Ohio. Elaine encouraged Laurel to get into the basket business, and I'm so glad she did.

For the past 19 years, Laurel has excelled with Longaberger and has worked hard to build her business into a successful enterprise. The thing I love is the way the company treats its people, especially its independent national sales force. Every company should take a page out of the Longaberger book on acknowledging employee efforts. The company's mission statement is "To Stimulate a Better Quality of Life."

Longaberger is a family-owned company that began making baskets in 1896. J.W. Longaberger wove maple into quality-crafted baskets that were used at home and on the job. In 1973, Dave Longaberger revitalized the basket-weaving trade and turned the family tradition into a booming business. Dave was a visionary who put his heart and soul into making Longaberger the class operation it is today. Tami Longaberger, Dave's oldest daughter, has done an excellent job of carrying on her father's passion by continuing the trademark high-quality craftsmanship as well as encouraging new product development that has resulted in a vast line of home furnishings. Tami's family business of basket weaving has branched into pottery, fabrics, beautiful wrought iron products and creative home furnishings.

My first taste of this royal treatment was in August 1993, when Laurel earned her first incentive trip for two to Cancun, Mexico. Longaberger's award package included individualized itineraries, personalized luggage tags, plane tickets, transportation services, hotel accommodations, planned activities, and elaborate meals cooked every morning and evening. We also found surprises and gifts in our room throughout the trip. The goal of Longaberger's staff was to recognize these hard-working women and let them know how much they were appreciated. As Laurel's husband, I got to tag along for the fun.

When we arrived at the Fiesta Americana Condesa in Cancun, Longaberger had prepared a deluxe reception party around the pool with the Caribbean Sea as the backdrop. It was my first time south of the border and it was absolutely spectacular. You could feel the warm constant breeze that continually cleanses your face while palm branches slowly sway to the music and yellow and green coconuts hang like chandeliers above you. The Caribbean Seas colorful hues of blue, green, and aqua-blue mixed with lime green and royal blue was unlike anything I had ever seen; each color exposing the varying depths and beauty of the Sea. This place was first class and five stars – Longaberger style. The reggae band played classic Bob Marley music and the sound of the waves along with the warm August sun was completely breathtaking and beyond what I had imagined. Anytime reality surpasses your imagination, you know you're part of something special. Longaberger's staff excels at exceeding your expectations.

After the band finished "Stir It Up," I asked if they knew the song "Sitting Here in Limbo" by Jimmy Cliff. The leader of the group looked at me kind of indifferent, so I started singing the first stanza to jog his memory. Then all of a sudden the lead singer said with a classic South American accent, "Go to the microphone *mon*." I stared at him in shock and he repeated again, "Go to the microphone *mon*." All I was trying to do was request a song – not sing it to hundreds of people. The next thing I knew, the band started playing my request and I was the lead singer. It was an experience I will never forget. Singing Jimmy Cliff music in a surreal setting with a polished reggae band was incredible; it was karaoke at its best. I felt like I was in limbo. The 1972 song goes like this:

Sitting here in limbo, but I know it won't be long,

Sitting here in limbo, like a bird without a song,

Well they're putting up resistance, but I know that my faith will lead me on,

Sitting here in limbo, waiting for the dice to roll,

Sitting here in limbo, got some time to search my soul,

Well they're putting up resistance, but I know that my faith will
lead me on,

I don't know where life will lead me but I know where I've been,
I can't say what life will show me but I know what I've seen,
Tried my hand at love and friendship but all that is past and gone,
This little boy is moving on.

Sitting here in limbo, waiting for the tide to flow,
Sitting here in limbo, knowing that I have to go,
Well they're putting up resistance, but I know that my faith will
lead me on.

The trip was like a second honeymoon and so much more. It was timeless and so romantic. As we sat along the beach and the daylight disappeared, I watched as the Caribbean Sea slowly faded into the night, but the sounds of the waves crashing the shore never ceased; forever painting that image in your mind. And as the evening fell upon us, one by one the stars appeared in the sky. The Milky Way grew more brilliant with each passing moment, to where the black canvas was suddenly dotted with stars that shone like glistening endless diamonds, basking in their infamous beauty. This place was special!

Two-way Street

As someone who has known Laurel for nearly 20 years, I contacted Tami Longaberger and asked her to include something about Laurel. She was kind enough to send me the following letter:

Comments from Tami Longaberger, chief executive officer and
president of The Longaberger Company.

Dear Bill,

*First, let me thank you for the opportunity to participate
in this wonderful book. It is an honor to offer comments on
Laurel. It also is refreshing to know that Longaberger has had such
a strong, positive impact in Laurel's life and on your family. She is
a true reflection of what we're all about.*

Best of luck with the book. Thanks so much for thinking of us.

*P.S. Glad you like the Kickoff Basket and will find good use for it
this Packers season! As you might expect, I'm getting mine in Ohio
State colors.*

*"Women like Laurel face a myriad of challenges and
responsibilities. As a wife, mother and business owner, she
certainly has her hands full. She is a companion to her husband,
caretaker of her family and, as a national sales leader with The
Longaberger Company, is responsible for her own business
along with mentoring teams of other consultants to grow their
Longaberger businesses. This is no small feat.*

*But Laurel handles it with dignity, grace and a smile. And, she
gets tremendous results. Her Longaberger career is filled with
milestones, from promotions and awards to strong personal sales.*

*Some might wonder how she does it. I happen to know her secret. It
is her attitude. Her soft spoken nature gives way to a larger-than-
life spirit that lies within. She is extremely positive and upbeat. She
loves what she does with passion and is committed to building her
Longaberger teams in a nurturing and loving manner. She is the
first to offer help, believing nothing is too big or too small for her
to tackle. Where others might give up, she forges ahead.*

*Laurel is a gem of a person and a great example of leadership
in our sales field. I consider it a pleasure to have her part of the
Longaberger extended family."*

Sincerely,

Tami

I believe going on trips with your spouse is one of the healthiest things you can do for your marriage. Vacations allow you to get reacquainted and offer the perspective you both need to step outside your daily routines, evaluate how things are doing, refocus, recharge your batteries and make halftime adjustments. It is medicine for your marriage!

Travelin' Clan

While on vacation in Mazatlan, Mexico, our family took a charter boat to a nearby island to swim and play on the beach. The skipper said his name was Captain Crunch and his first mate was Mike Tysone. While we were enjoying the warm Pacific, the kids decided they wanted to go on a family banana boat ride. Tysone drove the boat that pulled the inflatable banana and before I got on, I handed my digital video recorder to Captain Crunch and asked him to record the ride. I was the last one on; and as soon as we left the shore, I knew it was going to be a drag. The six of us were bouncing up and down as Tysone was speeding across the water. It felt like I was riding a bucking bronco, because the back end of the banana was constantly lurching four feet up out of the water and then slamming back into the sea. I was amazed that I didn't fall off! Then Tysone suddenly took a hard right turn, and the craft tipped over and we all went flying into the Pacific Ocean.

Everyone was startled, and my wife and kids were concerned about what lay beneath in the deep salt waters. We scrambled back onto the slippery yellow banana and bucked our way back to dry land. When we reached shore, I limped along the sand en route to my beach towel, as I had severely pulled my left hamstring when we crashed in the water. It really hurt and left me with a vacation limp and a bruise on the back of my leg the size of a football. The last thing on my mind was that I would get banged up on a family boat ride. And neither Captain Crunch nor Mike Tysone ever said the banana ride would be, *dainurous* or dangerous!

Bill, Laurel, Meghan, Elizabeth, Joe, and Michelle in
Mazatlan, Mexico in 2008

That evening, we were all sitting in the living room of our Mayan apartment and watching the recording of the banana boat ride. Once we took off, you could see my body bouncing up and down like a rag doll as we sped away from the camera. When we wiped out in the water and everyone scurried back on the big yellow banana, you could hear Captain Crunch laughing as he zoomed in on the action. Then, in beautifully spoken broken English, he said, *"Careful for dey chark – Dey chark is coming!" "Careful for dey chark – Dey chark is coming!"* I replayed the video over and over again, and the six of us laughed harder every time.

One of my favorite trips that Laurel and I took was a cruise to the Eastern Caribbean. We set sail from San Juan, Puerto Rico, on the Monarch of the Seas. The ship's manifest was booked with Longaberger women from around the country … and a few husbands. When our massive cruise liner docked in St. Thomas, we boarded a shuttle boat and sailed into Megans Bay. This magnificent cove, located in the heart of the Caribbean, had soft, white-sand beaches and the clearest, warmest, most transparent water I had ever gazed upon or swam in.

As we walked ashore, Laurel and I were romantically holding hands, enjoying each other's company and taking in the beauty, in search of a place to spread out our beach towels and set up shop on the beach. This place was heaven on earth. As we strolled along the shore, we came upon a Chinese woman, topless, sitting on the sand and leaning against a palm tree. She had her knees up with a hardcover book propped on top, and her arms were extended outward as she steadied the book. It looked to me like her boobs were reading the book too!

As we walked past, an idea came to me. I grabbed our Longaberger-issued instant camera and asked the gal, "Would you mind taking our picture?" Laurel couldn't believe my choice of amateur photographers. She nudged me and said, "Stop it, you're joking!" But it was too late. The attractive, petite woman set her book down and stood up wearing only the bottom half of a white bikini. I handed her our camera and showed her where to aim and shoot. Laurel and I stood side by side with Megans Bay in the background; it was the perfect shot. She was the most beautiful photographer I had ever seen as she held the camera up to her right eye and focused. She was a very pretty woman with a Caribbean tan and surprisingly large breasts. After she handed the camera back to me, I thanked her for helping us capture the moment as she sat back down on her towel and continued reading her novel. I don't remember Laurel thanking her. Actually, now that I think of it, I don't remember Laurel saying anything for the next 20 minutes.

The picture was priceless; judging by the look on our faces, you would think we were looking at two different things – as I was looking at two identical things. My excited expression was exactly the opposite of Laurel's frumpy frown. I was just trying to create lasting memories and mix things up a bit - and it worked.

Memorable Moments

One of the greatest joys I have experienced four times is witnessing the birth of our children. It is an exhilarating feeling that launches you high into the sky, and you don't come down for quite a while. The admiration I felt for my wife was incredible! The day after our daughter Meghan was born in April 1995, I decided to do something fun and different for my wife and new mom as she left the hospital. As we exited the main entrance, a tall chauffer, complete with driving hat and jacket, greeted Laurel and held her hand as we walked a red carpet to the car. When he opened the door, Biz, Joe and Michelle were sitting in the back of the white stretch limo waiting for their mom and new baby sister. The nurse, Kathy Dewitz, who had been pushing the wheelchair with Laurel and baby Meghan was moved with emotion. She said with tears in her eyes, "In all my years of working in pediatrics and escorting new moms and babies out of the hospital, I have never seen anything like this. Every mom should leave the hospital this way after going through childbirth." It was a special surprise for everyone. I was taught to treat your wife like she's a queen – because she is.

In July 1995, Laurel was heading to Columbus, Ohio, for the BEE, the annual Longaberger convention. Thousands of excited woman from around the country swarm to Ohio to see new products and get buzzed … about the company's bright future. That meant I would be responsible for our 8-, 7- and 4-year-olds, and 3-month-old, while she was away. The only way you can appreciate what your wife does for your children is when she's gone and you're the mom and the dad. It puts everything in perspective. This was a special year for Laurel because she was being recognized on the big stage for being No. 1 in her directorship as a national sales leader and national recruiter; both coveted awards only few women achieve in the same year.

When Laurel left for the Minneapolis airport, we all gave her a hug and a kiss and waved goodbye as she drove down the street. Now the chase was on: Operation Be Surprised! I quickly packed up the kids clothes in little suitcases and put together a baby carry-on bag filled with baby diapers, baby wipes, baby formula, baby bottles, baby powder and baby clothes for baby Meghan.

3 year old Elizabeth in the kitchen

Elizabeth was a great help getting everybody packed up. She has always been a kind elder sister to Joe, Michelle and Meghan. I love her instinctive thought process and the ahead-of-their-years trait that most firstborn children possess. When Elizabeth was three years old, she had the same voice as Thumper, the adorable rabbit in the Disney classic "Bambi."

Five minutes after Laurel left, we packed up the Calavan, the Callaghan van and I drove as fast as I could down to Milwaukee to catch a Midwest Airlines flight to Columbus. We arrived at Mitchell Field with 45 minutes to check in, go through security and board the plane. I got some pretty funny looks from other travelers as we ran through the terminal to our gate. The kids loved it. Once we made it to our assigned seats, I recall some of the moms on the plane kept looking at me and smiled; it was almost as though the instinctive mother in them wanted to help me. I must have looked like I was in way over my head. The expression on their faces was, "This guy is flying to Ohio with his three little kids and a 3-month-old baby - how brave." I felt like I was on a new reality show called "Survivor/The Amazing Race."

We arrived in Columbus and taxied downtown to the Crown Plaza

144

Convention Center. Phase one of the stealth mission was complete. Phase two was much easier. Since Laurel was staying at The Drury, all we had to do was hunker down in our hotel room on the 12th floor, go for a swim, take naps and maintain a low profile so none of Laurel's basket friends would spot me. I had met quite a few of these gals and some of their husbands on annual Longaberger trips, and they would certainly wonder what I was doing out there with our little kids.

We got up the next day, had breakfast in the room, got showered, dressed and headed for the Columbus Zoo. Going on the trip with my young family was such an adventure, and what I noticed the most was how my kids are such close friends and very kind and considerate of each other. They made my job of being the mom and the dad so much easier.

Before we left for Ohio, I called LuAnn, Laurel's director at the time, and told her that I wanted to surprise Laurel at this year's event. She liked the idea and helped coordinate the surprise.

That evening, we waited for our cue outside a gigantic convention hall. The kids ran all over the place while I fed Meghan a bottle. It was crazy! I couldn't help but think, "It's remarkable what moms do every day." The back door finally opened and I saw Laurel on a big stage with LuAnn, being recognized in front of thousands of women.

"We have a special surprise for you, Laurel," LuAnn said. "There are some friends in the audience tonight who would like to come up and congratulate you on this wonderful achievement and say hello."

A spotlight found us at the back entrance and followed us to the stage. Once the kids spotted their mom, they ran toward the stage and up the stairs to Laurel. I was still making my way down the aisle, holding baby Meghan with a bottle sticking out of the back pocket of my shorts. Laurel couldn't believe we were there to cheer her on. The kids were jumping up and down on stage, hugging and kissing their mom. The emotion in the room was breathtaking.

There was a hush in the room before the "awes" and tears began flowing. As I looked through the bright lights and into the audience, I saw many women and moms wiping away tears.

It was a very special surprise for everyone in attendance – especially Laurel! Operation Bee Surprised was well worth the effort and turned out better than I could have imagined.

Laurel's Parenting Perspective

Hi,

When Bill asked me to say a few things about moms and some things I've done as a mom for his book, I said "sure". As I thought about moms there are so many things to say and so many facets of life that I really don't know where to begin.

I know! I should start with the pregnancy test, "yup, it's the little + sign." Right there all the feelings begin..."Oh, my gosh!", "Oops!", "I've waited so long"! "I can't believe it"!, "What am I gonna do?" Women have the ability to feel so many emotions all at one time, … anxiety, excitement, fear, doubt, anger, joy, happiness, sadness, compassion and numbness. As mother's we can feel 10 different emotions in a 5 minute time slot. We can show empathy while fixing a scraped knee, happily sing to "Row-Row Your Boat" while making cookies, cry during a sad movie, laugh hysterically when your sister calls. It's one of the gifts God gave us. As mother's, we see and feel everything our children see and feel.

The childhood we had and the experiences we've gone through (like high-school, first job), make us who we are today!

So, what makes up Mother's then? Is it patience, compassion, giving time, attention and love? …sometimes totally unappreciated? Is it sleep deprivation when the kids were young, multi-tasking…doing 8 things at once while the kids are in school, squeezing your child so tight they might throw-up when you find out they are all right? Maybe it's surviving when everything is falling apart, worrying until you hear the garage door open and know the kids are safe, learning to let-go when you want to hold tighter, or is it cooking, cleaning, doing home-work...actually what makes up Mother's is all in her heart.

It's what we know in our hearts, that we became the moms we are today. You know the saying, "Mother knows BEST!" or "If momma ain't happy, ain't nobody happy!"

Every mother truly tries to do the very best for her children. At different times in our parenting we have experienced "helicopter mom's" who always make sure their kids have everything they need to a fault. The "tough love mom's" who have to set strict rules for their children and carry out difficult decisions, all the while crying inside and praying to God that their kids will be safe and obey. The "critical mom's" who want their children to be perfect and perfectly-behaved, only to find themselves drowning for solutions when the kids become resentful and rebellious. The struggling mom who works double shifts to put food on the table, always struggling and over-coming obstacles only to find children who are survivors themselves.

And in the end, we are all mothers only trying to do the best we can for our families. Mother's are nurses, pizza makers, accountants, tax collector's, heroes, budget makers, drill sergeants, supervisors, housekeepers, cooks, dare devils, race car drivers, exotic dancers (when they need to be), lovers, movie stars (in their kids eyes), cheerleaders, debaters, bargain hunters, gamblers, counselors, sellers, smart shoppers, gymnasts, monsters in scary movies, snuggly stuffed animals, mail carriers, and the beautiful graceful ballet dancers! "Now, I'm on a roll!"

Mother's are a force, a team! We need to support one another, encourage and help one another, lighten the load for one another, laugh and pray together. We will not be conquered! We will fight! Fight to the Death!

"And to all mothers... get your tennis shoes on and tie them tight! We got things to do! You go girl!"

I'll start with "Lessons Learned and actions taken". Some of these I learned by observation, trial and error and several from my own mother and father, my sisters and my friends. In the following pages, I'll cover topics such as; creating an atmosphere for growth, listening at the right time, finding the potential in every child and enhancing it, looking in the mirror, courage is a tremendous thing, kindling friendships, keeping the little things little, organizing chores and paperwork, organizing life long habits and dinner's on.

Creating an atmosphere for Growth

Here's a hypothetical example:

It's December 17 and the Hansen family is getting ready to go to 16-year-old Valerie's school Christmas concert. Mrs. Hansen has prepared supper ahead of time so things will run smoothly. Just as they sit down to eat; Valerie's 11-year-old sister Carly spills her milk all over the dinner table. Her brother, 13, starts yelling, "There's milk in my food and I'm not going to eat this anymore! You're so stupid!"

Mom hops out of her chair and is busy trying to clean up the counter, the floor and the milk dripping down the cabinet. Valerie says in a very condescending tone, "Carly, you're such a klutz! Now look what you've done; I'm going to be late for my concert! You idiot!" Dad stands up and reaches toward Jack who is now loudly complaining about milk in his food, when the vinaigrette salad dressing tips and spills on Valerie's concert outfit! Now, fuming dad says to mom, "Why do you still use this huge dressing holder anyway. I suppose because you got it from your wonderful brother, who always buys weird stuff!" His wife glares at him and diligently tries to clean both the milk and the vinaigrette.

At that point, Dad tells Jack to shut his mouth and eat his soggy food. Then Valerie gets up and runs to her room in tears while her father is yelling after her to quit saying mean things to her little sister. Mom is not saying a word but is now clanking the dishes into the sink, while Carly is watching the entire situation explode without saying a word.

By now, it's time to go to the concert, which goes from 6:30 to 8:00. No one has eaten, the dishes aren't done, Valerie won't come out of the bathroom because her dress is ruined and her eyes are too red and she wants to skip the concert. Mr. Hansen's blood pressure is probably 150/98 and yells forcefully for everyone to get into the car. They head out to the school.

The concert was great and after listening to the beautiful Christmas music, everyone was feeling a lot better. However, as the Hansen family returns home, the mood returns to gloom-and-doom. The dirty dishes and food left out on the counter staring them right in their faces is reminder of the hurt feelings and brash words exchanged. The energy in the home again remains unhappy and negative.

At this point, the parents can keep the tension in the house, which will result in a negative atmosphere, which harbors negativity in family members, which leads to more doom and gloom, eventually ruining self-esteem and creating unhappiness. Constant negative energy will drain a person three times faster than a person who exerts positive energy to make a change.

The parents need to get the doom and gloom out of the house immediately. It's like opening a window and letting cool, fresh spring air circulate throughout the house after a long, cooped-up freezing winter with all the windows shut. This will take positive energy and creativity, but it's well worth it. It starts with a positive attitude and freeing of the mind, mixed with positive actions and intervention.

Sometimes the change may simply be for one parent to *not react*, saying nothing and just listening. That means listening with an open mind; no eye-brow raising, mouth gestures, smiles or smirks, head raisings, nodding, and absolutely no sighing or heaving breathing. Listen with a pleasant expression and an attitude of understanding and really try to bring the home back to a place of warmth and love where all can relax and grow.

Another change is for one parent to *react* by setting the mood while in the car or upon entering the house. A statement such as, "I feel so good listening to those Christmas songs; let's all work together to get supper ready and get things straightened out. The rest of the night will be fun!" At this point, someone needs to start getting rid of the mess. It only takes one person to be a positive catalyst and turn the entire situation around.

These transformations don't just happen overnight. They require baby steps toward what you want your home to be like. You need to think it, visualize it and anticipate the laughter and the peacefulness in your home. Then slowly your actions will affect the entire family and the mood lightens. Have you ever tried lowering the tone of your voice during difficult times? Amazingly, everyone listens and understands things better; a sigh, a whisper and eye contact were more effective then raising your voice. That's a huge lesson I learned, and I still have to practice it, even the dog cocks his ears when I speak softly. It's the little things that make the difference.

With three children in elementary school all at the same time and one in pre-school, you can image when they all got home at the same time after school and were just so hungry, ravenous! They'd come into the house and make a BEE line to the refrigerator, freezer, cup boards and just grab food of any sort. Wrappers were left out all over the place - ice cream bars, crackers, popsicles, peanut butter and cookies, fruit roll-ups and granola bars, to name a few. They were like scavengers and could eat a box a fruit roll-ups, a box of chewy bars, a jar of fruit cocktail and a box of popsicles in less than 10 minutes. OK, I'm kind of exaggerating, but you get the picture.

This scenario had to stop! I finally figured out that if I wanted them to have healthy snacks, I would have to have it ready when they came home. Light bulb moment! Working parents can set out a box of cereal, bowls and an apple before leaving for work. It seems like the first food item they see when they get home from school; they'll usually reach for and eat. So, I kept fresh fruit out and had a little basket with healthy snacks that were just for after school. Sometimes, I'd made the snack before they came home. I'd pour little bowls of apple sauce, set out a paper plate with crackers and cheese on it along with maybe yogurt, or a bowl of cereal, carrots, popcorn and maybe a rice crispy bar. They'd race home to see what snacks I had put out; eat them with fury and move on to the day's next venture feeling great. Such a small change made a big difference!

One of the greatest lessons I learned wasn't just to listen to my kids, but to listen and be available when they were ready to express themselves. Not when I had the time to listen, but when they were ready to talk. That really seems like a "no brainer" but one that deserves mentioning. In most homes, a great place to gather and talk is in a cozy spot, usually the kitchen. There are also prime times to be available to listen, like after school and right before bed. These prime time periods only last for so long also. Those brief periods of time give you peace of mind and satisfaction that all's right with the world in your kid's eyes!

There's going to be times your not going to be available, and that's okay. No guilt! Just try to create those time slots where you can give your undivided attention to your child. You don't want to miss out on what's been happening in their lives, or the ability to give ideas or strength to your kids.

Kids need reassurance that they are doing the right thing and these are precious times to give that reassurance. I remember my daughter Elizabeth telling me a story of a friend getting laughed at and what she did about it. She was feeling so sorry for her friend and really needed to expound on it! She needed to hear, "You did the right thing!" When we miss the time when our children express themselves, then were missing opportunities for teaching and praise.

Every once in a while this happens when Bill comes home from work. He's tired and probably thinking about a million other things, but he'll say, "Just a minute Joe, give me 10 minutes."

He'll put down his brief case and go up stairs for 10-15 minutes and he'll give his full attention to Joe's story. Once again, this wasn't the best time for Bill to listen, but it was Joe's time to talk. They close the door and nothing interrupts this precious time. If the phone rings, they'll have to call them back or let the answering machine pick it up.

Just a quick addition; Sometimes I interrupt and don't allow the kids to tell the whole story, because I am asking for more detail and questions. Then they sometimes lose their train of thought and they never get to finish their story.

For example; when the kids came home from school (elementary, middle and high school) they were usually busy telling stories and sharing things with each other about classes, tests, teachers, friends, events and just about any subject you could imagine. It's a great opportunity to interject, ask a short question, to give a short praise statement or to just laugh and listen. The kids will enjoy sharing stories and will want to make sure your included in future stories. The secret here is to allow them to continue the story with as few interruptions as possible. We don't mean to squelch the opportunity to hear about interpersonal relationships they have with other people. But by asking too many questions, the child can't finish the story! As parents we sometimes feel like we need to teach a lesson or give a lecture during this time because it is a "teaching moment!" Then the conversation ends quickly with, "Well, I better get started on my homework."

Another prime time to listen is when the kids come home from a sports event, an evening party or after get-togethers with friends. They want to tell you who was there and what happened that night. As a parent those are your golden times to be a part of their lives. Stories are told that are heart-warming and heart-wrenching. It's also a great time to give your kids confidence, "You know what you're doing," "Your sister knows what's going on," "That was a great idea!" or "Your brother knows what to do." It's a time for approval, confidence-building and support!

A lot of times parents think and say; "My kids need to work around my schedules! I don't work around theirs, they work around mine! They'll listen when I say to listen. They'll be quiet when I want them to be quiet. We'll talk when I'm darn good and ready to talk!" That may work for many other things but in order to really hear what your child wants to say, and have them share the details, you need to listen when they are ready to share the events of their lives. If you're too busy watching TV or playing on the computer they will probably get something to eat and drink and go to there rooms. Another lost opportunity to listen when they were ready to talk. Those brief five and ten minute conversations may unveil alarming things that may allow us to encourage better choices. They may stop an action that may be detrimental or they may create opportunities for us and our kids to set goals together, and help fulfill dreams that we maybe didn't know about, if we weren't listening.

Keep the doors of communication open when they are very young and it will continue when they are as old as you. The moral of the story is to listen when they are ready to talk. Develop Ears for your Children!

It's amazing …this listening thing has gone on for years! They even wrote poems about it! Read on…

My grandmother loved to write letters, wonderful letters to everyone, and she always expressed herself in a loving way. She'd out little quotes, words of advice and little poems out of the church bulletin or cooking newsletters, and mail them to me when I was in college. Some were funny, some were wise, some were reminders, but most were outstanding. The one I have kept for more than 35 years still sits at my desk. The edges are torn, the paper has faded and browned, but the message is timeless. This one's from my Grandma Thomas. Thanks grandma…

<u>Take a Moment to Listen</u>

To what your children are trying to say;

Listen today, whatever you do,

Or they won't be there to listen to you.

Listen to their problems. Listen for their needs.

Praise their smallest triumphs.

Praise their smallest deeds.

Tolerate their chatter. Amplify their laughter.

Find out what's the matter.

Find out what they're after.

But tell them that you love them every single night.

And though you scold them, be sure you hold

them tight. Tell them "Everything's all

right; tomorrow's looking bright!"

 Take a moment to listen today to what

your children are trying to say.

Listen today, whatever you do,

and they will come back to listen to you.

Children have many gifts; find the one they sparkle in!

I got some really great advice from a dear friend of mine that has stuck with me since I heard it over 5 years ago. My dear wise friend Connie once told me to find the one thing your child is good at and build that skill or talent to the fullest. Connie said, "Make sure your kids are really good at one thing so they can say, *"I'm really good at that!"*, and genuinely mean it."

My philosophy was to expose my children to several hobbies and sports and allow them to continue the ones they really enjoyed, excelled in and wanted to continue; not the ones I wanted them to be in, but the ones they wanted to really engage in. My third child, Michelle was in softball and could really swing the bat but didn't really want to pursue it. She wanted to be a dancer, but I never really knew a good dance school or how to get her involved. I actually had her take a ballet class at the YMCA when she was in kindergarten and that was the extent of her dancing experience. She was good at swimming, basketball and volleyball, but just wasn't really excited about any of those sports. She kept saying, "I want to be a ballet dancer!" It was pretty obvious that Michelle's one love was dancing!

The dancing story all began when my youngest daughter Meghan saw Emily, her close friend, dance in a huge recital. The room was filled with music, lights, beautiful, graceful dancers all with brilliant costumes, dancing ballet, jazz, hip hop, lyrical and many others gorgeous dances. After the recital, Meghan and Michelle both wanted to get involved in the same dance school. Little did I know that dance would make a major impact on their lives and become so instrumental in their growing years.

Connie, who also had a daughter in dance, encouraged me to have Michelle get involved in competitive dance, so she could really learn the dance moves. I was apprehensive because Michelle had only been in the Eau Claire School of Dance for about 1½ years and was a beginner. I wondered if she would be able to learn quick enough to compete with such little experience.

I'll never forget the night Connie said to me, "Laurel, look into my eyes, look at me," as she put her hands on my shoulders. "Find the one thing that Michelle is excited about and good at and grow it! Every kid should have one thing that they are really good at! Every kid should be able to say, 'I'm a great at _____ or I'm really good at _____.' Give her the best opportunity you can at what she loves! Dance! "

What great advice! Find the one thing your child is really good at, foster it, build it, enhance it… it doesn't matter what it is, fishing, hunting, bowling, hockey, math, baseball, spelling, debating … whatever it is, find it because it will impact their lives, boost their confidence, self-esteem, self-worth and feelings of accomplishment!

I enrolled Michelle in competitive dance, just as Connie had encouraged me to do and she just improved and excelled with the competitive classes. Several years passed and the exciting part is that I got to watch her dance on the varsity high school team and competitively compete in Orlando, for the Universal Dance Association. Her team took eleventh in the Nation!

No Quitters Allowed

Sometimes finding that one thing kids are good at, gets a little to complicated and a little to hard for the kids and they want to quit! When my son, was in fifth grade he was on a baseball team and the loved it! Just as he was starting to be a really good hitter and could belt the ball way out in left field he got hit by the ball. Then when he was up to bat, he got hit again in the same game. Hard! The next game he was apprehensive and do you believe it? He got hit in the arm again at that game. That was it, he wanted to quit, but he didn't! Instead, he showed up at the next game! What courage he had! I told him he was courageous and very brave!

It takes hard work to be good at anything and its important children don't become quitters. "You are not a quitter!" "You and they will overcome!" That reminds me of the wimpy guy on "Lost in Space", his name was Dr. Smith. Do you remember him? The robot would swing his arms and say; Warning! Warning…Will Robertson! "CRUSH, KILL, AND DESTROY!" Warning! Warning…Will Robertson! "CRUSH, KILL, AND DESTROY!" All Dr. Smith ever wanted to do was run and save himself! He didn't care about Will Robertson or the others. He was the epitome of a quitter!

Just like Dr. Smith, when hobbies and anything worth doing got hard he'd quit. With our children, try to talk it out despite the tears. It's a huge lesson for your children; if they overcome tough, difficult times they will feel great pride and a sense of accomplishment that they overcame obstacles. Keep your children serving others and doing things for others that is when true happiness is experienced! This is a true example of raising your child with praise, which will help them overcome adversity in the workforce, in college and in marriage.

Mirror Images repeating itself

As parents, we need to allow our children to dream of a wonderful future and to be the best they can be. That means we need to be the best we can be! When they look in our mirrors do they like what they see? Children observe the way we talk, eat, think and dream. They watch how we perceive our lives, our jobs, our families, our chores, and they usually share our perception because of our influence and values.

Have you ever heard your child repeat something publicly, that you said privately? For example, at student evaluations, it's just the teacher, your spouse, your child and you! The teacher is speaking, "Mrs. Hansen do you realize Cory has been late to class eight times in the last three weeks?" Cory says to the teacher, "My dad says, your underwear must be on way to tight, it's not a big deal!" CAUGHT! REALLY CAUGHT! How's that mirror image look that you gave your child? When you complain about your job, your kid may be thinking "Why would I want to do what my parents do?" or "Why should I even go to college?" It's amazing what thoughts go through those little brains, and people don't realize how perceptive they are. My dad used to say, "You can do whatever you want to do, just make it matter. Make a difference in the world. Have a mind of your own. You can be whatever you want to be if you set your mind to it. Do it right or don't do it at all. Play hard and study hard but don't get the two mixed up!" The moral of the story; Mirrors don't lie and your kid is painting one of you! What examples are you painting for them to follow!

My mom and dad gave me courage by kind words but also with assertiveness. I was taught to stick up for myself, compliment others, and be kind and respectful to the elderly. When I picked up a quarter that someone dropped or held the door for someone, they'd give approval by a little wink or a gentle squeezing of my hand. Dad would hold my hand just firm enough that I knew I was safe and to stay close, yet loose enough I could let go and get away. It's the little things that sometimes give the most reassurance and love.

There goes 3 year old Susie, carrying a full pitcher of cherry kool-aid to the opposite side of the room. Her older brother says, "STOP! GIVE IT TO ME, YOU CAN"T DO THAT! YOU'LL SPILL!" Mom says, "It's okay, she knows what she's doing!" Susie is thrilled with her mother's approval and confidence in her. She becomes courageous at this point, stands up and does it again, this time beaming with smiles. When she begins to spill, Suzie quickly looks at her mother for disapproval or approval. Smiling at her, she continues to try and accepts small spills and moves on to better and bigger things. Another version would be to turn your head and act like you didn't hear or see the spill. Don't react! Sometimes as parents we need to close our eyes to innocent mistakes or act very non sealant about things.

When you say…"Show me what you got!" "You know what to do!" They believe in themselves. Kids need us to believe in them. Sometimes we need to walk away and let them make mistakes too! Just look the other way, don't react much and say, "Gee Susie, what are you going to do now?"

Another example: Mary is getting ready for Halloween and can't find the shoes she wants to wear for her costume. She searches and searches knowing they were just in her room last night. It's getting closer to the time when she has to leave with her friends and Mary starts to panic and yells for someone to help her find her shoes. After looking for a couple minutes her mom says, "Mary, why don't you just wear those green tennis shoes?" Mary who is frustrated rolls her eyes and says under her breath, "How weird is she?" Now the courage for the parent is to be non sealant, able to act like they didn't see it. You'd probably want to tell her to go to her room, but instead you act like you didn't see or hear it. Mary leaves with her friends wearing black shoes instead of the shoes she wanted to wear and is thinking she is getting away with rolling her eyes and mumbling a hurtful phrase to you. Later, after the Halloween party is over and your daughter is home, you sit down with her and tell her how surprised you were when she rolled her eyes and heard what she said. In a very quiet but stern voice you can tell her "Not to do it again and that the comment was very hurtful and when she ready to give you her apology." This is way more effective than catching her right at the time she is rolling her eyes because so many things were going on at the time she was looking for her shoes. She has time to think about it and isn't distracted by her friends, shoes or time. We had to look at the situation and have the courage to NOT REACT every time.

Just food for thought...Have you ever seen a friend tell another friend, "You are so stupid and you can't do anything right? Just kidding!" Sure, they might be teasing, but consciously they still mean it! Have you ever had someone tell you that you're fat? Then they say, "Just kidding!" First of all the person asking the question had to first think your fat in order to even mention it in the first place. Secondly, by saying just kidding, they realized they were wrong in saying it or couldn't believe they just said it, or will take the wrath of the friend, so they say "just kidding!"

Friendships allow you to get along together in the World!

Friendships are priceless. Every friendship teaches your child something. They learn sharing, understanding and competition. They learn to like themselves and they even learn to defend themselves. Having friends also prevents your children from thinking only about themselves. It creates an atmosphere of creativity and imagination.

It seems like friendships started in pre-school. I'd have a play day and invite pre-school kids over and we'd make home-made pizzas and go to the pool or go places together, but a child with friends is a happy child.

We had one rule in our house about sharing! When the kids were smaller and if they were fighting over the same toy, it was a rule in my house that neither of them got to play with the toy. It was put on the mantle where they could see it but couldn't play with it until they learned to share. Everyone who came over to "The Callaghan" house knew the rules about sharing. Consistency in discipline allowed everyone to know the right way and the wrong way, without saying a word.

Prudent Poetry

One of my favorite poems about life, "Children Learn What They Live," was written by Dorothy Law Nolte. The poem is about what children learn, but I think it's for all ages. The poem is a tremendous reminder for us all.

CHILDREN LEARN WHAT THEY LIVE

If a child lives with criticism,
he learns to condemn.

If a child lives with hostility,
he learns to fight.

If a child lives with fear,
he learns to be apprehensive.

If a child lives with pity,
he learns to feel sorry for himself.

If a child lives with ridicule,
he learns to be shy.

If a child lives with jealousy,
he learns what envy is.

If a child lives with shame,
he learns to feel guilty.

If a child lives with encouragement,

he learns to be confident.

If a child lives with tolerance,
he learns to be patient.

If a child lives with praise,
he learns to be appreciative.

If a child lives with acceptance,
he learns to love.

If a child lives with approval,
he learns to like himself.

If a child lives with recognition,
he learns that it is good to have a goal.

If a child lives with sharing,
he learns about generosity.

If a child lives with honesty and fairness,
he learns what truth and justice are.

If a child lives with security,
he learns to have faith in himself and in those about him.

If a child lives with friendliness,
he learns that the world is a nice place in which to live.

If you live with serenity,
your child will live with peace of mind.

With what is your child living?

Household Duties

Laurel's advice: Don't let the little things become BIG things. I really shouldn't be offering advice because there are times when I am in way over my head and let the little things become big things. So I have learned from being there and have learned a few things that may make a difference for others. I believe in systems, routines and organization. If things are organized you have more time to spend with your family.

Try to find a place for everything. The first step to organization is having places to put things, especially the little things that drive you nuts when you search for them, like car keys, remote controls, scissors, nail clippers and wallets. Have a specific spot or container or basket to keep them in. It may take a little behavior modification and reminding to keep them there, but it will really help.

Take for example the PS3 Video System for kid's games. Put the system, the games, controllers and all the cords in one place. When your kids are finished playing with it, remind them where it belongs. If they forget, put the PS3 system and its components in the spot you have created. Over a period of time it will become known that the PS3 system goes in that particular spot. Also, have a location where you always put your pictures and camera and all of its components. It will save a lot of time and frustration.

Paperwork! Paperwork! Mail! Mail! It never stops! I'd really encourage you to get a basket or tray for only the important mail such as bills, bank statements and letters that require attention in the next week. In another section, place schedules and rosters. Have you ever searched for a roster to call a coach or to find the time of a game and the roster is gone? I remember one time when Michelle had to be at her softball game at 6:30, it started at 7:00, and it was 6:15. I have pile of paperwork and couldn't find the roster. I had fifteen minutes to find the roster which had the directions to whatever field we were playing on. When I finally found the directions I was sweating, the children were broiling in their coats and on the schedule was written that it was my turn to bring the team treats and beverages.

The next section is for paperwork that requires action. For example, an invitation you need to respond to, a statement you need to clarify, a form you need to re-mail or something else you have to do with that piece of mail. I also have a separate spot for coupons. Another for business cards and passwords is a good idea as well. I keep business cards of everyone that has serviced my family. I can reference the names and phone numbers of the electrician who serviced us four years ago, the plumber, the garage door guy, and our orthodontist with the flick of my wrist. Otherwise I'd forget the information in a few years (actually a couple of months, but who's counting?).

Another organizational tip is to have a standing file where you can slide information into. The four slots are 1. To do, 2. To read 3. To mail and 4. To file.

Every day, no matter what, certain things had to get done. If they didn't, I'd pay the consequences later. It's like brushing my teeth, I just do it! Coffee is always first! Music helps most of the time! Then, roll up my sleeves and get to work. I load the dishwasher, throw in a load of clothes, hang up towels, do another load of clothes, and put a load away. That had to be done each day!

Every day I'd try to clean or organize one shelf or drawer somewhere in the house. (Don't cheat; it has to be a different shelf each day.) You can tidy up the bathroom and the shelves that were done last week, but a new shelf needs to be straightened that wasn't the day before. (I know you're thinking that you could clean the same shelf everyday and it'd still be messy the next. That's OK, that's just the way things are. You just need to accept that and tidy up that same shelf over and over again.)

These are the little things that need to be done each day so they might as well be done with some fun! Basic work must be done each day just to keep up; it's like brushing your teeth. Completing such daily tasks helps you survive and maintain sanity. It creates order and consistency so life doesn't become overwhelming. Music makes it easy and fun most of the time! When things are fairly organized, you can think straight, relax and enjoy your children and the little things they say and do, without feeling like you have to do something or be somewhere else.

When you keep up with daily chores, you accept things for what they are! Acceptance that there is toothpaste in the sink each morning, that dirty socks are always found at the bottom of the bed. Acceptance that you have to clean the same shelf every day because it never stays clean, that the floor needs to be cleaned every day because the dog and the kids bring mud in the house and forget to take off their shoes. If you can accept these things as normal, you have taken baby steps to creating a happy home.

It's easy to complain every day about the mud in the kitchen and raise your voice and sigh, but you're only frustrating yourself. No one else really cares! Sorry, I know that's hard to hear, but they don't care! So, Quit beating yourself up; it doesn't help anyone. Just clean it up and mark it off! Complaining usually causes your children to "tune you out" and pull away. They don't want to be around someone who is complaining about the same things over and over. Those feelings of frustration come from disorganization and non-acceptance.

Kids can tell when you accept them despite their faults and love them anyway. You can see it in the sparkle of their eyes when you notice who they are becoming and what they have accomplished. Raise with praise comes from gentle reminders - a soft touch, hugs and squeezes - they get from you each day, plus the interest you have in them. Accept them just the way they are with unconditional love. I always said to my children, "I may not like what you've done and no matter what you've done, I will always love you! Tell me the truth and I will try to help you!"

When kids are young, it is harder to find time to get it all done, but you will find a routine that will work. We used to eat breakfast, play games for about an hour, go for a walk around the block or play outside and get cleaned up. Sesame Street was a lifesaver because they'd watch it while I made lunch. I'd tape Sesame Street and Blue's Clues so I could turn on the TV when it was appropriate for my schedule and on the Callaghan's timeline, not the television station's schedule. After lunch we'd play for a while and then it was nap time. It's amazing how much a mom can get done in 1½

164

or 2 hours while the children nap. I recall running around the house like a maniac getting things done that couldn't get done when the kids were awake!

Just don't get hung up on perfectionism and try to do too much! Just tighten your belt and so something…anything! Because I had washed the clothes, Joe's T-ball uniform was ready for the morning game; because I'd organized the bathroom shelf, I noticed we needed more toothpaste and deodorant, plus I found Michelle's toothbrush that had fallen into the hairclip container. The little things done each day create some sense of harmony.

Also, there are weekly routines that you may want to try. For example; Monday is dusting and floor day. Dust and clean all floors, hardwood, bathroom, vacuum carpets… This is so funny! Several years ago I was complaining about the kitchen floor needing to be cleaned. I really don't like to wash the kitchen floor; I'd rather clean the bathroom than the kitchen floor. I was putting it off and putting it off until finally, after several days of feeling irritated that the floor was dirty, I cleaned it. It took me about one minute to get a bucket of hot water, some cleaning detergent and a rag and another nine to actually clean the floor. I probably complained to myself and felt irritated for probably five total hours, when it took me only about ten minutes to clean the kitchen floor. I felt so good having it clean. So the moral of the story is to just *attack* the kitchen floor. Attack it! Now I clean the floor with a whole different attitude. It takes a lot more energy to procrastinate than to just do it.

Tuesdays are great days for working in the laundry room and bathrooms. Put all the towels and clothes away that didn't get put away and clean the shelves in the laundry room. Disinfect all bathrooms! Remember the floors were done yesterday. The faster you work the more time there is to have fun! How many of watched the game show "Beat the Clock." I loved that show! The host would set a timer and contestants needed to accomplish several tasks, like emptying three garbage cans, putting four logs in a pile or stacking 12 books and dumping water on someone's head,

165

within 90 seconds. It was hilarious. Look at picking up your house in that manner. Set the microwave timer for 15 minutes. When it beeps, you're done.

Wednesday's are great for office organizing and sorting all day long! Pay bills, go through all mail and do something with it or pitch it! Take those collapsing piles of stuff and get rid of them. It's paperwork day! After this day...everything is downhill for the week. Thursday's are bedroom cleaning days, and grocery shopping. Friday's are great days to do something for each person in your house. Make a favorite recipe for your husband, cookies for your kid's, clean the quilting room for yourself. Saturdays are fun days with the family and Sundays are outdoor yard work and fun!

Check out the website www.flylady.com the site suggests not letting things get too bad or difficult and cleaning a little in all areas of your house each day. My sister, Elaine turned me on to the site and it's great! Thanks Elaine!

Now don't laugh! I like to de-clutter my house in 15 minutes so I can clean easier each day. If you did this each day for only 15 minutes you'd have a cleaner house in one week! I call it speed cleaning my house! Take 15 minutes each day and go from room to room and put things in their place. You'll find things that don't belong in the living room so put them in a big, sturdy basket. Then you're off to the family room to tidy up; put items that don't belong in that room in the basket. Then you may find things already in the basket from the living room that belong in the family room that you got from the living room, so you take those things out of the basket and put them where they belong. Then you go to the bedroom and de-clutter things that shouldn't be in the bedroom and put them in the basket, then tidy-up and so on...

You may be thinking it would take 15 minutes to just clean the dining room table. That's OK! At least you're able to see a clean spot on the dining room table in 15 minutes and you're that much closer to a clean home! A happy home! Just take one thing at a time and put it where it belongs. Then the next day take 15 minutes and clean just the tables in the living room. The next day take 15 minutes and clean the dining room table and living room again and tidy up and organize the pantry with the time that's left. *Slowly* but surely you'll get a grip on things.

Prioritizing

I like to prioritize things into three categories; 1. Important / urgent and 2. Important / non-urgent and 3. Non-urgent and not-important.

Important and Urgent. Examples are: time-sensitive deadlines, emergencies and high-priority tasks. For example, property taxes needing to be paid by July 31 so you avoid interest and fees and it's July 31st; paying bills on time; having your airline tickets with you arrive at the airport; making sure your power-point presentation is completed by its deadline; getting to your child's doctors appointment on time; putting out a fire; running your child to the emergency room with a burned finger. This is what I call the "panic mode" category.

Important and Non-urgent. Examples are: prevention, activities in line with your values, identifying possibilities, planning strategies, relaxation and keeping the home clean and healthy. For example, keeping your gas tank full, having yearly exams and health physicals, taking your kids to the playground and planning a family vacation, having healthy food in the pantry so meals can be made. I call this my safe and productive category, the all's right with the world category, because I know that accomplishing things in this category will prevent complete chaos and keep me away from the panic category.

Non-urgent and Not-important. Examples are: getting on the computer to check something and two hours later your still on the computer, talking on the phone, watching TV, taking naps for hours, golfing, fishing, quilting, taking a bath for way to long, listening to music….

If you spend most of your time in the second category, you'll have time for yourself, your family, your husband and be able spend that time in a positive way because you're caught up and not drowning in things you have to do. You'll have more time to listen to your children and address the needs of your spouse and have time to tell stories and laugh and create a loving environment.

These are extreme analogies, but just think for a minute if you didn't change the smoke detectors batteries and a grease fire started in the stove. The smoke detector wouldn't go off because the batteries are dead and suddenly there are blood-curdling screams coming from the kitchen. If you would have changed the smoke detectors batteries as a routine task, it would have stayed in the #2 category (the everything's under control category); instead it raced to the #1 (emergency) category.

Let's take visiting your grandparents or keeping in touch with family members, which is a #2 category; it's a non-urgent but important thing to do. There are always other things to do and you think your grandparents will understand your busy schedule, which they probably do, but they still want to see you. Time passes and they call and you say you'll visit soon. They don't complain that you don't visit but they call and say they miss you and again you tell them you will visit soon. They say you haven't visited for six months now.

Time passes, you have other things to do and you just don't make it a priority to see them as a year passes. You no longer hear from them, but you think about them. Then your parents tell you they are ill and want to see you. Your #2 category just changed to a #1 gotta-see-them-within-a-month category. If you would have seen them three months ago, you would have stayed in the #2 category (the everything-is-under-control category).

I think life would be much easier if we spent zero time in the #1 category (which is completely unrealistic, but one can hope), 75 percent in the #2 category, and 25 percent in the #3 category. That's how I feel right now. I may change my mind in the next

10 minutes, but right now that sounds pretty good. After all, I'm getting to the age when I have to think and rethink and change my mind at times!

The Dinner Bell

My mom was the master of whipping together a great meal in minutes. She taught me well, and I'd like to share a few of the ideas that have helped me. There are a few items you should always have on hand, like a master grocery list of staples in case you don't know what to make for supper. This could include canned tuna, canned chicken, Bisquick, hot and regular cereal, peanut butter, potatoes, rice, canned vegetables, muffin mixes, nuts, canned fruit, flour, sugar, oil, spices, noodles, spaghetti sauces, Worcestershire sauce and other seasonings, mustards, kidney beans, tomatoes, spinach and sauerkraut to have on hand for Reuben's … just add the cheese and corn beef and slap on bread. Yum!

I always have the ingredients on hand for some of my favorite dishes: tuna wraps, spaghetti, cheese steak sandwiches, chicken, Patti melts, fajitas, stir fry, and Rueben's. Having these things on hand prevents my family from eating out and allows us to have healthier meals. Chicken is always in my freezer and also in cans in my pantry. When I prepare chicken, I always cook an entire three-pound bag of breasts, seasoning them with garlic salt, pepper and sometimes rosemary.

The first night we eat a chicken dinner with potatoes and all the fixings. The cooked chicken I have left just needs to be heated for a chicken Caesar salad or chicken parmesan with noodles and marinara sauce with parmesan cheese on top the next night. Leftovers can be placed in a freezer bag and frozen to be used later. I like to buy my meat in large quantities when it's on sale, so I usually have pre-made hamburger patties, fish and pork chops ready to go in the freezer. The night before a meal, I just pull out the meal and allow it to thaw overnight. When I cook up the ground chuck for chili or whatever I'm making, I cook all the meat with garlic salt, pepper and onions. Whatever is left over from that meal, I will put in 1½-pound increments in the freezer for a rainy day. When we want spaghetti, the meat is ready to go and all I have to do is cook the noodles. It really saves time.

Potluck dinners seem to happen quite frequently at my house, so I usually make my favorite, a pizza hot dish similar to lasagna. Just being prepared with the ingredients and knowing I can whip it up in 20 minutes is a huge relief. Sometimes I'll also bring grapes, strawberries and watermelon to potlucks. Just knowing a few favorites when potlucks arise is helpful. Planning ahead alleviates a lot of tension, makes it fun and allows you to look forward to an event.

I'd encourage you to Hug yourself and love yourself. Live within your budget if possible! Be proud of your family and accept its members for who they are. Take care of yourself; try to get enough sleep, take vitamins, exercise and laugh everyday. Laugh some and then some more! Talk less and listen more, because less can be more.

Simplify your home and your life and try to get organized. Be sure to get extras, like an extra set of house keys and an extra set of car keys. Bury them under your rhubarb or another unique location. Pray for strength and for God to bless you! That's all you need. He's in charge and knows everything. All will be according to His plan and not ours anyway. Every night love yourself a little more. Sing, sing louder! And don't ever lose the kid in you!

In closing, below is one of the most beautiful stories written about Mother's, it's called moms! For those who are lucky to still be blessed with your Mom, this is beautiful. For those who aren't, this is even more beautiful. I received it from my sister, Michele and I have to share it with you all! Thanks Michele!

God Bless You!

Laurel

The young mother set her foot on the path of life. "Is this the long way?" she asked. And the guide said "Yes, and the way is hard, and you will be old before you reach the end of it. But the end will be better than the beginning." The young mother was happy, and she would not believe that anything could be better than these years. So she played with her children, she fed them and bathed them, taught them how to tie their shoes and ride a bike, and reminded them to feed the dog and do their homework and brush their teeth. The sun shone on them and the young Mother cried, "Nothing will ever be lovelier than this."

Then the nights came, and the storms and the path was sometimes dark, and the children shook with fear and cold, and the mother drew them close and covered them with her arms and the
children said, "Mother, we are not afraid, for you are near, and no harm can come."

And the morning came, and there was a hill ahead, and the children climbed and grew weary, and the mother was weary. But at all times she said to the children, a little patience and we are there."

So the children climbed and as they climbed they learned to weather the storms. And with this, she gave them strength to face the world. Year after year she showed them compassion, understanding, hope, but most of all......unconditional love. And when they reached the top they said, "Mother, we would not have done it without you."

The days went on, and the weeks and the months and the years, and the mother grew old and she became little and bent. But her children were tall and strong, and walked with courage. And the mother, when she lay down at night, looked up at the stars and said, "This is a better day than the last, for my children have learned so much and are now passing these traits on to their children."

And when the way became rough for her, they lifted her, and gave her their strength, just as she had given them hers.

One day they came to a hill, and beyond the hill they could see a shining road and golden gates flung wide.

And Mother said: "I have reached the end of my journey. And now I know the end is better than the beginning, for my children can walk with dignity and pride, with their heads held high, and so can their children after them." And the children said, "You will always walk with us, Mother, even when you have gone through the gates. And they stood and watched her as she went on alone, and the gates closed after her.

And they said: "We cannot see her, but she is with us still.

A Mother is more than a memory. She is a living presence. Your Mother is always with you. She's the whisper of the leaves as you walk down the street, she's the smell of certain foods you remember, flowers you pick and perfume that she wore, she's the cool hand on your brow when you're not feeling well, she's your breath in the air on a cold winters day. She is the sound of the rain that lulls you to sleep, the colors of a rainbow, she is your birthday morning. Your Mother lives inside your laughter. And she's crystallized in every tear drop. A mother shows every emotion... happiness, sadness, fear, jealousy, love, hate, anger, helplessness, excitement, joy, sorrow and all the while hoping and praying you will only know the good feelings in life. She's the place you came from, your first home, and she's the map you follow with every step you take. She's your first love, your first friend, even your first enemy, but nothing on earth can separate you. Not time, not space.......not even death!

Chapter 6
Just a Spoonful of Sugar

In my opinion, the best times in life are when you are a kid and you have no worries, no responsibilities, and all you have to do is just enjoy growing up.

Two movies that rank high on my list of all time favorites are "The Sound of Music" and "Mary Poppins" – both rated Four Star by the motion picture industry. The music in both shows is filled with timeless lyrics and beautifully composed melodies that bring back memories of being a kid in the 1960's.

While writing this book, I realized a stark similarity with both films. Each blockbuster tells a similar story of children longing for their parents' affection and selfish parents who don't seem to have time for their kids. The fact that Julie Andrews starred in each film is remarkable; she reminds me so much of my sister Margaret. As Fruelein Maria, she brings color, life and love into a home that was run by an Austrian naval commander who summoned his children with a dog whistle.

Baron von Trapp eventually admitted to Maria that he didn't know his children very well and that he didn't spend much time with them. Maria taught Captain von Trapp and the children about hope and optimism through her gift of music:

"Girls in white dresses with blue satin sashes,

snowflakes that stay on my nose and eye lashes,

silver white winters that melt into springs,

these are a few of my favorite things...

...When the dog bites, when the bee stings,

when I'm feeling sad,

I simply remember my favorite things,

and then I don't feel so bad."

Maria brought the sound of music and happiness into a cold, heartless, regimented boot camp and helped the children and father reunite.

Mary Poppins arrived on a magic umbrella to answer the advertisement from Jane and Michael Banks. Their parents, George and Winifred, employed nannies to run their house and raise their kids, while they were busy keeping a schedule, making money and wrapped up in the suffragette women's lib movement; each running from their responsibilities as parents. Mary Poppins showed them how to enjoy their children and laugh again and ultimately to direct their attention towards their children and not themselves. The Poppins woman left the Banks family flying a kite together in the park and feeding tuppins to the birds. In the end, the children became the focus of the parents.

The message in both films: Get to know your kids while you can by spending time with them whenever you can.

If you want to know how you're doing as a parent, take a look at your kids; they are a direct reflection of you. Our children may inherit our eyes, nose, dimples, laugh and smile, but they also become heir to everything from our disposition to our attitude. We set the example for them to follow. We are their first and most influential teachers.

Nothing is more upsetting as a parent than to watch your children argue and fight with each other. Consequently, nothing is more upsetting and unsettling to a child than to watch their parents argue and fight with each other.

The way we are raised has everything to do with the type of person we become as well as the peace of mind and level of happiness we enjoy throughout our life.

My theory is that the reason why God gave children an abundance of courage when they are born is because he knew parents would knowingly or unknowingly discourage their kids throughout their young life. And not just parents, but siblings as well. Younger siblings look up to their older brothers and sisters with great admiration. I know I did and still do. Unfortunately, there are some older siblings who don't realize how much they are adorned or understand that what they say and do has a major impact on their younger brother or sister's self esteem.

I believe what happens is that a person can only handle so much criticism (some more than others) and after awhile, the constant put-down and discouragement eats away at that God given supply of inherent bravery. You become unsure of yourself, depressed and eventually an unhappy soul. All that negative input leaves a lasting effect that is difficult to shake.

The last thing you want to see as a parent is for your child to become constantly worried, confused, rejected, lonely, fearful, paranoid, or isolated.

I know some people my age and older that look back on their childhood and still long for the affection from their parents and still harbor deep resentment from parental guidance or lack thereof. Poor parenting can have lasting effects.

How strange it must be for some people to go through life and have no respect for their mother or father, much less an ongoing relationship while they're still alive.

Constant discouragement, whether it be verbal, or through negative body language, will erode a person's self confidence and greatly diminish their self worth.

In 1971, Albert Mehrabian's research, (currently a Professor Emeritus of Psychology at UCLA) concluded that,

"There are three elements in any face-to-face communication: words, tone of voice, and body language. These three elements account differently for the meaning of the message, words account for 7%, tone of voice accounts for 38%, and body language accounts for 55% of the message."

If communication is over 90% about tone and body language, we should watch how we say what we say to our children.

Encouragement will only add to a young child's self esteem and help them feel glad about who they are. If you treat your kids with respect and tell them you love them and that you are proud of them at the appropriate time, you can't help but build their self confidence. You will have instilled in your children a major asset that will help them throughout their life and give them the inner strength to accomplish anything they set out to do.

My parents made a conscious effort to raise me with kindness and a supportive tone. When I made a mistake, they looked at as an opportunity to show me how to do it right. Not focus on the wrong.

If your child accidentally drops a cup of grape juice on your living room carpet, do you freak out because the carpet might stain, raise your voice in anger and begin to reprimand your child? Or do you rise above the dilemma, and understand that it was an accident and begin the cleanup process? How you react is so critical.

I don't think parents realize how much their kids observe, analyze and idolize their every word and action. Many parents seem to react like the child was purposely trying to cause a problem. For example, your child accidently wets his bed and needs your help to clean up the linens. He's already embarrassed about waking up in another puddle of piddle and is disappointed in himself for wetting the bed for the umpteenth time. He walks in your room and says, "Mom, Dad, I wet my bed – again!" If you react with an upset irritated tone and scold your child, you blew it! You had a chance to be understanding and helpful, and instead you only made the situation worse by thinking about yourself (and the work it will be to clean the sheets and air out the stained mattress) instead of your child. Don't be a reactive parent.

I know all too well because I was that kid who wet my bed constantly. My parents' proactive approach included a plastic mattress protector and infinite patience. But their tone and body language was never condescending.

How you handle unexpected events with your children is so important, and we know that body language and tone of voice is everything when it comes to interpretive communication. When you yell at your kids, they become defensive and tune you out.

My son Joe came home from grade school one day and said, "Dad, I really like my 4th grade teacher." I asked him why and he replied, "She never yells at us, even when we make a mistake." The teacher's name was Miss Lee (Gerry Lee Langer), who reminds me a lot of my sister Mary, always kind and understanding and easy to be around. Miss Lee taught simple things like when the class was going on a field trip and a student needed a permission slip signed by their parent, she instructed them to wait until the parents aren't busy or distracted and then explain the event and obtain their signature. Her teaching skills were exceptional.

How fortunate for those kids to have a teacher like Miss Lee who can enjoy her students, maintain control in the classroom and not have to raise her voice and yell to be heard. Teaching a room full of 10-year-olds must be trying. I'm sure her 4th graders constantly tested her patience, but she rose above the challenging situations and maintained her composure and tone at all times. Parenting is no different.

My daughter Michelle came home from Meadowview Elementary School one day and gave me a round sticker that simply said "Listen and Learn." I find it interesting that God gave us the ability to perform many functions at the same time, but one thing we can't do very well is talk and listen at the same time. I stuck the message in the inside of my wallet so that I would be reminded of that fabulous advice.

When our kids were young, I remember asking them to clean up their toys in the play room or organize their bedrooms, and they would react as though I had just pulled out a glowing green rock from the planet Krypton. The mere mention of cleaning up or performing manual labor knocked them to their knees and eventually glued them flat to the floor. I suppose I could have gotten upset and scream, *"I told you kids to clean up your rooms so get moving right now!"* - But why do that? Seeing my three oldest children - Elizabeth, Joseph and Michelle lying on the floor and hopelessly pleading their case with no effect was actually humorous to me. I would just laugh out loud and then scrape them off the floor one by one and send them to their rooms to start cleaning up. I suppose I could have bribed them and said *"If you clean up your rooms right now, then I will take you to Dairy Queen and give you an ice cream cone."* But why would I do that? My parents never bribed me as a kid. If they wanted me to do something, they would simply ask. Nor did they ever pay me to do work around the house. They taught me to be helpful to others and if work needed to be done – then do it. I actually think if I was bribed or got paid to clean around the house, it wouldn't have been as rewarding.

I was fortunate and surprised that our youngest daughter Meghan didn't suffer from the kryptonite-like effects that affected her older siblings. In fact, of our four children, Meghan was most helpful when it came to cleaning up around the house. From a typical birth order profile, the youngest usually lets everyone else do the work for them, but not her. She would clean the kitchen, organize her bedroom or do a load of laundry without being asked.

At a young age, I noticed Joseph had a knack for approaching anyone and making new friends with people, no matter the age range. He felt comfortable talking to anyone from five to 95. Oftentimes, I would find him carrying on a conversation with someone in the store or in the doctor's office that he had just met. He was born fearless – like the rest of us!

When Joe was eight years old, we attended a New Year's Eve celebration at the Eau Claire Convention Center. One of the many activities for kids included karaoke auditions. Joe walked up to the Rock & Roll To Go champ, who was about 28 years old and asked him if he had the song "Dreamer" by the English band Supertramp. When the DJ told Joseph that he didn't have that song in his vast library, Joe said "No problem, I'll sing it anyway." The DJ seemed startled by this young contestant's plan and said, "You want to sing it without the words or the music?" Joe smiled at him and said, "Sure!" So without the words on the monitor or the accompanying music, Joseph stood up on stage with himself and the microphone and sang:

Dreamer, you know you are a dreamer

Well can you put your hands in your head, oh no!

I said dreamer, you're nothing but a dreamer

Well can you put your hands in your head, oh no!

I said 'Far out, - What a day, a year, a laugh it is!

You know, well you know you had it comin' to you,

Now there's not a lot I can do,

If I can see something

You can see anything you want boy

If I could be someone

You can be anyone, celebrate boy.

Well if I can do something,

If you could do something,

If I can do anything -

Well can you do something out of this world?

I was so proud of Joseph to stand up there in front of hundreds of people and wing it. It told me a lot about the confidence that he had in himself. He's a born entertainer!

When he was a toddler, baby Joe had severe speech and learning delays. His fine motor and gross motor skills were way behind the average 14-month-old, so much so that he didn't walk until he was 20 months old. One strength Joseph did have on his side was the tremendous courage he was born with. Prior to walking, he improvised by hopping about the house on his knees. I remember watching my son leap along with red carpet burns on his knees and being amazed at his determination to get around – wanting so badly to walk. At times it made me cry. Thanks to Laurel's intuition and pediatric training, she enrolled Joseph into every early intervention program available through the Eau Claire public school system as well as the programs offered through the UWEC. Laurel took Joe to see Early Development Specialists and speech therapists that helped him develop these critical life skills. Because of talented specialists like Carol Hossman and Judy Harrell, you would never know Joseph had speech delays when he was young. In fact, he is a master of many voices and wants to get into the voice-over business someday.

My daughter Elizabeth gave me a book last Christmas titled "101 Reasons God Made Dads" copyright 2007, Family Christian Stores. It's a compilation of classic sayings wrapped into one book. I wanted to share just a few:

God made dads so they could show their kids how to…….Remain Calm.

"One of the nice things about problems is that a good many of them do not exist except in our own imagination." Steve Allen

"Worry and anxiety are sand in the machinery of life; faith is the oil." E. Stanley Jones

God made dads to help kids learn how to…….Be Happy.

"The happiest people in the world are not those who have no problems, but the people who have learned to live with those things that are less than perfect."

James Dobson

God made dads so they could show kids…..How to make things happen.

"He who waits until circumstances completely favor his undertaking will never accomplish anything." *Martin Luther*

This book is a story about raising children in a positive light, a beautiful concept my parents adapted when I was born. Children are a gift from God; and as parents we are entrusted with that gift and given the huge responsibility to raise our children to the best of our ability. It is up to us to help them to learn right from wrong, as well as to teach them how to be responsible and have strong morals and instill important concepts such as common sense. We only have them under our guidance for a brief time and have to make the most of each day they are in tow.

We must encourage our children and treat them with respect and allow them to develop into considerate responsible adults. We have to teach them to be kind, understanding and respectful of others. The late Paul Beyer, a dear friend of mine from Milwaukee, told me that his father had a note that he kept in his wallet that read, *"The three most important things in life are: 1. Be Kind – 2. Be Kind – 3. Be Kind."* And Paul was the epitome of kind!

"Treat people how you would want to be treated" was what I often heard from my parents. They simply wouldn't tolerate their children talking down other people and finding fault with others. Another popular saying around our house was *"If you have nothing nice to say, don't say anything at all."* As a result, I was purposely taught not to be critical of others.

The most important thing in life to me is the health and happiness of my family. I thank God often for the blessing of good health. I'm so grateful that my wife and kids, my parents, siblings, nieces and nephews are all alive and well. I have accumulated so many family members and friends to pray for that when it comes to the petitions during mass, I have too many people to be thankful for and never have enough time to squeeze them all in.

So many possibilities exist for sickness and poor health that are out of our hands and way out of our control that we can only hope and pray that everything will work out. But we do have the opportunity and ability to make a tremendous impact on our children's growth and happiness. I've noticed that watching my children grow up is a super subtle slow process – that happens really fast.

McCartney wrote a beautiful song the year my son Joe was born about a father- son relationship that at times has brought tears to my eyes. "Put It There" was written in 1989 and appeared on the "Flowers in the Dirt" CD.

Give me your hand I'd like to shake it

I want to show you I'm your friend

You'll understand if I can make it clear

It's all that matters in the end

Put it there if it weighs a ton

That's what the father said to his younger son

I don't care if it weighs a ton

As long as you and I are here put it there

Long as you and I are here put it there

If there's a fight, I like to fix it

I hate to see things go so wrong

The darkest night and all its mixed emotions

Is getting lighter sing a song

My wife, Laurel, and I have enjoyed raising our four children very much. Parenting is such an awesome responsibility, and I find it fascinating that you really don't know how to be a parent until your kids start showing up. To make that transition from husband and wife to mom and dad all the more challenging, there's a 100% chance that you were raised differently than your spouse. That means you must blend together the way you were both raised, find common ground, and learn how to raise your new family together. Kids only seem to expose the obvious differences between the ways you were both raised. You have now created another unique family unit because no two are alike.

I know that when I was married in 1986, I was learning so much about being a husband and just getting used to the married life that I wasn't thinking about being a dad. Then, in no time at all, it seemed like five minutes after our honeymoon, we had four children.

All of a sudden, my wife and I had to learn how to be parents, which has been a wonderful ongoing discovery and a work in progress. Kids change your life. Doors that you used to go through seem to disappear – your focus changes from yourself to your kids in an instant. Life is no longer about you! Parenting is an adaptive, fluid process and a never ending learning experience.

The oldest kids in the family have the toughest job growing up because they are the ones who have to teach the parents how to be parents. As a result, these first born are heavily scrutinized and oftentimes take the brunt of the parents' learning curve. The kids born at the tail end of the family benefit from parents who have now been trained and have a better understanding about raising their children.

The busiest time for me as a parent was when our kids were zero to ten years old, because they rely on you each day to fulfill their most basic needs. That's when you find out what you and your wife are made of and how effective your parenting skills are.

Wedding Day - June 14, 1986, at St. Patricks church in Eau Claire, Wisconsin. From left to right: Elaine Waldschmidt, Mark Wolff, Michelle Astrup, Bill Fox, Kelly Zender, Laurel, Bill, Matt Rupsis, Jesper Dinesen, Kathy Callaghan, Phil Cataldo, Renee Bewer.

When our oldest was ten our youngest was two and we had a six and eight year old in between. Our home seemed like a manufacturing plant – building and raising kids. Those days were nonstop from sunrise to sunset. And when I look back at the decade of the 90's (the major baby years), it mostly blends into a fog. Thank God I photographed and videotaped a lot of those years so I can hit the refresh button and recollect what was going on during what was the most hectic, demanding and exciting time in my life.

When Elizabeth was barely three years old, she was hospitalized with septicemia (infection in her blood stream) on three separate occasions and had IV's and IV antibiotics. Dr. Sazama, a Urologist at Sacted Heart Hospital, discovered that the urinary tract infection was caused by one of her flow tubes that incorrectly entered her kidney wall at an odd angle. He explained that this was something she was born with and they have a surgical procedure that can repair the problem. On one hand I was so relieved to know that Dr. Sazama and today's amazing medical technology can help our baby girl and yet I was apprehensive, to say the least, to see our first born going into surgery.

I'll always remember lying next to Biz in her hospital bed at Sacred Heart and watching "The Land Before Time" movie together, while Laurel was back at home with our two-year-old son Joseph and seven months pregnant with Michelle. Every time I hear the song from that movie, I immediately go back to that Sacred Heart hospital room in 1990.

We would take turns between staying home with Joe and staying with Biz at the hospital. I remember feeling so helpless as a parent while our daughter lay in her hospital bed with IV's and tubes everywhere. I could only put my faith and hope in the trained team of specialists and pray that they perform a successful surgery. The pediatric unit was so professional and most comforting. It also helped that Laurel was a nurse at Sacred Heart at the time, so many of her friends - fellow nurses and doctors checked in on us all the time.

After that amazing experience at the hospital, I realized how blessed we are to live in a time where influx surgeries such as Elizabeth's are commonplace with a high probability of success instead of certain kidney failure.

When Laurel's Grandma Thomas was alive, we used to take the kids over to Columbia Heights and visit her in the nursing home. Grandma Thomas was a classic French lady with a very sharp mind.

I hadn't been inside a nursing home prior to visiting Clair Thomas in Minnesota. I was amazed at the dying atmosphere as I walked through the halls. It had to be one of the saddest experiences I have felt. My heart went out to every one of those older folks who were basically there in a holding pattern or waiting to die. It was hard to watch. I'm glad we took the time when we had the time to visit Grandma Thomas in her late years before she passed. All in the family got to know her better and create lasting memories of a wonderful lady. And I wanted to teach our kids to spend time with their great grandparents by taking time out of our busy lives to be with them.

In 1988, my next door neighbor built his home a year after we moved in and included a separate living quarters within his home for his mother–in–law. Twenty years later, I'm still impressed with Greg Brandrup's giving heart and unconditional care for his extended family. Greg showed me how, by example, to make room for the older generation when and if the time comes.

The Mind of a Child

I'll always remember the time my daughter Michelle and I went for a walk around the block, and as we looked up to the sky there was a magnificent sunset going down. Brilliant pastel colors of pink, purple, yellow and blue in a sweeping design that spanned for miles. It was like a painting drawn on a grand scale. I said to little Michelle "Isn't it fascinating how God paints a different sunset at the end of each day and a new sunrise to start the day, just for us to enjoy?" As we were holding hands and walking slowly down the street, Michelle looked up at me and said "Dad, is the sky God's paper?" I thought to myself, what a clever question from my four-year-old daughter. "Yes, I said, the sky is God's paper." "Does he have all the colors?" "Yes, he has all the colors!"

When you are that age, you spend a lot of time coloring on white paper with an endless rainbow of colors. So I could see where she was coming from. The mind of a child is a wonderful thing – pure like a white piece of paper with an imagination as colorful as a box of crayons.

Ever since that walk in 1995, I look at a sunrise and sunset a little differently. Now I see a beautiful, original, one of a kind painting that's forever changing on a large canvas and Almighty God is the artist. Michelle has always been a deep thinker and is blessed with a keen awareness of the world around her. I was amazed at her cognitive thought process at such a young age.

The following song was written in 1995 and will always remind me of that special walk with Michelle:

Pocahontas - Colors Of The Wind

- Lyrics courtesy of www.stlyrics.com

You think I'm an ignorant savage
And you've been so many places
I guess it must be so
But still I cannot see
If the savage one is me
How can there be so much that you don't know?
You don't know ...

You think you own whatever land you land on
The Earth is just a dead thing you can claim
But I know every rock and tree and creature
Has a life, has a spirit, has a name

You think the only people who are people
Are the people who look and think like you
But if you walk the footsteps of a stranger
You'll learn things you never knew you never knew
Have you ever heard the wolf cry to the blue corn moon
Or asked the grinning bobcat why he grinned?
Can you sing with all the voices of the mountains?
Can you paint with all the colors of the wind?

Our children were born in odd number years from '87 to '95.
Each time a new person came into our family, the chemistry and
dynamics within our home changed dramatically. It seemed that
every two years a new child arrived into our world and before we
knew it we were out numbered. It was a four on two.

Laurel and I brought our kids with us everywhere so they learned
how to behave in public. It would have been much easier to get a
babysitter and go shopping without the kids, but those events were
opportunities to teach them about people, to behave, and to feel
comfortable in all settings.

'97 – Joseph (8), Meghan (2), Michelle (6), and Elizabeth(10)

Going to the grocery store with our four kids was always an adventure. With two kids in the cart, one in the cart seat and one riding out front, people would stop me in the aisle and tell me that I had a beautiful family and such well-behaved kids. Then they would say "enjoy your kids while they're young, because before you know it, they will grow up on you and these wonderful days will disappear." I could tell they missed their kids. At the time it sounded like nice conversation, but now I know what they meant. The time of raising young children goes by too quickly. Those people were so right.

I believe that the most challenging time as a parent is when your kids are between the ages of 16 to 23. The reason I say that is because once your kids get their driver's license, all bets are off because they are now exposed to many potential hazards that are out of your control. Sixteen is the age when you suddenly aren't with your kids as much and you need to ask God to watch over them and keep them safe. I still do ask God to guide them to do his will, to follow his ways.

Automobiles can be deadly and since you no longer are the one driving them around, you can only hope and pray that they will arrive to their destination safely. High school and college friends can be an excellent or a poor influence on your kids as well; especially if they mix alcohols, drugs, text messaging, cell phoning, and loud music with driving.

Laurel and I were at a Christmas party in December of '07 when we got a call from our 16-year-old-daughter Michelle. She explained how she was driving and changing radio stations and she slid off the snow-covered road and into the ditch. It all happened within seconds and fortunately she and her sister Elizabeth were unharmed. Michelle learned a good but safe lesson about the importance of attentive driving.

I know that guardian angels are keeping a close watch over each of my children, and I find comfort in knowing that God is in control of the situation.

I've learned from my own experience that roughly by the time you turn 23, you have a better idea of who you are and what you want to do with your life. By that age, you begin to think more maturely and have a clearer understanding of the career you plan to pursue. Relationships with the opposite sex become more serious. You really start to grow up. At that point in your life, you begin to settle in and consider big and bold decisions like getting married and raising a family.

As our children have grown up (now 22, 20, 18, and 14 years old) it seems that my life has been on fast forward the last few years. Sometimes my brain downloads more information and stimulation than I think it was designed to handle, with the fast-paced lifestyle that surrounds most of us. The multi-tasking and being electronically linked to seemingly everyone and everything in the world affects our ability to spend time with our children. If I could only find the remote with life's pause/play button and slow things down a bit. I must admit there've been times when I felt the Amish lifestyle looks pretty appealing.

We need to simplify our lives a bit more so we can really see our children grow – it is one of the most exciting joys a parent gets to experience. It just seems that the months and years are flying by.

Our "kids" are not children anymore. Savor every moment.

Have you ever had a moment as a parent when you look at your children and they appear older than they looked eight hours ago? Many times Joe would walk downstairs in the morning after a full night's sleep and he appeared taller. He must have grown a half inch overnight. Last year I dropped off Meghan at South Middle School in the morning at 7:40 am and drove to work in Osseo. Later that afternoon, I pulled up to school and waited on Hester Street to give her a ride back home. When she and her friend Emily walked across the street to get in the car at 2:40 pm, she looked at least a year older than she did when I dropped her off. She had definitely changed – and grown.

In today's world of parenting, you wouldn't think of missing your child's sporting events. In fact, many families plan their individual and family calendars around their kids' sports schedule. For eight straight years, from 1997 to 2005, I coached basketball at the Eau Claire YMCA on Saturday mornings. It turned out that I was able to coach each of my kids for two seasons. Despite our efforts, our record the first year with Elizabeth and last year with Meghan was 0-10. However, I thoroughly enjoyed the time I was able to spend practicing and coaching my children and their friends throughout the season.

On Wednesday evenings, our company sponsored a basketball team in the Young Men's League at the Y. The "Rollo-Mixers" roster included my brothers Hayes and Tom, and anchored by Eric Skoyen, Tim Popple, Rob Larson and Kelly Mulhern – all four of which were stars on the Osseo-Faichild basketball team during their high school years. I also recruited Rob Morrel and some of his black friends to round out the squad.

My team was a rare blend of Norwegian, African and Irish Americans. As we did on many occasions, Tom and I picked up Rob M. and his friends at their apartment, and drove them to the game. One night, we were heading downtown to the YMCA and listening to Millie Vanilli's "Don't Forget My Number" and Cool

Mo Dee, singing "*Wow, Wow, Wes* (Wild, Wild, West)." The guys in the back seat were surprised at my choice of music and also enjoying it at the same time. They were singing along as I was playing the funky music loud in the Calavan when one of my teammates shouted, "*Hey Callaghane, you Billy Vanilli.*" Tom fell apart! Apparently he wasn't used to seeing a white guy singing and grooving to '80s funk music - word for word.

We videotaped each game and immediately after a win, the guys would meet just a few blocks away at Houligans to drink beers, and Terry Weld was kind enough to let us watch the taped game on the big screen TV. Sometimes we would invite the opposing team to join us for the post game activities – which made the recap even more entertaining. The "Rollo-Mixers" had more fun than any other team in the Y league. We treated every game like it was our last!

In fact, on March 16, 1990, the USA Today sports section ran the following story after receiving a press release sent by my brother Tom:

WISCONSIN

Rob Larson scored 29 points as Ray's Place defeated the Continental Rollo-Mixers 54-52 in overtime to win the Men's Classic League basketball championship at the Eau Claire YMCA.

Raising a team

Boys and girls traveling teams have become very popular over the last 15 years in such sports as basketball, soccer, hockey and boys baseball or girls softball. These talent-laden teams compete locally and across state lines against some of the best upcoming athletes in the region. From Friday evening to Sunday evening, families will spend many weekends during the summer and throughout the school year to help their child perfect their athletic skills. I admire the parents and kids dedication, but my only problem with it was that we had more than one child. Our four kids were born within an eight year time frame and when Elizabeth was in 7th grade she wanted to join a basketball and softball traveling team. It didn't make sense to haul the other three kids around to hotels and gymnasiums or get a babysitter or take off and leave Laurel and the other three children at home – for many weekends at a time. It didn't seem fair to the rest of the family. Our chance to log valuable time together was usually spent during precious weekends together at home or on family vacations.

One of the parental lessons I learned was that while raising four little kids who are close in age, you do everything together – as a family. The opportunities to spend time alone with one child at a time seemed few and far between. If Elizabeth wanted to play outside in the snow or make a snowman, I automatically bundled up Joe, Michelle and Meghan and the five of us rolled up a snowman together. Unless I set aside a date and time to go one on one with any one of my children, it just didn't happen. We went everywhere, together! We were known as the "Callaghan clan!"

However, Elizabeth did play for the Danes in high school, a traveling girl softball team that made it to Nationals in North Carolina in 2004. I scheduled a business trip to North Carolina that same week and along with Rollo-Mixer meetings in Winston-Salem and Mocksville, I was able to see Elizabeth compete on a national level at this beautiful sport complex in Raleigh. They had four deluxe fields and comfortable box seats with a roof over our head. I know how much it meant to my daughter to look up in the stands from center field and see her dad cheering her on.

A Whole New World

In 1997, we decided to surprise our kids and take them on a family vacation to Florida; they were 10, 8, 6 and 2 years old at the time. We packed up individual suitcases with a week's worth of clothes and hid the luggage in the back of the Calavan. They thought we were going to the Mall of America (MOA) for the day. When we arrived at the Embassy Suites hotel in Bloomington, Minnesota, we could either take the shuttle bus to the airport or across the street to the MOA. Although our kids thought we were on the shuttle to the Mall, I privately instructed the driver to announce that their parents have decided to take them on a trip to Florida instead of the Mall because they are such fabulous kids. I remember everyone was so excited - except Michelle looked confused. She said, "Why aren't we going to the MOA, I thought we were going to the Mall today." Her older brother and sister told her that Florida will be much more fun and she warmed up to the idea once we got on the plane. Meghan wasn't old enough to understand what was taking place, but because of the joy she felt from her brothers and sisters, she flung her arms in the air, grinned from ear to ear and clapped. Happiness harbors happiness!

When we finally arrived at Disney's MGM Studios, we rented one of those blue strollers, packed it with diapers, bottles, sunscreen, baby wipes, etc., and held hands as we entered the park just past Mickey's huge magic blue hat. When I went to Disney World in 1971 (the year it opened) the only park at that time was Magic Kingdom. Now there are so many family parks to visit that it takes four or five days to take it all in.

As we strolled along this magnificent theme park, I noticed some parents had strapped a leash onto their kids like a pet and kept track of their kids that way. I'm sure a parent's worst nightmare would be to lose track of their children in a place like Disney World. But a leash! I don't know, it just didn't look right.

Then, as we walked down the middle of Main Street with seemingly everyone on earth, I heard this mom in front of me say to her son, "if you kick your brother again, I'm going to hurt you." I thought to myself, WOW, what a stupid thing to say to your child. Is she threatening to physically harm her own child as a form of discipline? Her husband was walking along-side her and didn't say a thing. It was pitiful. This lady's abusive attitude amazed me, which unfortunately I had to follow from the Little Mermaid to the Lion King. Her husband was probably afraid if he said something, she might sit on him with that huge samurai butt she was growing inside her pink stretch pants. She reminded me of Ursula the sea witch and her poor unfortunate souls.

I'm sympathetic for the children and husbands in the world who have to live with and put up with harsh, critical, controlling wives or moms. I have met too many women during my lifetime with these unflattering qualities. I'm equally concerned for children and wives who have to live with and deal with ungrateful, demeaning, demanding husbands or dads. For some reason, some of the nicest women I've met seem to attract professional jerks for husbands.

We eventually arrived at the Lion King Theater and walked through this endless maze of moving people. I had Michelle on my shoulders, Meghan in my arms and Laurel was walking ahead with Elizabeth and Joe. The procession seemed to have no end in sight and I was getting tired, so I started to moan "Moo, Moo" as we traversed back and forth past the same crowd and through the network of dividers. I felt like an animal being herded along to the auction house. Being from Wisconsin, I could do a pretty good cow impression. A young Japanese couple was following in line behind us in the maze; they appeared to be newlyweds on their honeymoon in Orlando. The surprisingly tall Asian groom leaned down to his new bride and said, " *Moo, Moo, Moo, Moo.*" The guy was mocking me in his pure native tongue. I loved it. I don't speak Japanese or any foreign language for that matter, but I know one thing for sure. The sound a cow makes in any language is "Moo!"

Later that evening, as we were leaving the spectacular Fantasmic fireworks show, this young family walking behind us was pushing a stroller with a crying child inside, when all of a sudden the father yells - too loud, "Quit your crying – I told you to stop crying." Of course the two to three year old kept crying. I can't remember a time I told my kids to stop crying and then they stopped crying. I wished I hadn't witnessed what happened next. The irritated dad leaned into the stroller and slapped his son in the face three times. The startled boy never saw it coming and was now screaming at the top of his lungs and in obvious pain; the Mom just stood there and watched and didn't say a word. I was amazed at the physical reaction! The young dad's response was uncalled for and so poor; it actually stopped me in my tracks! His abusive actions were so foreign to me. My blood pressure immediately spiked and my heart went out for the crying child. I was furious! Why wouldn't he take the time to figure out why his son was crying in the first place? Maybe he could have picked his child out of the stroller and carried him for a few minutes. Maybe his son was hungry and wanted something to eat or maybe he just needed his pants changed. I'm sure the little boy wasn't purposely trying to irritate his father. Everyone, kids and parents, were exhausted after a long day at the park; I know I was.

All I could think of was that the dad was once a little boy himself and was probably raised by abrasive parents. Maybe he doesn't know any other way! But now he is teaching his family how to react (the same way) as he was taught. He obviously didn't know how else to deal with the situation, but physical abuse is not an acceptable method of discipline or a way to quiet a crying, defenseless child. It is demeaning, harmful, uncalled for and disrespectful. And it is a learned behavior that is passed down from one generation to the next. It is a terrible cycle that has to be broken. I was so upset that I wanted to confront the guy, but that probably wouldn't have solved any long term problems. It was sad to see. God bless the parents who don't know any better!

I searched the subject of child abuse and found the following on Wikipedia:

Child abuse *is the physical, psychological or sexual maltreatment of children. The Centers for Disease Control and Prevention (CDC) defines child maltreatment as any act or series of acts or commission or omission by a parent or other caregiver that results in harm, potential for harm, or threat of harm to a child. Most child abuse happens in a child's home, with a smaller amount occurring in the organizations, schools or communities they interact with. There are four major categories of child abuse: neglect, physical abuse, psychological/emotional abuse, and sexual abuse.*

Child abuse can take many forms:

- *Neglect, in which the responsible adult fails to adequately provide for various needs, including physical (failure to provide adequate food, clothing, or hygiene), emotional (failure to provide nurturing or affection) or educational (failure to enroll a child in school).*

- *Physical abuse is physical aggression directed at a child by an adult. It can involve striking, burning, choking or shaking a child, and the distinction between discipline and abuse is often poorly defined.*

- *Child sexual abuse is any sexual act between an adult and a child, including penetration, fondling, exposure to adult sexuality and violations of privacy.*

- *Psychological abuse, also known as emotional abuse, which can involve belittling or shaming a child, inappropriate or extreme punishment and the withholding of affection.*

According to the (American) National Committee to Prevent Child Abuse, in 1997 neglect represented 54% of confirmed cases of child abuse, physical abuse 22%, sexual abuse 8%, emotional maltreatment 4%, and other forms of maltreatment 12% According to a UNICEF report on child well-being in the United States and the United Kingdom ranked lowest among first world nations with respect to the well- being of their children. This study also found that child neglect and child abuse are far more common in single-parent families than in families where both parents are present.

The effects of child abuse vary, depending on its type. A 2006 study found that childhood emotional and sexual abuse were strongly related to adult depressive symptoms, while exposure to verbal abuse and witnessing of domestic violence had a moderately strong association, and physical abuse a moderate one. For depression, experiencing more than two kinds of abuse exerted synergetically stronger symptoms. Sexual abuse was particularly deleterious in its interfamilial form, for symptoms of depression, anxiety, dissociation, and limbic irritability. Childhood verbal abuse had a stronger association with anger-hostility than any other type of abuse studied, and was second only to emotional abuse in its relationship with dissociative symptoms.

If the United States ranks lowest among first world nations when it comes to the well being of our children, I would say in general that we as a country are failing our kids miserably.

One of my favorite parks in Orlando is SeaWorld. I have always marveled at the world of sea creatures God has created and how beautiful life is under the sea. We sat in the Shamu stadium, outside the splash zone, and listened to the whale trainers explain their process of teaching these 6000 pound entertainers. The staff talked about working with dolphins, walruses', sea lions, and whales and said their training is based on positive reinforcement, which they have found was the most effective way to train. I thought it was interesting that positive reinforcement is a proven teaching method that works for all God's creatures especially human beings. Among other things, I learned that dolphin's and humans are the only creatures God made that have sex for pleasure, which I found fascinating.

I have talked to many parents who seem to look forward to when their child turns 18 and moves out of the house. Oddly enough, the tone of the conversation is almost one of "good riddance." Then there are other parents who wish that day never comes.

Last summer, I was talking to one of the moms at my daughter's high school graduation party. Her oldest child had also just graduated and was going off to college in the fall. As she described how hard it will be to not have him around, tears began to roll down her face. I felt for her. I listened to her lament about how she is going to miss him so much and I could tell that her heart was troubled. I told her something that I read some years ago: *"Don't cry because it's over, smile because it happened."* She looked at me somewhat confused at first and then began to smile and thanked me for pointing out a different way to look at "graduating." She continued telling me stories of her son and how proud she is of him. Parents have to graduate along with

197

their "kids" and allow them to move on.

My wife shared with me the following phrase written by an anonymous author: *"Worry looks around. Sorry looks back. Faith looks up."*

Why people waste their time and energy dwelling on the past is beyond me – life is too short as it is. Be glad for all that has come to pass and the precious time that you have had to spend with your kids. Be grateful for what has been and focus on the future - you can't change the past. It is sad to see them go, but you have to let them grow!

Since infancy, as parents we have encouraged independence starting as early as potty training, cheering your infant on for being successful and non-dependent on diapers. Just as baby birds need to grow strong wings, we need to allow our children to develop strong wings so they can soar high like an eagle.

Raising Kids

"For Raising Kids, Eau Claire ranks No. 1." That was the title to a story written by Andrew Dowd that appeared on the front page of the November 12, 2008, Leader Telegram. Here is an excerpt:

Eau Claire topped a trio of Wisconsin cities included in the second-annual ranking of the Best Places in America to Raise Kids published last week by BusinessWeek magazine.

Mount Prospect, Illinois, was declared the best place in the U.S. to start a family based on affordability, safety, school performance and other "quality of life" measures, but Eau Claire was declared the best in Wisconsin, followed by Appleton and Racine.

First and foremost, people move to follow jobs, said Rob Kleven of Eau Claire- based Kleven Real Estate, but they also consider safety, education and other factors. "One of the biggest things they're looking for is the school system," he said. Other amenities that bring people to Eau Claire include the city's variety of retail and services.

"It's real interesting that Eau Claire is a typical small town. Our neighbors help out each other, and it's a friendly town," he said. "Yet it is a regional medical center with Sacred Heart and Luther/ Mayo and has a university."

New York-based OnBoard Informatics crunched the numbers on behalf of BusinessWeek for all U.S. municipalities with at least 50,000 residents and a median family income between $40,000 and $100,000. For Wisconsin, that meant 13 cities were up for consideration, from Sheboygan with about 50,500 people, to Milwaukee, which has a population of more than 590,000. Then the analysts narrowed the list using statistics on school performance, household income and spending, crime, air quality, job growth, diversity, and local amenities such as museums, parks and theaters.

Safety and school performance were given the most weight, according to the article. But the main principle of the list was to identify affordable places to live. The median selling price of a home in Eau Claire County was $136,200 in the second quarter of 2008, compared with $190,000 in the Milwaukee metropolitan area and $215,900 in Dane County, home to Madison.

In the latest list, BusinessWeek described Eau Claire as a former logging and manufacturing city that now includes high-tech, health care and university jobs. The Eau Claire metropolitan area, which includes Eau Claire and Chippewa counties, ranked second in the 2007 CQ Press ranking of the safest cities in the U.S. That annual ranking considers only FBI crime rates for murder, rape, robbery, aggravated assault, burglary and vehicle theft.

Eau Claire is a great place to raise a family and foster your children's friendships.

Our daughter Meghan and her friend Emily have known each other since they were four, when they first met in pre-school at Chapel Heights in 1999. They are both the youngest in the family; both were born in the fourth month of the year and only 4 days apart. And because of their close friendship, Laurel and I have become close friends with Emily's parents. It's wonderful how your children will introduce you to future friends. And in fourth grade, Emily introduced Meghan to dance at the Eau Claire School of Dance and the two of them have been dancing together ever since.

CSI – Eau Claire

One of the fun pranks that high school kids like to pull off in Eau Claire is sneaking out in the middle of the night with their friends, going over to the grocery store and loading up on multiple rolls of toilet paper; so they can toilet paper the crap out of someone's yard. I know kids are just having fun, but I think it's ridiculous – as a home owner, I look at it as defacing personal property – and I'm not a lawyer. I feel for the parents when they discover that their son or daughter's "friends" trashed their front yard. No doubt it is a pain in the butt to clean up. Endless rolls of toilet paper unraveled and draped throughout the beautiful trees and all over the yard. If you don't collect it before it rains, your lawn and trees will be coated with papier mache. For some reason it doesn't sit well with me. Throughout my time growing up in Milwaukee, I never saw anyone's private property get papered.

I've been told that the reasons for getting toilet papered include: the celebration or recognition of making a school athletic team, like making the varsity dance team or the JV football roster. Or maybe your son or daughter did something stupid causing retaliation from their friends, or maybe it's something the parents did or said that got the toilet paper champs attention. I've also heard that it could be a result of your kid's "popularity" or maybe it's simply done out of pure boredom.

One of my goals as a parent was to have all four of my children get through high school without having our house toilet papered once. I vowed that if it did happen, I would hunt down the individuals responsible and make sure they would be the ones to wipe it up.

When my oldest daughter Elizabeth graduated from Memorial high school with no TP attacks, I was thrilled. But unfortunately that feeling was short lived. Just days after school ended for the summer, I was sleeping in on Saturday morning, only to be woken up by my wife with the dreadful news that our house had been toilet papered. I thought I was having a bad dream and went back to sleep. But she woke me up a second time and wanted to show me the damage. When I walked out the front door, my front lawn resembled the middle of winter and appeared as though we had just got hit by a major snowstorm – but it was June 8, 2006. The blue spruce trees, birch trees, Norwegian pine tree and the box elder tree were all completely covered under a blanket of toilet paper. It looked like a professional hit. I told my kids that oftentimes the perpetrators will return to the scene of the crime the next day, so they can check out their nocturnal artwork in daylight.

As I walked around the yard in disbelief, I spotted four empty packages of toilet paper by the edge of the street. Each one was a 24-pack. When you do the math that meant these teenage ass-wipes spread 96 rolls of TP over my trees and throughout my entire front lawn.

Now I was on a mission and determined to find out who did this – not so I could call the cops and tattle, but to see that the culprits clean up their mess. These guys fogged with the wrong house and soon they would find out that Inspector Callaghan had been assigned to the case.

I got in my car and drove over to Copp's Food store, one of two grocery stores on the south side of Eau Claire, and went in to see if their stock of toilet paper was missing any bundles of "Soft & Gentle." It turned out that the shelves were stocked full and the manager assured me that they were filled early Friday evening. After ruling out Copp's as a source of the WMD's (Weapons of Mass Destruction), I drove over to Festival Foods to see what their toilet paper inventory revealed. Sure enough, the "Soft & Gentle" supply had been depleted. I got a hold of Mr. Walker, the store manager, and asked him if he would do me a favor and take a look at last night's security tapes from the surveillance cameras and see if they show any high schoolers making late night TP purchases. I told him to look for some teenage kids with their pants at half mast and their hats turned around backwards, walking to the cash register and packing four cases of S&G ammo. I asked him to narrow the search from between 11:00 pm and 1:00 am. It was just a hunch. He said he would check into it later that day. In the meantime, I headed out to Hillcrest Country Club to play golf with my brother Tom.

After playing 18 holes on a beautiful Saturday afternoon in the summer sun, I got a call on my cell phone as I was heading back home. It was Mr. Walker from Festival Foods. *"Con – Sonar, I've got them on screen sir."* At least that's what it sounded like to me. He went on to say, "I'm looking at three high school kids, just as you described, entering the checkout lane at 11:24 pm with four-24 packs of "S&G." What do you want me to do?" I told him that I'm on my way over and should be there in about 10 minutes. When I got off the phone, I called my son Joe at home and asked him to meet me over at Festival Foods so he could help me identify the champs caught on camera. Joe was well known throughout the school and would most likely be able to recognize the three stooges. I figured it had to be either one of Elizabeth's or Joe's "friends" involved in the attack. I know it's possible that these guys didn't head to my house with the TP and went to someone else's house that night, but I had a strong feeling that these were the kids I was looking for. This was too much fun.

While Joe was backing out of the driveway en route to Festival Foods, a car with three teenagers rolled down the street and slowly approached our house and then came to a stop when they spotted their friend Joe pulling out into the street. Joe later told me the conversation went something like this: "Hey dudes, what's up?" "Oh, not much dude, we're like driving around doing nothing, dude." "Dude, where are you going?" "I'm driving over to Festival Foods to meet my dad and see if I can help him figure out who trashed our place with toilet paper. He's got three dudes on video buying four loads of toilet paper late last night." "Like, no way, dude! Oh my gosh, dude. Dude, like, it was us, dude. Tell your dad not to call the cops; tell him we'll clean it up."

I was waiting outside the front door of Festival when Joe finally rolled into the parking lot. As he drove by me, he leaned his head out the window with a big smile on his face and said, "Dad - I know who did it." I was wondering how that could be since we hadn't looked at the video tape yet. As we walked up the stairs towards Mr. Walker's office, he told me what had just happened back home. Joe and I laughed hard as we watched his friends on camera walking through the check out aisle with an S-load of "S&G."

I realize nobody meant any harm and it was all in good fun. Actually, it was all in great fun for me! All I wanted to do was find the kids who blew out my place with TP and have them clean it up – which they did!

My children are fortunate to attend school in the Eau Claire K thru 12 school systems. Wisconsin has some of the best rated schools in the country, and Eau Claire is highly ranked in the state. That means my kids have been able to attend one of the best educational curriculums in the country, from pre-school through high school. This is a wonderful benefit of raising children in Eau Claire that most of us Eau Claireans take for granted.

Put in a Jam

When Joe was starting his second semester as a junior at Memorial High School, I got a call from the attendance office and was informed that Joe had been suspended from school for a day. I asked her what he did, and she said he is being suspended for inappropriate behavior to a faculty member. I thought that doesn't sound right, Joe wouldn't say or do something inappropriate to one of the teachers.

Laurel was out of town in Columbus at the annual JAM (January Advisors Meeting) with Longaberger and I called her later that evening and told her about all the things going on at home with the kids. After I told her about the incident at MHS with Joe, she wasn't receptive to the suspension ruling and suggested that I go in and tell the principal that Joe is going to go to school tomorrow and can't afford to miss a day of school. I told her, "that's easy for you to say from Ohio - but I'll do my best."

The next morning, I dropped off Meghan at South Middle School (SMS) and Joe, Michelle and I drove on to Memorial.

Prior to my meeting with the staff, I asked Joe to tell me what happened. My kids know that if they tell me the truth, I will try to help them. If they tell me lies, I can't help! Joe explained, "I was talking to Brittney Buckley outside of class between 5th and 6th hour and she told me to sit down across the aisle on the floor. Seconds later, miss S came walking out of her classroom and nearly tripped over me as she strolled by. She stopped and looked down at me and said "What are you doing sitting on this side of the hallway, you know you're not supposed to sit there." So I realized Brittney had set me up for a problem and I looked right at Brittney and shook my head and said - I smell bitch! Miss S thought I said it to her and dragged me down to the principal's office and they suspended me."

While we drove down Fairfax Street from SMS to MHS, Joe kept saying to me, "Dad, it's no use, you're wasting your time - they will not let me back in school today – they don't reverse suspensions!"

I had Joe wait in the car as I walked into school to plead his case.

When I entered the assistant principal's office, I was introduced to Miss S, Mr. K, and Joe's guidance counselor, Mr. H. I listened to the four of them explain the altercation between Joe and Miss S and I was told that once they make a ruling to suspend a student - it is final. When they finished laying out there case, I told them Joe is waiting out in the car as we speak and has his homework done and is looking forward to attending school today. I told them that what happened yesterday was a complete misunderstanding and that Joe was directing his "I smell bitch" comment to Brittney, not Miss S. They weren't convinced, but I was unwavering in my goal to reverse the suspension.

I said, "Today is a new day, and I want you to make an exception in this particular case and revoke his suspension. I knew what I was asking was not easy – reversing a suspension won't look good if Joe comes waltzing back into school and brags about overriding the sentence to exile island. Everyone in the room knew Joe well and they knew he didn't have the immunity idol. I guaranteed them that Joe will not tell anyone about this morning's discussion and keep it between his ears. I assured Miss S that Joe likes her and doesn't think she smells like a bitch. I told her I don't even know what a bitch smells like!

I stepped out of the room for only a few minutes as they made their decision quickly and then they opened the door and I sat back down and rejoined the group. They said they will reverse the suspension and to go get Joe out of the car and bring him in to see them first - before he goes to first hour. I walked out to my car which was parked underneath the Eagle and got in and said, "Joe, grab your backpack, you're going to school today!" He was actually shocked that they let him back in. I told him to go to the attendance office and see the principal and that he wants to talk to you and have an understanding before you go to your first hour class. In all my years of taking Joe to school, I've never seen him so excited to walk into MHS. I could tell he felt like Lazarus.

As I was saying earlier, Joe has always been an entertainer. It's one of the gifts God gave him! He shines in front of an audience and despite his early disabilities, he has forged ahead. Joseph recently put together a voice-over tape for agents in NY and LA titled "The Duck Hunter." Joe does the voice of the late Steve Irwin as he hunts down Donald Duck in Walt Disney World. Pete Wittig, Joe's cousin, taught Joe and his sisters how to do Donald Duck when they were little kids. The CD is a collection of 17 different voices Joe performs, thus illustrating his range of voice characters he can do. I got to work with Joe on writing the script during the month of March, 2009, and the finished product turned out better than we thought. I felt like Lennon and McCartney as we worked together to compose the story line.

Weekend Double Header

On June 20, 2009, I celebrated my 49th birthday with my family. We sat in the living room as everyone watched me open a few presents. Laurel gave me a couple of nice golf shirts and then the kids had me open their presents – in a particular order. The gifts were used as symbols to see if I could guess the real present. First I opened a wooden cane, then a box of Crayola Chalk. I didn't catch on until I opened the third present and it was an English Derby Hat. As I put it on, I immediately felt like George Banks.

That's when I realized the present was exactly what I hoped for, two tickets to see Mary Poppins at the Orpheum Theatre in Minneapolis in September. I started singing, *"Yust a spoonful of sugar helps the medicine go down."* Ever since I went to Mexico in 1993, I get my J's and Y's backwards all the time. The fourth present was actually a spoon coated with sugar. Then Meghan handed me a black umbrella and when I opened it up, I found two golden tickets taped to the underside. All I could think of was:

"Chim chimmery, chim chimmery, chim chim charoo,

I does what I like and I likes what I do."

On June 21, 2009, (the next day) I celebrated my 21st Fathers Day – and now that I think of it, it was my Golden Fathers Day!

Laurel, Meghan, Joe and I went to 11:00 mass and then went out for brunch at the famous Norske Nook restaurant in Eau Claire. When we arrived back home, Meghan handed me a homemade Father's Day card that read:

Dear Dad, I love you so much!

You're the best dad! You help me with anything I ask for.

You always make me laugh!

You're my dad, and that's the coolest thing on earth!

Love – Meghan

Then Joe handed me a Father's Day card and on the inside cover were two tickets to see "Star Trek" at the Oakwood Mall. What a Father's Day gift! Joe and I went to the 4:00 show and it was fabulous. For someone like me who has followed Star Trek since I was seven years old, it was wonderful to see the writers follow Gene Roddenberry's mastery of exploiting human behavior and thus the human condition. Gene was light years ahead of his time! I loved watching the movie with my son. The closing scene shows the Enterprise flying off on a new mission with a young Captain Kirk at the helm. Then you hear Leonard Nimoy's legendary voice:

"Space, the final frontier – these are the voyages of the Star Ship Enterprise, its ongoing mission – to explore strange new worlds, to seek out new life and new civilizations – to boldly go where no one has gone before."

The hairs on my arms where standing straight up as chills ran through my body. I was suddenly transported back in time to the sunroom on Menlo in 1967. I felt seven years old all over again.

What a weekend. On Saturday, I was given two tickets to see Mary Poppins, went out for dinner in Chippewa Falls, and then played beer pong in the basement for the first time. On Sunday, I got to sing "Be Not Afraid" at the 11:00 mass, work on the finishing touches to this book, and see "Star Trek." Wow, am I blessed!

Chapter 7

Mixing the Family's Business

*Rollo-Mixer in Osseo, WI plant, set-up and run-in
prior to shipping to Moses Lake, WA*

On March 8, 1979, Otis Nelson, Sr. and I headed west in our '76
International truck with blueprints, tools and a new electronic
weigh-blend system for mixing fertilizer for the wheat fields in
the great Northwest. I had been home from college a few months
and was between factory jobs in Milwaukee. My father needed
someone to help with the long drive to the state of Washington,
so I volunteered. Our job was to deliver and install a new four-
ton capacity Continental Rollo-Mixer at Simplot Soil Builders in
Moses Lake, Washington. The ride out West was an adventure and
education in and of itself. We drove through Minnesota, North
Dakota, and through the Rocky Mountain range in Montana and
Idaho before finally entering eastern Washington - about 1,775
miles from Osseo, Wisconsin.

I don't know about Otis, but I felt like Lewis and Clark as we explored and absorbed this magnificent section of America while driving up and down the Rollo-coaster highway. Every mile west past Billings and Laurel, Montana, was breathtaking. We drove our flatbed truck around the Absaroka Range on Interstate 90, just north of the Tobacco Root Mountains. As I looked out the driver's side window, I could see Granite Peak, which rises more than 10,000 feet above sea level. The sheer size of these massive mountains made me feel small in a way that I had never felt before. I was floored by the beauty of the moving picture that surrounded us. We continued our journey northeast past Missoula and through the Bitterroot Range into Idaho.

Ever since I was a kid, I was always intrigued by the fact that Continental Products Corporation (CPC) had become a national manufacturer of mixing equipment with applications throughout the U.S. It appealed to me that my father's business allowed him to travel the country and work directly with his Rollo-Mixer customers.

And how fortunate was I to be on a trip with Otis Nelson, who had worked at the plant since 1960. He is the one who told my father, *"That's a pretty good mixer"* when my dad was deciding whether to pursue the mixing business in 1960. Otis was originally from Montana and worked for the railroad out West before moving to Osseo in the late '50s with his family. He was a man of few words, but those words were always worth hearing. He was also a jack of all trades and unparalleled in this ability to fabricate and install Rollo-Mixers.

When we arrived in Moses Lake, Washington, the western sun was setting over the Interstate Inn – our final destination. The next morning, we drove to the plant and unloaded the Rollo-Mixer with two forklifts on each side of the truck that lifted the 10,000-pound machine off the truck bed as Otis drove out from underneath. We lowered the blender onto four machine rollers. It took only three people to push the mixer down the main aisle. Then we located the unit in the blending room as called for in our installation drawing. I had two years of mechanical and two years of architectural drafting in high school, so I was able to interpret the blueprints with Otis. Continental's engineering department, Frank, generated all the machinery drawings; I was impressed the equipment fit just as it was drawn.

The application involved a four-ton capacity mixer that sat on four electronic load cells and received raw material ingredients by gravity from a cluster of overhead bins. Simplot bought the Rollo-Mixer to uniformly blend field-grade NPK (nitrogen, phosphorous, potassium) and spray herbicides onto the granular fertilizer. The mixer's discharge chute extension had to telescope through a hole in the concrete wall to feed a bucket elevator that sat just outside the plant. Once the batch is mixed, 8,000-pounds of blended fertilizer flows down the chute extension and is lifted up the bucket elevator leg and gravity-fed into large fertilizer spreaders. These specialty fertilizers are used to feed and protect miles of wheat crops and potato fields. The learning experience was nonstop.

Everything Continental manufactured was running smoothly, and the last thing to do in the installation was to bolt on the chute extension, which usually takes about ten minutes. The problem was the old building had reinforced concrete walls and thick rebar throughout the structure that made it difficult to jack hammer through the 14-inch-thick wall. We needed a 24-by-36 inch high opening carved out of the west wall, and the front of the Rollo-Mixer was only 15" from the wall. Lars Larson, the fertilizer plant manager at Simplot Soil Builders, was losing patience with the lack of progress as workers chiseled away the concrete. He called in a demolition expert to blow out the opening with dynamite. "This is going to be cool," I said to Otis.

Lars asked me if the Rollo-Mixer could withstand a blast at such close range. We had already bolted the mixer to the floor and connected the inlet hopper above, so moving the blending equipment away from the wall was not a viable option. I was surprised Lars would ask my opinion, so I looked at Otis for guidance but, unsurprisingly, he said nothing. He did sort of raise his head and peer at me with a curious smirk on his face, which I interpreted as "you bet." In Osseo this means, among other things, "Sure, no problem." I told Lars we don't run our machines through these types of tests, so we couldn't offer any guarantees that the explosion would not damage the new system.

Otis and I watched the pyro-technician chalk a 2-by-3 foot rectangular window on the outside wall and drill four strategically located cavities inside the target. He then placed red, five-inch sticks of dynamite in each hole. He wired the four charges together and connected them to a single spool of wire that he unraveled as we all walked about 300 yards away from the plant. After he connected the two wires to the "Bridge-on-the-River-Kwai" type detonator, he sounded the horn on his pickup truck for 180 seconds - part of the safety procedure - and then pressed down the plunger on the little box. "KA-BLAM!!!!" The percussion from the detonation went right through my body, and a large dust cloud spewed from inside and around the plant. It was so exciting! When the dust settled, we returned to the plant to see if a hole was blown out of the wall. Otis and I were hoping the mixer was unaffected by the blast. As we walked through a thick cloud of fertilizer dust, we came upon a perfectly blown window through the building.

Otis and I stuck our heads through the opening and saw that the Rollo-Mixer, though covered in dust, was unfazed by the explosion. Otis just smiled; no words were needed. I was impressed with the quality construction and craftsmanship that went into the mixers and, at that moment, became enthralled with my father's business. It was an education on many fronts.

Learning Experience

One of my favorite composers and musicians is Ray Davies of The Kinks. He and his brother Dave have created classic rock music for more than four decades that I have been fortunate to enjoy. The following song excerpts chronicle man's progress.

The Kinks Present Schoolboys in Disgrace, 1975.

Education

In a deep dark jungle a long time ago
Lived a lonesome caveman
He was a solitary soul
And he spent his playtime
Chewing meat from bones.
He didn't know how to talk much
He only knew how to groan
Then he lifted up his hands and reached to the sky
Let out a yell and no one replied.
Frustration and torment tore him inside
Then he fell to the ground and he cried and he cried.
But then education saved the day.
He learned to speak and communicate
Education saved the day.
He thanked god for the friends he made.
'cos everybody needs an education
Everybody needs an education.
Black skin, red skin, yellow or white,
Everybody needs to read and write
Everybody needs an education.

Teacher, teach me how to read and write,
You can teach me about biology,
But you can't tell me what i am living for
'cos that's still a mystery.
Teacher, teach me about nuclear physics
And teach me about the structure of man,
But all your endless calculations
Can't tell me why i am.
No you can't tell me why i am,
No you can't tell me why i am.

In the 1965 movie "A Hard Day's Night," the fab four are touring around England and Paul decides to bring his grandfather (John McCartney) with them. In many scenes throughout the film, this witty Irishman is always stirring it up with everyone he meets and was constantly creating harmless mischief while on tour with the Beatles. During one scene, the five of them are riding in a train car and John Lennon looks across at Paul and asks in his classic Liverpool accent, "Paul, what's with your grandfather?" Paul casually replies "He's a mixer!" On another occasion, Paul is franticly searching throughout the studio for his grandfather and eventually finds him laughing and stirring it up with two younger women; and refers to him as a "King Mixer".

While I was watching the movie it dawned on me; my dad is a mixer! My father is a cross between Bob Hope, Fred Sanford and Archie Bunker. He's always having fun mixing it up with other people and has a special ability to put a smile on your face and brighten your day. It's a gift really.

The fact that in 1960 he started a mixer business is ironic to say the least.

Joining the Family Business

In 1979, Tom was working at Schlitz in Milwaukee after graduating from UW-Eau Claire with a degree in education, and my dad asked him if he could join Continental and whether he could start in October of 1979. Our family business was in dire straits and our dad needed help – fast!

After making 40 tractors a day at the West Allis manufacturing plant, I was laid off from the Allis Chalmers tractor division in January 1980 and decided to join the company February 1st. And I remember Tom asking me, "Why would you want to work at CPC, you don't get paid jack?" So I figured I had nothing to lose and joined Continental. Coyne, Jr. left American Motors after working in North Carolina and Oregon and came aboard The USS Continental in June of 1980.

Our father had rounded up three of his son's to help him out in a desperate effort to keep the ship afloat! And I remember our first meeting in the dining room on Menlo with Mom, Dad, Coyne Jr., Tom and myself, just after my 20th birthday. My father said, "I don't have much to offer you in the way of a paycheck, but if we can generate mixer sales, we can get out of debt and everyone can benefit from our success in the future – we need sales!. Without sales, we have nothing!"

August 1980, Tom and Bill replace a Mark III
Rollo-Mixer in Jefferson, Ohio

For twenty years, our Dad was the Salesman, Engineer, Marketing department, Management, and responsible for new Product Development. He was a one man band!

The first major project we worked on was in Plymouth, Indiana, erecting a huge blend tower for a customer who has used our equipment to mix recycled aluminum since the early '60s. It was one of the few mixing applications outside the animal feeds

214

and bulk fertilizer industry the Rollo-Mixer was involved in. We worked with Phoenix Steel (now PDM Bridge) in Eau Claire to supply components for a blend tower that included the massive super structure and multiple-bin clusters supported above our Continental Vertical Blend System.

In the fall of 1980, the manufacturing plant was building a 133-cubic-foot-capacity mixer for a company in New Washington, Ohio, and not much else. The economy was in a deep recession with interest rates at 22 percent and inflation at 12.5 percent. We were having a difficult time selling capital goods to our customers. It was a tough time for America. There was a sense of helplessness in the country. We had hostages in Iran, high unemployment, lines at the gas station; the country's spirit was really down. And no mixer sales! The U.S. was fortunate to elect a leader in Ronald Reagan who brought needed optimism and renewed hope for the people of our great nation.

My brother Tom and I drove Dad's green Buick down to Louisville, Kentucky, to change a mixer seal at a Ralston Purina plant. While we were working on the Mark IV Rollo-Mixer that was built in 1964, we explained to Don B. and Don H., the plant engineers, that we had improved the design of our mixer with the new Mark V. The Dons contacted their headquarters at Checkerboard Square in St. Louis and arranged a test to blend their calf milk replacer at our plant in Osseo.

At this stage of our business, testing was new, so the only available test unit was also the production unit being built for New Washington, Ohio.

The research-and-development folks from Ralston Purina arrived in January 1981, and we tested a typical batch of Chow 2000, which was a 3,000-pound batch of calf milk replacer. We mixed the batch for 35 minutes, stopping the mixer every half-minute to retrieve samples from the front, middle, back and to the left, center and right of the shaft, amassing well over 200 Dixie cup-sized samples to be evaluated at their lab in Missouri. It took a few months to get the results back from RP. When they called back, they were vague about the results, and they asked if they could run another test. This seemed strange. For one, what happened the first time we tested? Were the results good or bad? And two, we had shipped our most recent test mixer to Ohio two months ago.

We opted to build a new machine for the second RP test and hoped to sell it in the future. This wasn't an easy task, as we didn't have any capital to invest in the raw materials, but somehow we came up with the steel and drive components to build a machine. We tested again in late spring and this time the only difference was that Bill Braun, the director of manufacturing at RP, was in attendance.

The test results came back much quicker this time around – within two weeks - and the results were stellar. After the second minute, the lab analysis proved that we achieved uniformity in two minutes and did not waiver more than two-tenths of one percent throughout the 35-minute test. The test results mirrored the previous findings. The remarkable mixing data showed that during the trial, we added only 30 grams of a red iron oxide tracer to be distributed among 3,000 pounds of powder, and tracers were found in every one of the 200 samples.

What we learned as a company from the RP test echoed what Otis Nelson, Sr. told our dad back in 1960, *"That's a pretty good mixer."* Up to that point, our company's primary focus had been in agriculture-related industries - animal feeds and fertilizer. Armed with the eye-opening test results, we decided to pursue any market that requires uniform blending.

Opportunity Knocks

While Coyne and I were traveling back from a service trip to Turtle Lake, Wisconsin, in the spring of 1981, we were heading east on Highway 8 through the unincorporated town of Poskin, Wisconsin. The small town consisted of a feed mill, a church and a post office that doubled as a restaurant. Even though the Poskin Feed Store appeared to be a small operation, we stopped in to see if there might be an opportunity to sell a Rollo-Mixer. After meeting with the mill owners, we drove home with plans to draw up a 7.5-ton feed mixer and new elevator leg. After we designed the new equipment into the mill, I drove up to Poskin with my dad to sell them a new Mark V Rollo-Mixer and a 50' (or was it 60') elevator leg. We reviewed the drawings and equipment costs, and after we finished the negation phase, they decided to buy it! The whole process of finding the customer, designing a mixing process and then closing the deal was fascinating. I had just turned 21 and sold my first Rollo-Mixer. And the feeling I had was exhilarating.

Roughly two months later, we shipped the equipment on our flatbed truck and began the installation adventure. The crew was made up of Tom, Phil Cataldo, Dad and me. I was the design engineer and Tom was the on-site welder. With the mixer installed, sitting level and square on the wooden plant floor, we erected the long-bucket elevator in the parking lot so we could lift and install it as one. I was surprised when Tom showed me the drawing I had put together with five 10-foot elevator sections on the front view and only four 10-foot elevator sections shown on the side view. Since we had only built four sections in the first place, Tom and I agreed to go with the side view, which should have enough height to run downspouts to the mixer, bagging bin and bulk load-out.

And thank God it wasn't any taller because when the crane operator lifted the massive elevator leg high in the air and into position, the entire crane and load began to topple over the warehouse section of the mill and the boom laid on its side as it severely damaged the roof. As the crane tipped over, the elevator dropped on the railroad tracks on the other side of the mill. The disaster resulted from the operator forgetting to employ his four out-riggers before making the important lift, which should have been covered on the first day of Crane Operating 101.

At one point during the installation, my Dad slipped on the roof and appeared headed for a dangerous fall. I happened to be standing next to him at the time and, grabbing him by the coat with my right hand, I was able to pull him back up. He looked up at me with a smile and said, "Thanks. I was on my way down to the ground."

We recovered from both unfortunate incidents and completed a beautiful installation that is still in operation today. As we drove back to Osseo, Tom said, "You know, Bill, our company is going to make it."

Saving Menlo Boulevard

The movie "Star Trek II – The Wrath of Kahn" is in the top five on my list of favorite classic movies. Many lessons are cleverly woven throughout the script; including the Kobayashi Maru test, which is given to future starship captains. Among other things, this is a lesson in life. The test is a training simulation program that puts the ship in peril and, no matter what you do, you can't win. Kirk didn't believe in the no-win scenario and altered the computer program so he could rescue the ship. As Admiral Kirk explains, "It wasn't a fair test of my command abilities – I don't like to lose." Apparently he was the only trainee to pass the test and received a recommendation for original thinking.

When "The Wrath of Kahn" came out in theaters in 1982, I went with Phil Cataldo who is a great friend from Milwaukee and also a big Star Trek fan. Phil is half Italian and half Sicilian, which gives him the ability to look Klingon or even Romulan if he's sporting a goatee. While I watched the inspiring sci-fi classic, I realized that we, our company and family (Mom, Dad, Coyne, Tom and me) are playing out the Kabayashi Maru test.

While working in the office with Coyne, Jr. in early 1982, all we had operating at the time were the phones. The gas and power to the plant and office had been shut off because we were behind on the bills. I'll never forget sitting at my desk, seeing my breath as I talked on the phone to potential customers. It was tough. Talk about making cold calls! Coyne, Jr., Tom and I worked four years straight without receiving a paycheck.

The manufacturing plant had been closed since the first of the year because there were no machinery sales. Our workforce was laid off – collecting unemployment compensation. The IRS had taken my father to court for past due taxes and the judge said to my parents,

"You have 90 days to pay back your debts or lose your home; we will have a sheriff's auction on Menlo and sell everything." It was the no-win scenario! Tom said he had never seen Dad look so distraught.

How are we going to generate thousands of dollars by September 15, especially when we haven't sold any Rollo-Mixers for months and our workforce was disappearing due to extended layoffs? If my parents lost their home, where would they live? Where would John attend sixth grade in the fall? Where would we relocate Continental's home office? We can't lose Menlo!

Then in June, just two weeks after our meeting with the judge, we sold two identical Rollo-Mixers in Danville, Illinois, and a month later we sold another fertilizer mixer in Jewell, Ohio. We restarted the plant on July 21st and brought the men back to work. Frank had retired after working with Dad for 20 years, so I was the draftsman and, along with Tom and Dad, we were the engineering department. In September, needing the money to pay the IRS, we sold a new model, a 3-ton capacity feed mixer to Cloverleaf Farm Supply in Cadott, Wisconsin. That down payment on September 12 and the money Mom inherited from the passing of my grandmother Mimi allowed us to come up with the money required to pay back our debt. With no time left on the clock, we saved our parents' home and Dad's office on Menlo. We had beaten the "No-Win Scenario."

As a kid, I was taught to: Never say die! Never give up! Never quit! That lesson from my parents has helped me overcome adversity throughout my life.

Looking to shore up our engineering department, I hired and fired a full-time draftsman, who was often three sheets to the wind and didn't last that many weeks. I contacted Manpower to help me find a full-time engineering draftsman. What we got in return was a special individual who was a combination of Paul Bunyan's younger brother and the Angel Gabriel's older brother – all in the guise of John (Jack) L. Schintgen. He was truly a godsend!

Jack rolled into the plant parking lot in a refurbished school bus with his wife Kathy and six children. As they poured out of the bus, Jack lined them up in order from oldest to youngest, like Captain Von Trapp from the "Sound of Music." Jack was a giant of a man at 6-foot-6 and when we shook hands mine disappeared. As Tom and I shook hands with the rest of the family, one of the kids looked up, made eye contact and smiled. His name was James.

Jack adapted immediately to our family business and his contribution was immeasurable. We immediately put him to work designing the fabrication drawings needed for producing the Danville and Cadott mixers. He and I worked together in our engineering department for many years. Jack is one of the most heavenly souls I have had the pleasure to know. His son James has worked as a designer in our business for more than 15 years and possesses the same kind, humble, easy-to-work-with characteristics his father did.

Traveling the 'Continental' United States

In the mid '80s, we built a small demonstration Mark V Rollo Mixer that fit perfectly in the back of our Toyota SR5. The little mixer plugged into a 110-volt outlet and had viewing windows in the back to illustrate the unique mixing action. We actually used the original drive components from the Mark III demo mixer that our dad drove around in a VW bus in the '60s. And I would often use fragile bird seed ingredients to show off the Rollo-Mixer's gentle mix action.

On a trip to Connecticut, I was dancing and driving northeast on I-95, just past New Rochelle, New York, and listening to "Neutron Dance" by the Pointer Sisters. The song was a smash hit and also the opening number to the 1984 classic movie "Beverly Hills Cop." As I was flying along the New England Thruway, playing the energetic rhythm as loud as possible, I suddenly came upon a tollbooth and slowed down to a stop. I rolled down the window and saw a pretty black lady who looked like Beula May Pointer and reminded me of Margaret McBride. Really friendly! She had long fingernails and a happy smile. She loved the music blasting from my car and said, *"How ya'll doing?"* "I'm just burning, doin' the neutron dance," I replied and gave her a dollar. She handed me a receipt and said, *"I heard dat!"*

Neutron Dance   From www.songlyrics.com

I don't want to take it anymore
I'll just stay here locked behind the door
Just no time to stop and get away
'Cause I work so hard to make it every day

Whoo oooh, Whoo oooh

There's no money falling from the sky
'Cause a man took my heart and robbed me blind
Someone stole my brand new Chevrolet
And the rent is due, I got no place to stay

Whoo oooh, Whoo oooh

And it's hard to say
Just how some things never change
And it's hard to find
Any strength to draw the line
I'm just burning doin' the neutron dance
I'm just burning doin' the neutron dance

I wonder……..Did the Pointer Sisters sing this song about me?

The Right Stuff

One of my favorite stories and movies to date is "Apollo 13." There have been times in our business when we have been in survival mode. And somehow we made our way through.

There are so many aspects of the Apollo 13 mission that went wrong that it's astonishing that those three astronauts didn't wind up lost in space. The mission to land on the moon became a mission to bring three brave men back home to earth – alive. "Apollo 13" is a masterpiece! The drama between technology and human survival is incredible. I admire people like Gene Krenz, flight director, whose strong leadership and "failure-is-not-an-option" attitude helped NASA get through its toughest mission. When Krenz overheard President Nixon's people guessing the odds of bringing these men home safely, he responded with, "Gentlemen, this will be our finest hour!" And it was!

Many times I have felt like Gene Krenz when things in our business looked desperate and the odds were against us – only to see us miraculously recover and create opportunities from the adversity.

We were in one of those survival modes after 9/11. The fourth quarter of 2001 was eerily quiet, and we were having a difficult time selling our machinery (shades of the early '80s and '90s). We desperately needed an order before year end! On December 28, I called my friend Mike, who is one of our customers and friends in Ohio, and asked if he would purchase a Rollo-Mixer before the end of the year so we could meet some critical deadlines like; pay our health and liability insurance and payroll. The next day, Todd drove into Osseo in his Fed-Ex truck with a check and we were able to get out of 2001 alive. I am forever grateful to my friend Mike for coming to our rescue at a time when we needed it most! He's one of the finest and most giving souls I have ever met on earth.

Present-day Osseo

Ever since I can remember, my father has had to spell the name Osseo to many vendors around the country. To this day, I still hear him say in his Navy vernacular *Obo-Sugar-Sugar-Easy-Obo* spells Osseo!

Going to work in Osseo is wonderful. The city is a collection of 1,400 Norwegians who are friendly and a joy to work with. It's a town of Olsons, Andersons, Nelsons, Johnsons, Rongstads, Rightstads and Ottestads.

When I first arrived in the early 1980s, I thought of making a bumper sticker that simply read: "Osseo Later" (I'll See You Later).

Having a business in Osseo is like having a business back in the '60s, when the workforce was reliable and dedicated and everyone in town knew you by name. My son Joe says Osseo is like the Shire on Lord of the Rings. Everyone is so friendly and helpful.

Other companies in town, including Electric Cleaner Co., Titan Air, Osseo Plastics and Global Finishing Systems, are most gracious – often lending materials and services and expertise without an invoice. No unions, low corporate taxes, friendly, helpful people. As an employer it's hard to beat that combination!

From Marlene and Linda at the Norske Nook restaurant with award winning pie to Larry and Betty at the local Kwik Trip store, the hometown feel of being treated like someone special is what Osseo is all about.

One morning in early 2009, I stopped in the Kwik Trip to grab some fresh coffee and a Milwaukee Journal Sentinel. It was absolutely freezing outside as the mercury dipped to 27 below. As I piled my items on the checkout counter, I asked Betty, "Have you ever heard of an ass freezer?" Without hesitation or a verbal response, she pointed out the window and looked at me with a matter-of-fact "right out there" expression. "Exactly!" I said.

Necessity is the mother of invention

When Tom and I started Farm Equipment Repairs in the mid '80s, it was out of necessity to generate revenue for the company. We needed to supplement infrequent Rollo-Mixer sales. It also turned out to be a way to meet local dairy farmers living outside of town in the beautiful, glacial terrain of west-central Wisconsin. Since the manufacturing plant could sheer, bend, roll, drill, punch, cut, weld, sandblast or paint anything made of steel, we figured we could repair or replace just about any farm implement and went after the business.

We ran print and radio advertisement campaigns for two solid years to establish our presence, even though we have been cloaked in Osseo since 1960. In fact, we actually went full circle when we started Farm Equipment Repairs because the plant was originally built by the Osseo Industrial Development Corp. to serve local farmers who have breakdowns on the farm and need immediate support. The ads in the <u>Tri County News</u> and <u>Trading Post</u>, along with the 30-second radio ads that Hayes helped us create at TV-18, generated an instant response on many fronts.

Every piece of farm machinery you could picture began to roll into the plant - hay bailers, fertilizer spreaders, antique tractors, barn cleaner chutes, and odorous manure spreaders that left a stench at the plant for days. Even the steel in the racks smelled like manure! There wasn't enough air freshener at Waldo Johnson's Supermarket to mask the smell. When it came time to pay the bill, some of these champs would walk in the office with a smile on their face and knee-high cow crap on their overalls, often leaving remnants on the carpet.

One farmer said it was the smell of money; I knew it was the smell of s$#%. But in a way he was right, the farm repair business was created to generate cash flow and it turned out to be a successful move at a critical time for our business. But beyond the business, we got to meet some of the kindest, most genuine, hard-working, laid-back people you will find. These dairy farmers are the salt of the earth. They are truly the backbone of our great country and in my mind the spirit of America and all that it stands for.

And the stories they tell with a Norwegian twist are some of the best I have heard. Most of these guys don't know they are gifted standup comics who could give Seinfeld and Leno a run for their money. One of my favorite comedians - I mean farmers - is Don G. from nearby Strum, Wisconsin. He was one of our first customers and is still the same fun kid 24 years later.

Don tells the following story with a pure Norwegian inflection:

Two young brothers were lying awake in their beds one night and

224

the older one says to his younger brother, "Tomorrow, I think I'm going to use a cuss word." The younger sibling asks, "Oh, really, what word are you going to use?" The older brother says, "Hell." With that his little brother says, "I think I'll use a cuss word tomorrow, too." "What word are you going to use?" his brother asks. "Ass."

So the next morning the two brothers wake up, come downstairs to the kitchen and sit down at the table. Their mother asks the older boy, "What kind of cereal would you like for breakfast?" He replies, "Aw, hell, I'll have some Wheaties." With that, his mother grabs him by the ear and takes him out back for a lickin'. When she comes back into the kitchen, she asks the young boy, "And what cereal are you going to have for breakfast?" And he proudly answers, "You can bet your ass I'm not havin' Wheaties!"

Over the last twenty years, we have rebuilt just about every piece of farm machinery you could imagine, and some machines you couldn't imagine, like the AH-1 Cobra Helicopter that sits on display at the VFW Post in Strum, Wisconsin. This Vietnam era War Bird left our plant in 2005 looking like it did the day it flew off the original show room floor in 1967. During the refinishing stages, we found bullet holes throughout the fuselage from enemy fire while deployed on combat missions in North Vietnam.

The transition we made with our mixing technology; from Agricultural related markets to the inclusion of Industrial and Consumer goods was significant.

From 1986 through 1992, we sold Rollo-Mixers to multiple markets including food and beverage products, animal health products, soaps and detergents, lawn and garden fertilizers, agricultural chemicals, soy polymers, refractory products, pet care products, and building products industries. All the major recycling industries; aluminum, plastic, rubber, paper, metals and glass benefit from our ability to uniformly blend these waste products back to life in an effort to keep the earth clean and green. Since the early '80's, we have established fifteen defined markets we

225

specialize in. We have come a long way in developing the Rollo-Mixer to meet tomorrow's challenge.

***AH-1 Cobra Helicopter Project donated to
VFW Post 6550 in Strum, Wisconsin***

Remember Mathasar, the commander of the Protector from the hit movie "Galaxy Quest?" Regardless of the torment and problems his ship encountered, he often preached, *"Never Give Up – Never Surrender!"* Then he would smile. And like Admiral Kirk, I never believed in the no-win scenario!

Continuing Education

In October 2005, Tom and I drove our Ford van down to Clearwater Beach, Florida, to attend our first IBA (Institute of Briquetting and Agglomeration) Conference. We brought the Mark VI demo unit with us in the back of the van and showed off the Rollo-Mixer's unique free-fall processing technology – the ability to apply liquids on to dry particulates uniformly. The scene was unlike any demonstration I had been a part of, as we were literally on the beach and only 100 yards from the coast with the sound of the Gulf of Mexico rolling ashore. There's nothing like having a white sand beach and the warm Florida sun and the inviting blue water alongside the Continental Rollo-Mixer.

I wrote a white paper for the conference titled, "Exploring the Versatility of Free-Fall Processing." With John's help, I created a power-point presentation for the attendees of the bi-annual conference. Since I was the 11th of 17 speakers, I listened closely to those who spoke before me because I had never presented a white paper on the Rollo-Mixer before. The executive director of the IBA, asked me to participate in the event months earlier; an honor as I was among PhDs, professors, engineers, research chemists and inventors from a variety of industries.

The Japanese fellow who was tenth in line was very articulate and doing fine until he got hung up during a question-and-answer period. One of the bright individuals in the audience asked him a direct question to which he responded, *"I cannot esprain compretry, I steer have prarem with question."* Needless to say, that helped calm me down before it was my turn to get up and speak.

As I stood up in front of the group, I felt right at home exploring the versatility of our unique mixing and coating technology with the IBA. The next day, I was presented with the Neal Rice Award, or Real Nice Award, depending on how you look at it.

Established in 1979 to honor Neal Rice, a founder of the IBA and its secretary-treasurer from 1949 to 1977, this award is given to the author of the paper judged to have the best technical content and presentation at the conference, and delivering a paper with technical depth, newness and/or interest to the marketplace.

The IBA is a nonprofit organization of business and technical professionals interested and involved in the research, development and production of briquettes, agglomerates and other densified products. The meetings have been held regularly since 1949.

Making Ends Meet

I have worked through and survived four recessions with my parents and brothers: 1980, 1990, 2001 and 2008. As a manufacturer of capital goods, we are usually the first item scratched from our customers' budgets during difficult economic times. Regardless of the economy, we have 17 families that count on us to deliver a paycheck every Friday.

I'll never forget handing out payroll one Friday in the late '80s. I walked into the plant with the paychecks and handed them out to everyone. One of the employees, Steve, looked at his check, looked at me, and said in broken Norwegian, *"Okay focker, you and me, right now, oatside!"* I was shocked to say the least. Apparently he was short two hours on his check (an error on my dad's part) and felt like he was getting ripped off. I said, "Sit your Norwegian ass down and relax." I couldn't believe the guy wanted to fight over his errant paycheck. And this happened 20 years before "Meet the Fockers" came out.

I told Tom about the incident, and came up with a new insecticide that I wanted to develop called the "Okay Fogger!" I could already picture the animated Raid commercial!

I could write a separate book on the countless times we miraculously generated enough money to cover payroll in the plant. Over the 1,500 Fridays I have been working in the family business and sweating payroll, we have had to come up with creative means to make ends meet that included borrowing thousands of dollars, from just about every one of our brothers and sisters, to keep the ship afloat. Thank God for them and the unbelievable support from local bankers.

Without their faith in us over the last eight years, we probably would have been out of business after 9/11 went down.

Selling a Rollo-Mixer usually involves meetings/demonstrations, secrecy agreements, product testing, and system design and engineering before finally closing the deal – which I've learned can take anywhere from two weeks to 20 years from initial contact to the purchase order and down payment. So I'm told it pays to be persistent!

We have been fortunate to work with Schewe Trucking Co. of Clintonville, Wisconsin, to ship our Rollo-Mixers around the country. They too are a family operation and run a sound trucking business. Tom Schewe and his daughter Krissy sent me the following fax:

"It is such a pleasure working with everyone at Continental Products. It is so nice when the phone rings and one of the Callaghan's is on the other end. Everyone is so friendly, polite, genuine and caring. We feel so blessed to be working with a company that holds the same family values as we do. Mr. and Mrs. Callaghan must be so proud of the positive characteristics and values they've passed along to their children."

Close Calls

I was once navigating narrow roads through eastern Pennsylvania with a wide-load truck delivering a Rollo-Mixer to Shippensburg. It was 1981 and Otis, Sr. and I were only miles from our destination. I took a hard downhill right turn, lost touch with the right side of the road, rode on two wheels and nearly tipped over. How we didn't lose the load and crash I'll never know! Our company flatbed truck had outriggers, making us 10-feet wide, and the big, green Rollo-Mixer stood more than 15 feet tall. Our elephant-sized load was top heavy as the mixer weighed more than 12,000 pounds.

We were riding dangerously on only two wheels when either our guardian angels miraculously pushed the out-of-control pachyderm back on all fours or my advanced Hollywood stunt-driving skills saved us from catastrophe. I'll bet it was the angels. We tight-roped the center of the road as our right wheels were probably 18 inches off the ground and Otis was sliding toward me on the seat. I was surprised the chains held the large mixer to the bed of the truck and didn't snap from the stress of the suddenly awkward load. When we violently touched down, and I realized the thrill ride was over and that we were still alive and breathing, Otis looked at me, white as a ghost and out of breath, and said, *"You prit near tipped her over."* That said it all. If he had said, *"You pert near tipped her over"* it wouldn't have been as bad, because I've learned that *"prit near"* is much closer than "pert near."

I have driven back and forth to work for more than 25 years without an accident. The 20-mile ride to work from Eau Claire to

Osseo is usually a relaxing trip that allows me time to focus on things I hope to accomplish that day.

The ride to work on December 17, 2008, however, could have easily been my last. It had snowed about three inches the night before and the city streets were covered in white fluff. I started my car in the five-degree climate and let it warm up for ten minutes, while Meghan and I got ready to embark on a new day. I'm so fortunate that I get to drive Meg to school each morning on my way to work. It's one of those one-on-one times I get to spend with my daughter that I cherish so much.

After I dropped my youngest at South Middle School, I stopped back at the house and snow-blowed the driveway while it was still free of tire marks. The machine did the job in 20 minutes and I left for Osseo. As I merged onto I-94 at the Exit 68 interchange, the highway appeared clear and dry so I took the car out of four-wheel drive as I headed southeast into the morning sun.

I had just passed the Highway 53 interchange as the road gradually veers south just past Gander Mountain when the back of my car suddenly slid abruptly to the left on what apparently was "black ice." I quickly turned the wheel to correct my direction and when the car hit dry pavement it lurched left at an awkward angle and wanted to roll over.

At that point I knew I had lost control of the vehicle and remember saying out loud, "I'm going to lose this car - I'm going to crash this car!" The momentum of my Isuzu Ascender sliding down the highway at 70 miles an hour was out of control; I was a passenger on a terrifying roller-coaster ride. The car then swung to the right and tipped slightly but again did not roll as I crossed into the left lane just under and past the Highway J bridge – heading directly for the guard rail.

At the last second, my car slid around to the right on the snow-covered median and smashed into the rail, first with the front right corner of the car at probably 65 miles an hour and my car spun around and its back right corner blew up as I made an even deeper dent in the steel rail. When I realized I was going to crash, I held onto the steering wheel as hard as I could and braced my body against the seat, leaning into the driver's door. If I had missed the guard rail, my car would have continued through the median and into oncoming traffic.

The problem was that I wasn't wearing my seat belt and when you go from 70 to 0 in 3.5 seconds – you are bound to get hurt. After hitting the guard rail twice, my car slid further down the highway and stopped along the left shoulder, perpendicular to the left lane and only a foot away from oncoming traffic.

I looked at the clock - 8:15 - and my car was still running with the heater on. I looked over to my right only to watch a minivan hit the same patch of black ice and begin to swerve back and forth down the road. I was thinking, "Oh, no, she's going to slide into me." Fortunately, the van slid safely into a ditch off the right side of the highway.

All the windows were still intact and the air bags didn't deploy, but everything else in my car was disheveled and thrown everywhere – except me. I conducted a systems diagnostic check on my body starting at the top and working my way down. My neck worked fine. My back, shoulders, and elbows and wrists – all fine. My hips and knees and ankles – no problem. I wasn't hurt – not even a scratch or a bruise! I can't explain it, except that my guardian angel must have created an invisible air bag around me at the point of impact. I hadn't moved from my seat.

I sat there in my car and realized I had just been in a bad accident and watched each car and semi-truck whiz past, thinking they might slide into me. I watched as they drove over parts of my car spread all over the highway. Although I was in a dangerous spot, I didn't want to get out of the warm car and stand along the highway. The contents of a 16-ounce coffee I had just bought at Kwik Trip were all over the passenger-side windows and door panels. I found my cell phone in the back of the car soaked in java and disassembled the phone so I could dry out the battery and call for help. After several failed attempts, I finally got power and a signal on my Blackberry. I called the plant and told Coyne I wiped out on the interstate and ruined my black Ascender - but for some reason I wasn't hurt. Coyne said I hit a guardian angel rail.

I had waited in my car for more than 15 minutes before a state patrol car came from the other direction and turned around to help the lady in the minivan. Moments later a yellow plow-truck showed up fully loaded with salt. It covered the deadly sheet of glass with a heavy dose of ice melt. It wasn't until 8:40 a.m. when a dark-blue Suburban cop car pulled up behind me and a nice gentleman came over to check on me. He asked if I was Okay and if I hurt anywhere. I told him I was fine but a little shaken from the ordeal. Later I realized I was in shock and didn't know it. When the tow-truck arrived, the driver said, "That's what I like to see - shiny side up." "What does that mean?' I said "You did a nice job of preventing the car from rolling over," he answered. "I didn't do anything; it was beyond my control," I said.

I jumped into his cab and watched as he winched the damaged Isuzu onto the bed of his truck. The car was a wreck but somehow all of the fluids were in their proper place, which explains why the engine continued to run. I asked him if he could give me a ride to work and drop off the car at Nelson's Collision Center in Osseo. I was riding a heavy adrenaline buzz and was still amazed I walked away from the accident unscathed, but I went to work that day like it was any other day. I should have been seriously injured, at the very least in critical care, but somehow I survived the crash even though the car was totaled.

That evening, when I was instructing my eighth-grade religion class at Immaculate Conception school, I told my students I was in a bad accident that morning and, like a fool, wasn't wearing a seat belt. I told them never to drive or ride in an automobile without a seat belt on because you never know when something unforeseen like black ice may suddenly appear and change your life in a matter of seconds. I explained that if my car had gone into a roll, the odds of surviving the accident, without wearing a seat belt, were not good.

As I finished my story, Mike Stage, who works with me as a catechist, told the eighth-graders that he had gone out that day to buy gifts for everyone in the class and for some reason had bought a Christmas present for Mr. Callaghan – unaware of what had happened earlier that day. He was so excited for me to open the gift that he couldn't wait until Christmas. I opened the present in front of the class. It was a beautiful piece of stained wood with a morning sun carved out of the top left corner and the following message engraved in italics:

Good morning,

This is GOD.......

I will be handling all your problems today. I will not require your help.

I read it to myself at first and then almost cried as I read it out loud to the class. I could feel waves of tingling vibrations reverberating throughout my body. I was moved with so much emotion. The plaque hangs on our kitchen wall where my whole family can read it each day.

I am very fortunate and blessed to have walked away from the auto accident. My car was totaled while I was unharmed! Ever since that morning, I have a renewed appreciation for every moment of every day. I feel like I was given a whole new lease on life and that God must have a few things he still wants me to accomplish - like finishing this book.

While watching the History Channel in a New Orleans hotel room, I happened to catch an episode of Modern Marvels titled "Dangerous Roads." It was a fascinating documentary for someone like me who travels thousands of paved miles per year to earn a living.

I was surprised to learn that in the U.S., more than 40,000 people die on 4 million miles of road per year, or five motorists every hour. The show explained how guard rails are designed to absorb impact and prevent vehicles from continuing into oncoming traffic.

One of the computer simulation programs used for designing guard rails showed what happens when a vehicle at high speeds crashes into a steel barrier. As I sat in my hotel room watching the show, I felt like I was driving the simulation car because it looked too much like the accident I had. Thank God for safety design engineers!

FYI – Did you know that if you smash into a guard rail, you are sent the bill to repair the damage? I just found out cause I just got the bill!

More than 1.5 million weather-related crashes occur per year in the U.S. and 75 percent of those are due to wet (or frozen) roads. Globally speaking, most accidents occur at intersections and the highest automobile death rate is in China – 2.5 times more deaths per year than in the U.S. And even though China accounts for only 2 percent of the world's drivers, it accounts for 15 percent of auto-related deaths. One expert concluded that there is "no car culture heritage" in China as the automobile is a fairly new concept. In the U.S., we have come a long way in designing safer roads and automobiles as the death rate in 1909 was 32 times higher than today.

Better Times

In all my travels, I think my favorite moment in time is driving into my hometown of Milwaukee and smelling apple cider oozing from the Ambrosia Chocolate factory as I drive under the 27th Street Bridge. And as I head East, I can see the glowing amber light high atop the Gas Company building on my left and the Train Station on my right. It is great to see Lake Michigan growing larger in the windshield straight ahead. I'm listening to "Bloody Well Right" from Supertramp's Crime of the Century CD as loud as possible and playing the "piano" with both hands on the dashboard. And I'm hitting every note on my dash (key)board. The piano is my favorite instrument; one day I may to take lessons and learn how to really play.

One of the daily drives that had to be taken while growing up in Milwaukee was the morning ride downtown to pick up the company mail at the U.S. Post Office, which is located next to the train station. Usually my mom made the trip, and I always went along so I could check out the great Lake Michigan as we drove along its pristine shores. The journey along Lincoln Memorial Drive was and still is one of my favorite tracks – it gives me the feeling of truly being home.

In the 1960s and early '70s, Milwaukee's harbor operated the Clipper, a car ferry that traveled between Muskegon, Michigan, and Milwaukee. I had always wanted to drive my car onto the Clipper and sail across the lake, but the ferry service ended before I was old enough to drive.

Then in June 2004, the Lake Express opened service, linking the two locations and thus saving travelers from the obnoxious drive through traffic-jammed Chicago. The high-speed Lake Michigan voyage takes just 2½ hours from Wisconsin to Michigan.

On July 12, 2006, I was able to make good on one of my childhood dreams. I had an important meeting with a customer in Holland, Michigan, and brought my 15-year-old daughter, Michelle, and her two friends Lauren, and Emma on the business adventure. One of our customers was finalizing an order to purchase two Rollo-Mixers to blend automotive pigments used in the interiors of new cars being manufactured around the world. My job was to design a new state-of-the-art blending and packaging system with the process and project engineers for their new plant in Apodaça, Mexico

We left Eau Claire in the morning and drove to Milwaukee to see my parents on Menlo. After Michelle gave Emma and Lauren a quick tour of the house, we followed Mom and Dad to the newly built boat terminal next to the Summerfest grounds. My folks watched from outside their car as we drove aboard the ship with 45 other vehicles. We quickly walked to the top deck to wave goodbye. As we shoved off, a thick cover of clouds engulfed the port, and we watched as Massa and Dadzo (my Mom and Dad) evaporated into the mist.

Michelle, Lauren, Emma, and Bill at the beach
in Holland, Michigan

The three girls were having too much fun doing cartwheels on the sun deck as the boat sped above the water. The driving winds would blow you off your feet if you didn't watch your every step. At one point, I was down below in the main cabin and could hear the pounding of the girls' footsteps dancing above. They had a ball!

Michelle, Lauren and Emma had the time of their life during the quick ride, and it was so fun watching the three of them jumping around like little kids. In no time at all, we arrived into the port of Muskegon as the sun set into our wake. We returned to the Ascender and continued our journey to Holland.

The next morning, I left for my meeting, while the girls hung out by the pool. The meeting was most successful as we were able to redesign the process to fit two Rollo-Mixer blend systems at the existing facility in Mexico.

I picked up the girls at the hotel, and we drove a few miles south to Holland State Park to check out the beach. As a child growing up in Milwaukee, I spent many days swimming in Lake Michigan at Atwater Beach, so I was always curious what the other side of the lake was like. When we got out of the car, I was surprised to see a bustling beach filled with hundreds of sunbathers, swimmers, Frisbee throwers and powerboats just offshore. It was like I had traveled back to Atwater Beach in the 1960s. One of the things I miss most about Milwaukee is Lake Michigan.

It's not a job – it's an adventure

I have been fortunate to journey throughout 45 of the 50 United States in my 29 years with Continental.

My job sends me on adventures many times a year, about twice a month on average. As I arrive in a new city, it takes me about a day to become acclimated to the new town and its surroundings. When I'm on the road, I am on a mission to accomplish a specific goal and create new business for our company. I love absorbing the various parts of our country and the unique cultures that make up this great nation. Just as I've settled in and adjusted to a new environment, usually two or three days at a time, I find myself back at the airport catching a plane or driving back to my beautiful part of the world in Eau Claire, Wisconsin – home!

In my travels, I've always been intrigued by the many accents of the English language that exist throughout the U.S. The East Coast has its own unique sound, kind of a cross between the Sopranos and the old Aardvark cartoon character. In fact, when I was in London with my wife, Laurel, in 1999, we were standing in the lobby of the Grosvenor House hotel, and I heard a familiar-sounding voice stored deep in my memory banks. I locked in on it and realized it was the Aardvark – I mean Jackie Mason. I looked around the crowded entrance and, sure enough, spotted the fast talking toon having a spirited conversation with an Irish friend. I closed my eyes and felt like a kid again; watching Saturday morning cartoons!

I have been told that people from the Midwest have a distinct tone, but I don't notice it much because I live in the heart of the region. But the purple people from *Minnesoota* tend to drag out their Os when they verbalize. After I migrated to west-central Wisconsin in the early '80s, I met many friendly Norwegians who possessed a Norsked language that could be considered broken English on some farms. During my early days in Osseo, I remember asking this fella if the UPS Truck had been here yet and he replied, "*I seen where one time he come by, so ....*" And I remember thinking at the time, "Who's teaching English at Osseo-Fairchild High School?"

Natives in the south-central and southeastern parts of the U.S. certainly have developed a different version altogether. I have toured the South on many occasions, throughout Alabama, Georgia, the Virginias and the Carolinas. One day it dawned on me why people from the South sound so different – it's all in the vowels. Long "I"s are short "O"s, short "I"s are long "E"s and vice versa. For example: "*If ahm feexin to play golf in Alabama, first odd make a tee tom.*"

My friend Larry Baker from Sylacauga, Alabama, would call and say, "*Beely, odd lock to bah another meexer.*" Larry and I became good friends while working on several Rollo-Mixer projects. I'll never forget when he said to me, "*Beely, won't you be surprozzed when you arrov at the pearly gates and St. Peter say's, 'Hey ya'll, where you been?'*" "Larry, there's no way St. Pete was from Alabama!" I replied.

I think he is as entertained when I open my Yankee mouth as I am when he articulates his southern version of the English language. When I first visited Sylacauga in 1987, I walked into the reception area of Parker Fertilizer to meet Larry and this pretty southern belle greeted me at the door. We talked for a few minutes. I asked her what her name was and she said, "*Peeny.*" I told her that I had never heard that name before and asked how it's spelled. She looked at me somewhat puzzled and said in a sweet, soft southern voice, "P-e-n-n-y." "Oh – Penny," I said. Then she said, "*You tauwk funny.*" I thought to myself, *I* talk funny.

I have come to the conclusion that Huckleberry Hound was from Georgia.

Larry is one of the most gracious and accomplished individuals I have met in all my travels. He is a tall-walking man with snakeskin boots, blue jeans and usually a long-sleeve shirt with the initials "LB" above the shirt pocket. Larry has a southern sense of humor that won't quit. I have the utmost respect and admiration for him and look forward to seeing him again on my next trip to Alabama, along with Fred Carney, Tim Orton and David Pursell, all of whom have become good friends from the South. Ya'll are great people!

In fact, when I jetted down to New Orleans in 2009 for the golf industry trade show, I ran into David and Fred, and later found Tim Orton working in a booth. It was a great surprise! The show was perfect for me as I saw current customers and potential customers from the U.S. and Canada. In the 24 hours I was in town, I was able to speak, face-to-face, to a majority of our customers in the lawn and garden and agricultural chemical industries - all under one roof. I saved months of traveling time and thousands of dollars by attending the golf show, which is sponsored by the GCSAA (Golf Course Superintendants Association of America).

Perks of the Trade

In 1993, I flew to West Virginia to start up a new Rollo-Mixer at the enormous DuPont facility in Parkersburg. The vast complex was bigger than the town of Osseo. Richard, the project engineer, worked closely with us on the product testing and design specifications. He met me at the guard shack and escorted me onto the grounds. We met up with the maintenance and safety group and ran through the mixing process with the operating personnel who would be responsible for the Rollo. The mixer performed well from start to finish. We finished earlier than expected so Richard drove me out to a gorgeous golf course that was carved out of the rolling and undulating mountainous terrain.

When I entered the clubhouse to rent some clubs and a cart, the attendant told me everything was complimentary of DuPont. The royal treatment made me feel like a king, and I realized that all I needed was something to drink and I was on an adventure - playing a new track in West Virginia. I asked the gentleman if I could get an ice water to go. He looked at me with that same puzzled look Penny had given me and began to search around the restaurant and clubhouse, even though the Styrofoam cup, ice and water were right in front of him. When he finally re-appeared, he said, "*Sir, we don't have a fly swatter!*" "No problem – I'll just take an ice water and be on my way," I replied. When I got to the first tee, bugs were flying around my head, and I began to wish he had found a fly swatter.

Fortunately for me though, my friend, Tim Orton, taught me how to get rid of those annoying flies. He said he cuts a little round hole at the seat of his pants and the flies no longer distract him.

From Ada, Minnesota, to Miami, Florida, or Valencia, California, to Summerville, South Carolina, my territory (the continental U.S.) has exposed me to so many wonderful people and places throughout these amazing states.

I recently flew into LAX, jumped in my Budget rental car and drove up the 405, leaving the city of Los Angeles in my rearview mirror and heading for Bakersfield, California.

"Light My Fire" by The Doors was on the radio:

"You know that it would be untrue,

You know that I would be a liar,

If I was to say to you,

Girl we couldn't get much higher – Come on baby light my fire."

As I sang the song as loud as Jim Morrison, I went back in time to when that song was bigger than life in California and around the country.

Then I merged onto the 5 and headed north along the golden-brown San Gabriel Mountains, which look like enormous sand dunes in late October. I looked out the driver-side window and saw a flock of sheep grazing in the elevated fields at 11:00 high. It was a breathtaking sight on an absolutely grand scale. It's the kind of striking image that car crashes are made of.

I flew down the winding Hot Wheels track highway from 4000 feet above sea level, past the "5 mile, 6% downgrade" sign and the runaway truck ramps. The mountains were closing in on me from both sides, and I spilled into the San Joaquin Valley, or more like the Garden of Eden. I had entered America's refrigerator, which was filled with every seed-bearing fruit and vegetable you can imagine - fields with miles of fertile grape vines, cotton plants ready for picking, walnuts waiting to be shaken from their trees and groves overflowing with ripe, vitamin-filled oranges. I have traveled through southern and central California many times but have yet to get used to the depths of her splendor.

Overwhelmed with excitement, I stuck my head out the window and yelled "WOW!" at the top of my lungs as I drove by hundreds of hard-working Mexicans on both sides of the road surgically pruning the fields. I was overwhelmed by the beauty and variety of God's enormous bounty. The migrant workers probably thought I was nuts; seeing this gringo driving down the highway at 70 miles an hour, yelling with his head out the window. I just wanted to make sure God heard me!

The ride back was even better. I was 35 miles south of Shafter, California, and left the valley in a fog as the Tejan Pass awaited my arrival. While ascending up the mountain in a thick cloud, I looked to the east and noticed the top-third elevation bathing in sunlight. At first I thought it was snow-covered terrain and then realized it was the sun glistening off the mountain tops. I felt like I was on another planet or on the Holideck aboard the Starship Enterprise. The scene was surreal.

Time is a Teacher

When I started working at CPC in 1980, I knew very little about the Rollo-Mixer and the many facets of operating a business. Today, I am involved in many aspects of our company and have learned so much about the art of solids processing in multiple industries. I especially enjoy the freedom that comes with working in a family business with my parents. They are a joy to work with and show up every day for work! Remarkable!

Working with my four brothers has been a wonderful learning experience as well!

Left to right: Chris Westphal, Tom, Bill, John, Otis Nelson, Jr., and Terry Burchell

Coyne Jr. and I have been writing up and selling new Rollo-Mixers together since the early '80s. Coyne is ten years older than me and very astute.

Tom and I have been designing tomorrow's Rollo-Mixer together for almost 30 years. CPC had only one Rollo-Mixer design when we started, and we now have five different versions! Tom is five years older and very innovative.

Jim and I work closely on the business finances and special teams projects. We complement each other well. Jim is three years younger and very intelligent.

John and I designed a state-of-the-art website together that went from the third page of "batch mixer" search results to No. 2 in just one year. Our website **www.continentalrollomixer.com** has become a resource library for the solids processing industry. John's mastery of website design and search-engine optimization has us at the top of the charts! John is ten years younger and very creative.

Over the years, we have received letters like this from our customers who have enjoyed working with our family's mixing business.

To all The Callaghan's,

On behalf of all of us at X-Calibur, I would like to thank Bill, Coyne, Tom and Coyne, Sr. for all you did during our visit last Tuesday. It was gratifying to see how all of you pitched in with the project. Please extend our appreciation to Terry and Scott for their help and suggestions.

The back bone of the American economy is the family business and it was wonderful to see one family business working so well with two other family businesses.

This was an interesting task to undertake. Scott, Tom and Bill Callaghan had read up on the procedure, but none of them had actually performed the steps in the process. Everyone contributed a great deal to move this test forward. On the day after the test I spoke with Jack regarding what had transpired during our visit. I used an analogy that we can all relate to in describing the day. I told him that what had been accomplished on Tuesday is equated to reading an article on how to play golf and then going out and playing golf. BIG DIFFERENCE!!!! The physical appearance of the product sure seems as if we had a very good first round.

On a personal note, the three of us would like to thank you again for the Cheese Tray you sent to the hotel as well as the outstanding lunch. Bill, you did not oversell the restaurant. The apple pie at the Norske Nook was the best I have ever had. I really should have taken one home.

We will be in contact with you as soon as we hear the results from the Germans. Their lab results will determine what direction we need to go. Should you have any questions or additional input, please feel free to contact us. We look forward to working with you in the near future.

Thank you,

Dennis Salettel

Working directly with our customers has allowed my family and I to meet many people throughout the country and develop many friendships.

The following is an e-mail exchange between myself and a customer from Minnesota who attended a Rollo-Mixer factory authorization test at our manufacturing plant in May of 2009. Brandon and his wife had 10 children between the ages of 13 and 6 months old and we immediately hit it off. Imagine raising ten children!

Bill,

Thank you very much for a wonderful visit on Friday - I can't thank you all enough.

Please send me a note when your book is available as I would like to pick it up and see how close our two families are alike.

Take care and thanks again for everything - Brandon

Brandon,

I enjoyed meeting you and the others last Friday as well. We are loading the Rollo-Mixer on the truck right now and it looks beautiful. My book is due out in November, and I have added your e-mail info to my master list. It was fun telling stories about our big families at the Norske Nook.

Kindest regards - Bill

Bill,

I completely agree, it was pretty funny at the Norske Nook, and I look forward to seeing your book. I am hoping to pick up pointers from the book and do some laughing as well. Thank you for adding me to your list - I greatly appreciate it.

Best Regards - Brandon

We received this letter from Doug VanDerVoort after he visited our test facility in 2008:

I really enjoyed meeting your parents and brothers. Fathers and sons that work well with each other are always a pleasure to see. I work with my boys much better than I worked with my dad so maybe I learned a little. To be able to work as closely as you all do with your Mom and Dad earns them my respect and admiration.

Having given parenting some thought, I developed a humorous presentation titled, "Experimental Parenting." It makes the point that we really are not trained to be parents, but that as in any experiment, things work best if we plan our actions and evaluate the results. I recently came across an excerpt from an article discussing how humans develop machines for specific purposes and then those machines change our lives in ways we might not have expected, or in ways that we wish they did not. Sometimes we need to restrict the use of our technology or it can have serious downsides to society. The cell phone would be one example. At any rate here is one of that author's thoughts.

"Technology can be sublime, but machines aren't something that happens to us; they're something we make. They are less like meteors that come crashing into our planet than like toddlers. Sure, toddlers crash into you a lot, and they change your life, but they didn't come out of nowhere and if you set your mind to it, you can teach them manners before they get bigger than you."

Your Mom and Dad seemed to have "set their minds to it" with good results on both machines and toddlers.

Regards,

Doug VanDerVoort - Senior Process Engineer - Gelita USA

When people visit our facility and see all the brothers working together and meet our parents, I often hear comments like, "I could never work with my brother; I don't know how you do it" or "How can you work so closely with your parents?" My favorite, though, was from Mike Zinni who came from Niagara Falls, New York, to test a Rollo-Mixer. After meeting seven Callaghans at Continental that day he surmised, "This place reminds me of the Ponderosa."

Chapter 8

Today's World vs. MYOB

When Madonna proudly sang, "We are living in a material world, and I am a material girl," she was profoundly correct. I believe people are way too preoccupied with money, clothes, cars, homes and mo money, mo money.

I think money is overrated and ruins more people than it helps. Money has destroyed marriages, friendships and lives. We all need money to pay the bills but being preoccupied with the accumulation of wealth, in my view, is insane. Some people truly do make money their God. By doing so, they blow the First Commandment out of the water. And I'm not down on people who work their butts off every day to provide for their family and are rewarded handsomely for their efforts. But when you find yourself coveting your neighbors possessions, then it's time to stop and realize how blessed you really are for the many gifts you've been given.

I don't recall my parents ever discussing money or the price of something they purchased when they came home from the store. My parents' financial picture was not openly discussed in our home; it wasn't any of our business anyway.

From the time I can remember, my father's income was based on the success of his mixer business. While growing up, I didn't know if we were rich or poor; money was a topic that was rarely brought up. As I got older, I realized my father rode a financial roller coaster of feast and famine – mostly famine. Some years were more successful than others, but there were many years when it was difficult to pay bills and make ends meet. Cash flow was sporadic at best. But growing up, I could never tell the difference. My parents taught us not to glorify material possessions and constantly want more but rather to be thankful for everything we had. And we were. To ask my parents for something like clothes or my own anything seemed inappropriate in our house.

Years ago I remember hearing, *"He who is thankful for little – enjoys much."*

I'm so proud of my parents. I remember telling them that for the first time about 15 years ago. I just wanted them to know how fortunate I was to be their son and how grateful I was for all they had done for me. And more than that, I thanked them for not teaching me how to be critical and find fault in others.

We are living in a critical world, and I am not a critical dude! Why do we live in such a critical world? I have noticed that people are quick to criticize and complain, and it's rare when you hear someone admit they were wrong. You don't hear "I'm sorry, I made a mistake," "Please forgive me" or "I was wrong" very often anymore. These heartfelt phrases - admitting when you make a mistake - have been replaced with less meaningful ones like "my bad" or "I'm like, sorry dude." What's that? Who came up with "my bad"? That phrase seems so watered down, and it doesn't at all sound like a sincere apology. It's not even proper English; how can someone be "*like* sorry?"

Fortunately for my children, my wife and I are not complainers. The thing that really burns my butt, is how many people today talk negatively about their neighbors (each other). I am amazed at how often I hear parents my age or children my kids' ages constantly put down other people and find every fault possible about that person then ride them to no end. I can't stand it! I've noticed in the last few years it has became "okay" to openly discuss the personal problems of others and share them with whomever.

Pick a little, talk a little,

Pick a little, talk a little,

Pick, Pick, Pick, Talk a lot, Pick a little more!

It's as though nowadays it's acceptable and understood that gossiping, ridiculing and berating another person is routine behavior. The Eighth Commandment is "Thou Shall Not Bear False Witness Against Your Neighbor." Meaning: Don't tell lies about other people and don't spread negative news about other people. Can you believe there is actually a TV show called "Gossip Girl?" What are they selling? Try not to get caught up in that vicious circle.

When was the last time you told someone something unflattering about someone else? Every time you are about to say something that's not nice about someone else – Don't!

Bite your tongue! Nobody likes a false-witness-bearing champ. We've all had people criticize us at different times in our life, so we know how hurtful it feels.

In my view, the world has become filled with judgmental individuals who are pre-occupied with editorialized, condescending conversations about their neighbors. I overheard a high school girl recently expound, *"OMG - I'm like – did you hear what Courtney did last weekend at the party? She is such a skank!"* With today's instant communication tools such as text messaging, Facebook and *MyPants* and, unfortunately, the need to tell, that negative story about Courtney probably made its way around school before fourth hour hit – whether it was true or not!

Criticizing others has become an art form; it's so easy and so addictive, and it is a learned behavior. We weren't born with a critical tongue.

It has become standard practice to put people down on demand. We must realize that our tongue has the power to destroy relationships.

Life is all about building relationships – not destroying them. I'm amazed at all the negative commentary. It's no different than saying, "Hey, guess what? I heard that Paul has poop in his pants and it stinks?" "I heard he might also have skid marks!" All this rampant "false witness bearing" reeks and is so immature!

Media Mayhem

From his 1981 album "I Can't Stand Still," Don Henley perfectly summarized the sensationalism that has been oozing out of our country's national media with the song "Dirty Laundry" – that was 28 years ago and crap is still king, except now it has a stronger smell!

I make my living off the evening news
Just give me something - something I can use
People love it when you lose,
They love dirty laundry

Dirty little secrets
Dirty little lies
We got our dirty little fingers in everybody's pie
We love to cut you down to size
We love dirty laundry

Everybody has some kind of battle they fight, and we have no idea what others are going through or what personal difficulties they are facing; so why are people so quick to judge and condemn? Whatever happened to giving everyone the benefit of the doubt? Whatever happened to "love your neighbor as yourself" or "do unto others as you would have them do unto you"? And what ever happened to "Mind Your Own Business?" I can still hear Dad say, "Hey, it sounds like your nose is out of joint," when he heard someone knocking somebody else.

We have all seen the different movie ratings from G to R to NC-17. I actually think many movies and TV shows coming out of Hollywood today should be rated *S* for shit! I'm amazed at all the movies produced in Hollywood today desensitizing death and the horror movies that have reached a new level of shocking, graphic, disgusting detail with the aid of super-computer animation. My 14-year-old daughter tells me that her friends have sleepovers and watch R (restricted) - I mean *S*-rated - horror movies all night. They think it's cool to watch terrifying flicks like the "Saw" series, and "The Grudge" and somehow prove to their friends how brave they are, that they can stay up and watch this sickening form of entertainment.

My daughter doesn't go to those sleepovers anymore because she went once and those movies still give her nightmares. I'm still sorry I ever saw "The Exorcist," in 1973, when I was in eighth grade. I wish my brain never downloaded that fear-provoking movie. And now we have the low budget film, "Paranormal Activity", which apparently is scaring the S out of everyone who sees it. Fear begets fear!

Heavy sexual overtones seem to be commonplace in TV shows and movies in today's world. I think the message it's sending our children is fogged up. Kids don't get to spend much time being kids anymore because our society today has accelerated their childhood to become young "adults." I can't imagine how high school boys can concentrate at school when many girls are wearing high-definition jeans and sporting a new cleavage.

When I heard that the Writer's Guild of America had gone on strike, I was thrilled. We all needed a break from the adult bathroom humor and constant cynical commentary that was written into most primetime television shows. I only wish they were out of a job because we as a society boycotted their unhealthy product, instead of some compensation problem between the actors' unions and the big production companies. I find most of Hollywood's "entertainment" predictable, condescending "humor" that oftentimes insults my intelligence. It seems that most punch lines or laughter comes when someone is putting somebody down or knocking someone else or using God's name in vain. How poor.

During the NFL season, countless commercials promote Sunday evening's "family" lineup, with "viewer discretion is advised." Why is Sunday night TV filled with material that requires viewer discretion? Unfortunately, it is now acceptable to produce a TV show, especially animated shows, with borderline foul content disguised as humor and slide it into primetime as long as the public is warned in advance that the show contains lots of S.

I wasn't raised with criticism, so therefore I didn't learn how to be critical. Did you know that the antonym of criticism is praise?

As a lector at Immaculate Conception, I rehearse the first and second readings many times, before I'm called upon to deliver the Word of God to the congregation. It is something I take very seriously and I feel honored to be involved in that ministry with Father Klink and IC.

On September 20, 2009 (25th Sunday in Ordinary Time), I read the following letter to the Eau Clairians at the 9:30 mass.

A reading from the Letter of Saint James:
 James 3:16 – 4:3

Beloved:

Where jealously and selfish ambition exist, there is disorder and every foul practice. But the wisdom from above is first of all pure, then peaceable, gentle, compliant, full of mercy and good fruits, without inconstancy or insincerity. And the fruit of righteousness is sown in peace for those who cultivate peace.

Where do the wars and where do the conflicts among you come from? Is it not from your passions that make war within your members? You covet but do not possess. You kill and envy but you cannot obtain; you fight and wage war. You do not possess because you do not ask. You ask but do not receive, because you ask wrongly, to spend it on your passions.

In the "Workbook for lectors and gospel readers" Year B – 2009.; *Mary A. Ehle writes:*

In comparison to those who would be filled with selfish ambition and those who might not be able to control the use of their tongue in teaching others, James speaks of those who show the fruits of wisdom active in their lives by their humility. In so doing, they can be identified as a lover of God, not a lover of the world (4:4-10). The passion of the lover of God is submitting to God (4:7) and the passion of the lover of the world is judging their neighbor. The former brings peace, the latter division.

Fatherhood vs. Brotherhood

One of the signs in front of a Wesleyan Church in Eau Claire read, *"God's approval is more important than man's applause."* How true.

Many years ago I heard my father say, "Man no longer lives by the fatherhood of God, but by the brotherhood of man." As I reflected on that, I think he was saying that man has given up on God to provide divine guidance, and that man now relies on his fellow man for what only God can give.

The Wednesday before Thanksgiving 2008, Scheels Sporting Goods ran a half-page ad in the Leader-Telegram titled "Proclamations of Thanksgiving" by President Abraham Lincoln:

March 1863.

It is the duty of nations as well as of men to own their dependence upon the overruling power of God, to confess their sins and transgressions in humble sorrow, yet with assured hope that genuine repentance will lead to mercy and pardon; and to recognize the sublime truth, announced in the Holy Scriptures and proven by all history, that those nations are blessed whose God is the Lord.

We know that by his divine law, nations, like individuals, are subjected to punishments and chastisements in this world. May we not justly fear that the awful calamity of civil war which now desolates the land may be a punishment inflicted upon us for our presumptuous sins, to the needful end of our national reformation as a whole people?

We have been the recipients of the choicest bounties of heaven; we have been preserved these many years in peace and prosperity; we have grown in numbers, wealth and power as no other nation has ever grown.

But we have forgotten God. We have forgotten the gracious hand which has preserved us in peace and multiplied and enriched and strengthened us, and we have vainly imagined, in the deceitfulness of our hearts, that all these blessings were produced by some superior wisdom and virtue of our own. Intoxicated with unbroken success, we have become too self-sufficient to feel the necessity of redeeming and preserving grace, too proud to pray to the God that made us.

October 1863.

It has seemed to me fit and proper that God should be solemnly, reverently and gratefully acknowledged, as with one heart and one voice by the whole American People. I do therefore invite my fellow citizens in every part of the United States, and also those who are at sea and those who are sojourning in foreign lands, to set apart and observe the last Thursday in November as a day of Thanksgiving and praise to our beneficent Father who dwelleth in the Heavens.

Those words were spoken 100 years before I turned 4. They seem to be more pertinent today than ever before. I wonder how many people are aware that the Thanksgiving holiday was created by Abraham Lincoln as a day of thanksgiving to God.

Chapter 9
The Other Side of Famine

When I was just a little boy, my mom would sing the following song to me:

C - A - LL - A - G - H - A - N spells Callaghan,

proud of all the Irish blood that's in me,

devil a man to say a word agin me.

C - A - LL - A - G - H - A - N you see,

it's a name,

that a shame,

never has been connected with Callaghan,

that's me!

I have always been proud of my Irish heritage. In my mind, everyone should be knowledgeable of their family heritage. You will be surprised at what you learn!

While searching Last Name Meanings on www.last-names.net found:

O'Callaghan (origin: Celtic or Gailic) are the descendants or tribe of Callaghan, from Ciallach meaning; prudent, judicious, discreet.

This surname means descendent of Ceallachan who was the King of Munster from AD 935 until 954. The personal name Ceallach means "bright headed."

Coat of Arms: According to www.allfamiilycrests.com :

The O'Callaghan coat of arms came into existence many centuries ago. The process of creating coats of arms (also called family crests) began in the eighth and ninth century.

The sept arms of O'Callaghan:

Argent in a mount vert, on the dexter side a hurts of oak trees, there from issuant a wolf passant towards the sinister all proper.

The Latin phrase "Fidus et Audux" written on the bottom of the crest means: Faithful and Bold.

I asked my Aunt Corky when the O'Callaghans became Callaghans and she said, "Our brother Tom told us the story that when Grandpa Martin came to America, one of the inspectors said, O'Callaghan – that's too highfalutin a name for America – off with the O. That was it. And when I was real little, I asked Grandpa Martin what happened to the O and he said, Corky, when I was on the ship on the way over, I just threw it overboard."

I would love to have met Great Grandpa Martin Callaghan! I have heard my parents talk about the historical Irish Famine in the 1800's, and I remember reading about it in my social studies class at St. Roberts and Shorewood High. But I never realized the Irish exodus to America was so immense.

From: www.spartacus.schoolnet.co.uk:

At the beginning of the 19th century the dominant industry of Ireland was agriculture. Large areas of this land were under the control of landowners living in England. Much of this land was rented to small farmers who, because of a lack of capital, farmed with antiquated implements and used backward methods.

The average wage for farm laborers in Ireland was eight pence a day. This was only a fifth of what could be obtained in the United States and those without land began to seriously consider immigrating to the New World.

In 1816 around 6,000 Irish people sailed for America. Within two years this figure had doubled. Early arrivals were recruited to build canals. In 1818 over 3,000 Irish laborers were employed on the Erie Canal. By 1826 around 5,000 were working on four separate canal projects. One journalist commented: "There are several kinds of power working at the fabric of the republic - water-power, steam-power and Irish-power. The last works hardest of all."

In October 1845 a serious blight began among the Irish potatoes, ruining about three-quarters of the country's crop. This was a disaster as over four million people in Ireland depended on the potato as their chief food. The blight returned in 1846, and over the next year an estimated 350,000 people died of starvation and an outbreak of typhus that ravaged a weaken population. Despite good potato crops over the next four years, people continued to die and in 1851 the Census Commissioners estimated that nearly a million people had died during the Irish Famine. The British administration and absentee landlords were blamed for this catastrophe by the Irish people. The Irish Famine stimulated a desire to emigrate. The figures for this period show a dramatic increase in Irish people arriving in the United States - about a quarter of the population - had immigrated to the United States in ten years.

A census carried out in 1850 revealed that there were 961,719 people in the United States that had been born in Ireland. At this time they mainly lived in New York, Pennsylvania, Massachusetts, Illinois, Ohio and New Jersey. The Irish Emigrant Society tried to persuade immigrants to move to the interior but the vast majorities were poverty-stricken and had no money for transport or to buy land. They, therefore, tended to settle close to the port where they disembarked.

Thousands of Irish laborers worked on building the railroads in the United States. Some were able to save enough money to buy land and establish themselves as farmers along the routes they had helped to develop. This was especially true of Illinois, and by 1860 there were 87,000 Irish people living in this state.

Other Irish immigrants became coalminers in Pennsylvania. Working conditions in the mines were appalling with no safety requirements, no official inspections and no proper ventilation. When workers were victimized for trade union activity, they formed a secret society called the Molly Maguire's. Named after an anti-landlord organization in Ireland, the group attempted to intimidate mine-owners and their supporters. The group was not broken up until 1875 when James McFarland, a Pinkerton detective and Irish immigrant, infiltrated the organization and his evidence resulted in the execution of twenty of its members.

The Irish tended to support the Democratic Party rather than the Republican Party.

On the outbreak of the Civil War, an estimated 170,000 men born in Ireland joined the Union Army whereas only 40,000 were in the

*Confederate Army. One Irish immigrant, Thomas Meagher, became
a highly successful general in the war.*

Was it General Lee that said, "If we would have had more Irish, we
would have won the war?"

*After the Civil War over a quarter of the US population had been
born in Ireland, with most living in New York, Chicago and Boston.
It was now possible that Irish voters were able to get their
candidates elected to power.*

*Several Irish settlers became successful businessmen. Michael
Cudahy started a highly profitable meat-packing business in
Milwaukee, John Downey made a fortune in real estate as well as
being governor of California (1861-62) and Willaim Grace ran
a steamship company before becoming mayor of New York City
(1880-88).*

*In 1890 there were large numbers of Irish born immigrants in the
states of New York (483,000), Massachusetts (260,000), Illinois
(124,000) and Minnesota (28,000). There were also significant
communities in New York City (190,000), Chicago (70,000),
Baltimore (13,000) and the textile town of Lawrence (8,000).*

*During the period from 1820 to 1920, over 4,400,000 people
emigrated from Ireland to the United States; only Germany
(5,500,000) and Italy (4,190,000) came anywhere near these
figures. In 1840 Ireland had been the most densely populated
country in Europe. By the 20th century this situation had been
completely reversed.*

The following Interview took place in the fall of 2007, at the Plaza
Hotel & Suites in Eau Claire, Wisconsin with my parents, Martha
and Coyne Callaghan.

Bill: "Can you tell me about my great Grandparents?"

*Coyne: My Grandfather Martin Thomas Callaghan came over to
America from Ireland in 1876. He got a job working in the city*

pumping station at the Northeast corner of Chicago Avenue and Michigan Avenue. Strangely enough, the Chicago Fire of 1883 went as far as Chicago Avenue and stopped. The pumping station was not touched.

He started his job there as an oiler. With oil can in hand, he worked a given route oiling bearings. Martin wanted to bring his girlfriend, Frances Dougherty, over to America, but you couldn't bring anybody in at that time unless you had a job for them. So he went up and down Lake Shore Drive, known as the Chicago Gold Coast, and visited the big meat packers' residences of the very wealthy such as Field, Swift, and Armour. He landed Frances a job as a domestic (maid) with one of those homes and made arrangements for her to come to America, and she did. While she was working as a domestic, he was going to night school, studying to be an engineer. Imagine the dedication and tenacity of this guy – He went 11 years to get his degree in engineering. And when he finally got his degree, they transferred him to head up the pumping station at 73rd and Stoney Island. Later they promoted him as Chief Engineer. That's where he worked until he retired. Those people really had a lot of grit.

Bill : *"Was Martin an O'Callaghan when he arrived in America?"*

Coyne: They were all O'Callaghans. Do you know what "O" means in Ireland? It means royalty – or king.

My brother Marty used to work with my grandfather and say to him, 'Gramps, why did you drop the "O" and keep the silent 'g'? We always have to explain the 'g.' I wish you would have left the 'O' and dropped the 'g.'

My brother Tom was quite a student of naval warfare – it was his hobby - a brilliant mind in naval affairs. He had one of the few private libraries with the complete works of Alfred T. Mahan, father of the modern American Navy.

But I remember one time Tom brought our Grandfather to tears. At the time, we were trying to get Ireland to let England move their

259

Callaghan

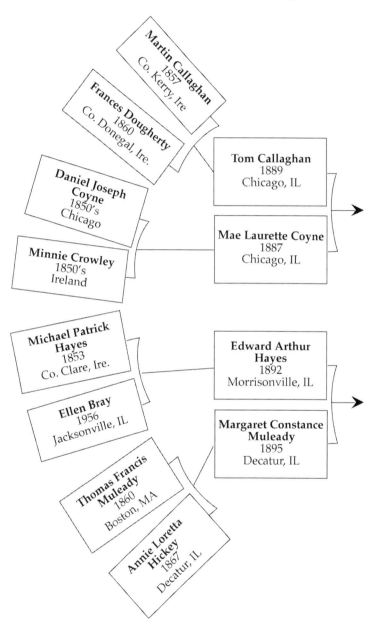

Martin Callaghan
1857
Co. Kerry, Ire

Frances Dougherty
1860
Co. Donegal, Ire.

Daniel Joseph Coyne
1850's
Chicago

Minnie Crowley
1850's
Ireland

Tom Callaghan
1889
Chicago, IL

Mae Laurette Coyne
1887
Chicago, IL

Michael Patrick Hayes
1853
Co. Clare, Ire.

Ellen Bray
1956
Jacksonville, IL

Thomas Francis Muleady
1860
Boston, MA

Annie Loretta Hickey
1867
Decatur, IL

Edward Arthur Hayes
1892
Morrisonville, IL

Margaret Constance Muleady
1895
Decatur, IL

Family Tree

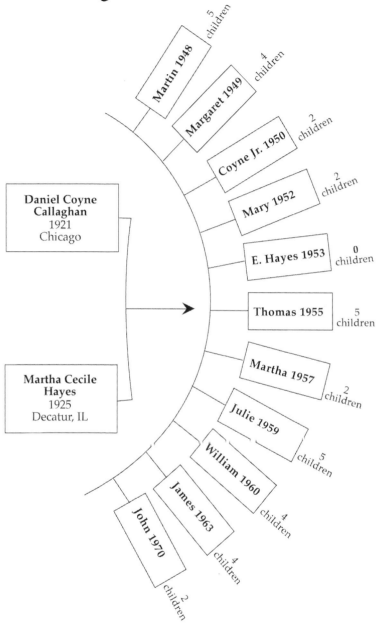

Daniel Coyne Callaghan
1921
Chicago

Martha Cecile Hayes
1925
Decatur, IL

Martin 1948 — 5 children
Margaret 1949 — 4 children
Coyne Jr. 1950 — 2 children
Mary 1952 — 2 children
E. Hayes 1953 — 0 children
Thomas 1955 — 5 children
Martha 1957 — 2 children
Julie 1959 — 5 children
William 1960 — 4 children
James 1963 — 4 children
John 1970 — 2 children

PLEASE NOTE: "While designing the Family Tree – I was not able to fit the long line of 35 grandchildren on the two page layout."……….....................................………Kathy O'Leary

261

Anti-Submarine base up from Scapa Flow. The move would have saved a day's sailing to establish a station there to monitor the submarine traffic. Grandpa Martin despised the Brits and would say "No, No, No! I don't give a damn. Once they get in – they'll never leave. You just can't trust the British."

Before Martin came to America, he left a little class warfare; they used to call the trouble. He owned a rifle and that was considered contraband. So he wrapped it in oilskins, oiled it and so on and he buried it in the bed of a river. When the trouble (British Rule) came up again, he was over here in America. Sympathetic for the cause, he wrote some friends and told them where he put his rifle, in case they would need it.

My other grandfather, Daniel Joseph Coyne, arrived here with several brothers. The exact year I don't recall. And he married Minnie Crowley, and he was quite an entrepreneur. As a matter of fact, my mother used to keep a scrapbook of all her kids. I was born the 27th of October, 1921. In my baby book, there was an article in the newspaper about the Chicago produce merchants on South Water Street. Daniel J. Coyne had two grandsons born within four days of each other, my cousin Dan J. Coyne III and me, Daniel Coyne Callaghan. And the article went on to say what a wonderful, successful entrepreneur he had been. The article mentioned, "Last year alone he earned $3 million candling eggs." He had a produce fortune in Chicago.

Bill: What is candling eggs?

Coyne: You take a piece of brown paper, you know, wrapping paper and you put an oil spot on it that gives a different clarity to the spot. When you pass an egg across that spot, the light reflects through the egg and shows whether the egg is fresh or fertile for marketing.

Martha: I've driven past the shop in Chicago. The awning came down, across the front window and out over a good part of the sidewalk.

Coyne: The leading edge of his awning barely cleared six feet. He loved standing on the sidewalk out there, talking to everybody walking by. If some passerby would bang his head on the awning, Papa Coyne would congratulate him, saying, "That's using your head." It was to get a little attention for the store.

One of Papa Coyne's brothers picked up my brother Marty at his baby christening and offended my mother by saying, (in a strong Irish brogue) "What a fine boy, the scrapings of the pot."

Bill: "How did the Callaghans and the Hayes families first meet?"

Coyne: Your grandfathers, Tom Callaghan and Ed Hayes, met in the Navy in World War I.

Martha: I think that part is fascinating. Talk about going back in history.

Coyne: Tom Callaghan was born in 1889 – so in 1910, at the age of 21, he had already been a secretary to one of the sons of one of the Swift family.

The only education Tom had was shorthand training in business school. Young Swift was the black sheep of their family and was kind of an arrogant, goofy guy – and my Dad was assigned to him. Dad got tired of his incompetence; this guy couldn't dictate a straight letter. He'd say, 'Callaghan, take a letter.' This letter's going to Jones, so and so, Meat Market so and so......... So my dad got tired of the fact he couldn't give a straight letter and he decided to straighten him out.

So the next time he took his dictation, he wrote down and typed every inflection, every offbeat change and handed it in for the signature. Needless to say, he was fired. Nevertheless, the older Swift brother gave my dad a good letter of recommendation, apologized and wished him good luck.

Then he went to work for the Michigan Central Railroad and became the general passenger agent. At 21, he was the youngest

general passenger agent for one of the major railroads in the
United States. When the war came he decided to go to war. He
wrote a letter to all the people he worked with and said 'I'm going
to serve my country.' He ends up at Great Lakes Naval Training
Station. And because of his experience, they commissioned him and
put him in charge of transportation.

Your grandfather, Ed Hayes,
got his legal training and
passed the bar from St. Louis
University. He started his law
practice in Decatur Illinois. In
1917, President Wilson asked
Congress to declare war on
Germany after the Lusitania was
sunk. Ed joined the Navy and
was commissioned as Ensign
and was assigned to Great
Lakes. Admiral Moffitt made
him his aide because of his legal
background. So Ed Hayes was
aide to Admiral Moffitt and my
dad, Tom Callaghan, was head
of transportation.

Ed Hayes in 1918 during World War I.

Martha: So Tom and Ed met in Admiral Moffitt's office in 1917.
Neither one was married at the time. After World War I, Tom
Callaghan headed back to Chicago and Ed Hayes headed back
to Decatur. But over the years they kept in touch. My parents
would see his parents when they'd go to Chicago and once the
Callaghans came to Decatur.

Coyne: Both families loved music. My mother, Mae Coyne, was
very capable. She was very popular in school - May Queen,
valedictorian of her class, etc. Everyone told me she was the life of
the party with her music. She could pick up a tune and play it. And
in those days that was your entertainment. You didn't have TV, so

we'd gather around the piano and she'd play it.

Martha: My mother, Mimi, was the organist at our church. She sang soprano and my father sang bass in the choir. And every party that was ever held at our place in Washington always ended up at the piano.

Bill: I understand Mimi was also from a family of 11 children. Tell me about her family.

From left to right: Aunt Cecelia Meara, Aunt Katie Cooney, Aunt Betty Kearney (lived with us in Decatur), Aunt Ag Walsh, Mimi (Margaret Constance Muleady) was born in 1895. Aunt Ann Muleady (never married), Aunt Julie Burtschi, and Aunt Mary Delaney.

Mom: "Well, Thomas Muleady married Ann Loretta Hickey and the two of them had 8 girls and 3 boys, James, Frank and Thomas – who became a Catholic Priest."

Bill: What about this picture of the Muleady sisters.

Mom: "This picture of Mimi and her sisters was taken in Mama Muleady's back yard. She lived at 960 E. William Street, in Decatur, Illinois. They were all in town for Mama Muleady's funeral in the early 1940's.

Bill: "I see that most of these gals married an Irishman!"

The following is an email from my first cousin Rich Martini to my second cousin Martha Welborne in November of 2005.

Dear Martha,

My name is Rich Martini - I'm your second cousin-grandson of Edward Hayes, son of Ann and Charles Martini. Mom told me you'd just come back from Liscannor, Ireland (North of Limerick in County Clare) and that you've found the Hayes' ancestral home. That's amazing! I've done my best to do some research into the family and have come up woefully short on the Irish side. She also just sent me a copy of the pix you took of the house - how did you find it?

I've been more successful on the Italian side, but that's another story. I forget where I heard that the Hayes family came through Roxbury, Massachusetts, at some point, not far from where I went to college at Boston University.

I'm sending along an interesting article that my mom sent me some years ago - it's the transcript from a local paper that interviewed Ed Hayes' father (your great grandfather) when Ed was named National Commander of the American Legion in '33. Our Great Grandfather Michael Hayes was born around 1853, and set out for the US around 1871, according to the article.

Rich Martini
PS - I just went to th www.ellisisland.org website and found a record of Michael and Katherine Hayes, from 375 N. College Avenue, traveling aboard the "Cedric"and arriving in NY in Sept 1923. He was 67 and she was 53. So Michael and his wife, our great grandparents, apparently went back to visit Ireland in 1923 to see the old stomping grounds he left when he was 14 and then returned to America aboard the "Cedric." They probably visited this little house that I'm looking at in your pix.

Here is the article that mom sent me about Michael Hayes, father of Ed Hayes and our great grandfather on the Irish side. His dad was Patrick Hayes, a boatman in County Claire according to the article, which is from the <u>Decatur Review</u> and written in August of 1933.

FATHER IS "MIGHTY PROUD"

Michael Hayes is Proud of His Youngest Son But Plays No Favorites Among "Five Fine Lads." by Robert A. Barracks, Herald Review Staff Writer.

I'm proud, mighty proud, of my boy Ed." Michael Hayes, father of Edward Hayes, new national commander of the American Legion rocked reflectively for a moment and then swung around with an admonishing forefinger uplifted.

"But I'm proud of all five of my boys. Don't get the idea that I'm playing favorites. I have five of the finest sons that a man was ever blessed with and it has been wonderful to see the fine tributes that have been paid to my youngest, but I'm just as proud of the rest of them."

"And to their mother goes the credit for making Ed and his brothers the fine boys that they are. She was a fine woman and she made fine men out of them." Thus proudly and modestly did the 76 year old father of Ed Hayes praise his wife and sons with never a word for his own part in the bringing up of the Hayes brood. Never a word of the long years of toil on the railroad that his sons might have the education he failed to get.
"I wanted the boys to have what I didn't and couldn't get," he continued. "I worked in the daytime and their mother raised the lads and taught them. She gave them the foundation for character and education that is beginning to appear now. Hers is the credit."

Michael Hayes, father of Ed, is a native of County Clare, Ireland, and the rich brogue of the old country still clings to his speech. He is the son of Patrick Hayes, a ship's pilot on the stormy Irish Sea, who kept his family of seven boys and two girls by piloting British boats in and out of the harbor and by fishing when sea traffic was slack.

Michael was the oldest of the flock. When Patrick lay on his death bed, he called his eldest to him. "It was father's dying wish that I come to America and make enough money to help my brothers and sisters," said Michael. "I promised that I would do it and I did."

At the age of 14 years, Michael set out alone on the long voyage to the new land. He had some cousins in the East, but he had an uncle, Patrick Fitzpatrick, who lived in Litchfield and was foreman of the section crew of the Wabash railroad. It was to this uncle that the boy Michael came."I started carrying water for the section crew of July 5, 1871," said Michael Hayes. I was 14 years old then. For two years I carried water and then for five years I was on the work train. Then they put me in charge of the section at Morrisonville."

In the meantime, Michael had married Miss Mary Ellen Bray of Jacksonville. Her father had built half of the houses in Jacksonville and had bought a tract of land near Raymond where Michael met his wife. Mrs. Michael Hayes was a woman of exception and refinement. She had attended schools in Jacksonville and the woman's college there. She was an excellent reader and elocutionist.

One by one the Hayes sons were born in Morrisonville. Ed, the youngest, arrived on Jan 5, 1892. When he was six years of age, Michael Hayes was moved to Decatur to take charge of the section for the Wabash. He moved to Decatur on his own request. "The boys were getting old enough to go to school - and the educational facilities at Morrisonville were not enough," he said. "I wanted them to have the best education I could provide for them."

"By the time Edward started to the convent school in Decatur, his mother had guided him through the second reader. He was a true student. He wasn't a baseball player and not much for sports. He preferred to stay at home and read. Music was the thing that he

loved next best, and he and his bothers all had fine voices. They
used to sing at home and for the neighbors, all five of them. Then
when Martin, the oldest boy, left, the four brothers sang together."
Edward finished his preparatory education in Decatur and went
to Browns' Business College. Then he went to St. Louis University
where he completed his education. He read law in Decatur law
offices, preparing for his future profession.
The mother, Mary Ellen Bray, who had reared the five sons, died in
1919. She lived to see them all grow into fine young manhood as a
tribute to her efforts.
Michael Hayes remarried in 1922 to Katherine Maloney of
Columbus Ohio. She is as proud of the boys as Michael Hayes.

Martha Welborne's email response to Rich Martini:

Hi Rich!

Great story! I will email you all the photos I took of the house,
including a few with me standing in front of it, and follow up later
with the story of our history adventure in Ireland. However, to cut
to the heart of the matter – discovering the Clare Heritage Centre
was the key. County Clare is very organized with their records.
When in Ireland, my husband John and I went there and they did a
bit of quick research that led to the house. I'll also include photos
of the pier that is immediately next to the cluster of houses of which
the Hayes' house is one. Great to hear from you!

PS – the website for the Clare Heritage Centre is:
www.clareroots.com.

Martha

The following interview took place in Northbrook, Illinois, on June 17, 2008 with my Mom's sister - Aunt Anthy Martini.

(Aunt Anthy showed me an old faded picture of the Hayes brothers)

Anthy: Let me tell you about the Hayes brothers. This is John (Uncle Doctor) right there in the middle. This is Martin, this is Tom, and this is Leo, and this is Ed, my dad. I'm not positive but I'm pretty sure he was the youngest. They also had a sister who died at an early age - her name was Estelle.

We called John uncle doctor because he was our family doctor. He raised his family in Decatur, Illinois, and his daughter, Mary Estelle, still lives in Decatur. And her daughter Martha, who was named after your mom, is a friend of Dicks out in California. And now this girl Martha (who married John Welborne) is an architect in a very well known firm out in Los Angeles. She went to Ireland, and when you are there, they have a number that you call and you say, "My great grandfather was born in Ireland - can you help me find out where he lived?"

So while Martha was in Ireland, she called that number and right away they told her where to go.

Anthy: And you know what, Bill? People named Hayes still live in that house in Ireland. And God knows the people who live there today would have to be like my grandfather's brother's great, great, great grandchildren - that kind of thing.

In January, 2009, two of my kids (Joseph and Michelle) were chosen to compete at the IMTA (International Model & Talent Assoc.) in Los Angeles. We flew our entire family out to California to share in the experience. I also made a point of meeting my second cousin, Martha Welborne, who worked on the 34th floor of the Union Bank of California building, which was conveniently located directly across the street from the IMTA event held at the Westin Bonaventure Hotel.

Martha Welborne in front of the original Hayes house
in County Clare, Ireland

Laurel, Elizabeth, Meghan and I went up to visit Martha (who was named after my mom) and share family stories from long ago. When I first laid eyes on her, she reminded me of my sister Mary – which wasn't surprising as they are both very pretty and born in the same year. Meeting my second cousin Martha for the first time was very special, and I was amazed at how quickly we became good friends. Sharing the same great grandfather (Michael Hayes) made that easy.

My favorite part about writing this book was during the research stage. If I had not interviewed my Aunt Anthy Martini in Chicago, I never would have met my second cousin Martha Welborne in Los Angeles.

During our trip to L.A., I was having breakfast in the restaurant of the Westin with my daughter Meghan and we met a happy Mexican waiter named Rogilio. He was most friendly and wore a smart looking goatee and had a pleasant disposition. He reminded me of Speedy Gonzalez. When I introduced him to Meg, he asked, "*Beel*, is this your *jungest*?" I said, "Yes, Meghan is our youngest!" And then when he realized we were from Wisconsin, he asked, "*Do you know Brett Far?*" What a great question!

Ten years earlier, in 1999, Laurel and I drove our family to Marco Island, Florida, for spring break vacation. We ran into a number of folks from Ireland "on holiday" who also happened to be staying at the Marriot Hotel. While our family was sitting in the hot tub together, we watched as these two leprechauns, filled with 100% blarney, verbally attacked each other. Finally, one of the Irish blokes had heard enough. He stood up, stomped out of the pool, and looked his friend straight in the eye and said, "*Póg mo Thóin*!" And then he walked away. I asked the other Irishman sitting with us what that meant in English and he shouted, "Kiss my ass!"

Believe it or not, the definition of blarney is smooth flattering talk. The blarney stone in Blarney Castle, County Cork, Ireland, is said to impart skills of eloquence and flattery to those who kiss it.

I think one of my great grandparents like Martin Callaghan or Michael Hayes must have left an indelible impression on that rock, because those same traits and skills have definitely been passed down and continues to be passed on to future generations. It is part of our Irish heritage since the Callaghans are from County Kerry and the Hayes family originated from County Clare.

Now that I think of it, the Irish have had such an impact on the world. I've always felt that God made the Irish so he could add some humor and laughter into the world! And brighten people's spirits along the way. My grandmother Mae Callaghan used to say, "People are the greatest show on earth!" And St. Patrick's Day is celebrated throughout the nation every March by all Americans, regardless of their ethnic heritage.

The Irish are known for, among other things, their rich tradition of alcohol consumption. For some reason, I was never good at drinking hard liquor. The last time I did was a few years ago at a Sunday night Packer game at Lambeau Field. After the game, we walked back to the Hilton Garden Inn and everyone I looked at had four eyes. They had a second set of eyes in their forehead! It got to the point where I couldn't look at anyone's face because they looked like one of the aliens from the Star Wars bar scene. They were the strangest looking people I had ever seen. For me, hard liquor is like liquid LSD – I don't see how anyone can drink it

– much less see straight!

I don't drink wine or even champagne for that matter. None of those fermented liquids appeal to me whatsoever. When I do drink, I'll have a beer, and not just any beer! New Glarus Brewery makes a special line of beers that are made available only to residents of Wisconsin. My favorite "Spotted Cow" is really the only beer I like to drink and it tastes great. Those other alcohols can be dangerous to your health and everyone around you - if heavily consumed.

My dad refers to alcoholic beverages, especially wine, as "blabber mouth soup."

One thing I have observed over the years is that when people drink too much champagne, it will act as a solvent and dissolve the elastic in their underwear.

Let's close this chapter with a prayer:

The Irish Prayer

May the road rise to meet you……

May the wind be at your back……

May the sun shine warm upon your face…...

May the rain fall soft upon your fields…….

And, until we meet again…….

May God hold you in the palm of his hand.

Chapter 10
Tell Me 'bout the Good Old Days

I never knew my grandfathers; they both died before I was born! But I've been blessed to see my father living into his late 80's. So I can imagine how his father would have been had I known him. I picture them as bright-headed, faithful and audacious gentlemen with a great sense of humor.

Through many recording sessions with my mom, dad, Aunt Anthy, Aunt Honey and Aunt Corky, I have been able to piece together the past and learn about my grandparents and aunts and uncles that I never knew. It was like unearthing the roots of our family tree.

These interviews were fascinating on many fronts. All five of the characters mentioned above are in their mid to late 80's and each one of them enjoy a remarkable capacity to instantly recall events from decades ago and bring them back to life!

The taped discussions took quite a bit of time to transcribe into word documents, but I was able to capture stories from the past so I could share our history with future generations. Don't let your family history fade away with the passing of parents and aunts and uncles – take the time to download the stories and the wealth of information that exists between their ears - before it's gone forever!

In 1985, the Judds struck a special chord in my soul with their smash hit "Grandpa." The mother-daughter magic created by Naomi and Wynona Judd is some of the prettiest sounding harmony you will find in any band. And the powerful lyrics of this song illustrate my desire for capturing my family's history.

Grandpa
Tell me 'bout the good old days.
Sometimes it feels like
This world's gone crazy.
Grandpa, take me back to yesterday,
Where the line between right and wrong
Didn't seem so hazy.

Grandpa
Everything is changing fast.
We call it progress,
But I just don't know.
And Grandpa, let's wonder back into the past,
And paint me a picture of long ago.

Did lovers really fall in love to stay
Stand beside each other come what may
Was a promise really something people kept,
Not just something they would say and then forget
Did families really bow their heads to pray
daddies really never go away
Whoa oh Grandpa,
Tell me 'bout the good ole days.

The following interview took place in Chicago on June 17, 2008, with my dad's two sisters, Aunt Honey and Aunt Corky:

Bill: What was it like growing up with my Dad?

Honey: "Coyne and I did everything. He'd come and see me at boarding school. I remember I was sobbing when I first went there and Coyne would come down the block and check up on me. I knew every day Coyne would be there for me and comfort me. He was at St. Joseph Institute and I was at Our Lady of Bethlehem(OLB) – both in LaGrange, Illinois.

We couldn't wait until after school because we always had a bag of fruit and cookies from home and we could have that after school - yum. We'd sit in the rectory, and I would say, "I won't eat your dirty food!" The nuns thought it was a scream; they told mom," she uses the word dirty like grown-ups would say damn. "I won't eat your dirty food" - and I wouldn't, I'd eat food only from home.

Tom Callaghan with Honey and Coyne in 1928 at boarding school in LaGrange, IL

St. Joe's and OLB boarding school wouldn't accept students until they were five. But my brother Coyne always says he was only four when he was sent away to boarding school. I'd say, "You weren't four Coyne", he says, "Yes, I was!" School began in early September and our birthdays being in September and October – so I guess we weren't quite five when we went away to school.

I found this letter that Coyne sent my parents from St. Joe's boarding school in 1927, when he was only 6 years old.

Dear Mother and Dad,
I am in Tom's room. I am fine. He is writing too! I love you very much. Tell Mary Francis I wish her a Happy Birthday.

God bless you all,
Coyne

I remember when we were little, Coyne played jokes on me all the time. We grew up on Crandon Street in Chicago and once when we were kids we went up the stairs and at the top of the stairs was our bedroom. Our parents said, "Go to bed, go to bed, time to go to sleep". So we'd be whispering and before you knew it we'd be talking out loud and we'd get a knock on the wall, "Go to sleep, go to sleep." So the next time it happened, Dad came into our room and my bed was closest to the door and all of a sudden I'd get a swat on my butt. "You two.......go to bed! I told you clowns to go to bed!" So I said to my brother Coyne, "Let's switch our beds around so he gets you first, and Coyne said "Oh no Honey, are you kidding me, I'm not going to switch with you!"

Bill: How did you get the name Honey?

Honey: Coyne named me Honey. Our parents had the two boys, Tom and Coyne, and then I was born. Mom and Dad were so happy and everyone would come in to see their little girl and say "Isn't she a honey?" Coyne would be standing in the corner, watching everybody, and then someone would come in again, "awe, isn't she a little honey?" And apparently he thought my name was "Honey," and that was it. He never looked at me and said anything but Honey. He named me! And we've been close ever since.

Bill: What is your real name?

Honey: Mary Frances

Bill: Aunt Corky, how did you get the name Corky?

Corky: I was born on October 16th on a Sunday and the comic Gasoline Alley was the biggest thing in entertainment on Sundays. And Gasoline Alley had a character named Skisics and he had a little brother who was named Corky. I was told by our mom that the nurse in the hospital came in and said, "Now you have a Corky, too." I got it the same day. On day one!
Bill: All these years I assumed it had something to do with County

Cork, Ireland. What is your real name?
Corky: Florence Therese

Bill: When I was little, my dad often called me Skisics, and I never knew the source of that name until now!

Honey: I was so excited when I knew my sister Corky was coming. I've got Tom, Coyne and Marty, but I wanted a sister. I remember Mom was going downtown and she took me with her, and I see a great big display of a baby girl. I said,"I want her—I want a sister". I said, Mom, "I want a sister." She said, "We'll take whatever God sends us." So I'd say, I picked her out! We've been together from Day 1!

Tom was so smart, Coyne was so smart, Marty was so smart. I'm hearing all this stuff, so one day I looked at Dad and said, "Dad I'm your dumb kid."
"Honey, I don't have any dumb kids!" he said in a loud voice.

Bill: How did your parents Tom Callaghan and Mae Coyne meet?

Corky: "They met in Chicago. Uncle Jim Whalen (Florence's husband) belonged to some Hibernian group, and he was going to a show and Dad was there and Mom and Aunt Florence were there. He introduced his friend Tom Callaghan to Mae. That's where they met."

Bill: The only grandparent I ever knew was Mimi, my mom's mom. What kind of person was your mom?

Corky: Vivacious and extremely wonderful!

Honey: "She was a very loving person and she was funny. She had some funny sayings. If you did something goofy it was "block that kick," good or bad. Another thing was we had to be at the dinner table at six o'clock every night of our lives, otherwise we'd be in trouble. Dad would chew us out! We'd do something silly at dinner and he'd say "Mae, we raised a bunch of monkeys." Or "Just a bunch of clowns." That was his way of letting us know we weren't so funny.

Remember, Corky, when we had to take those pills?

Corky: They were vitamins!

Honey: There were about 12 of them. Our older brother Tom would get to where he could pop them all in his mouth at once.

So then if the conversation at the table went to what you didn't want to talk about or something you just didn't want to discuss, Mom would say, "Let's talk about the orange groves in Florida," meaning, change the subject!

Corky: Another one of Mom's favorite sayings was, "You, whelp, you!" I didn't know what that was so I ran to the dictionary and found out that it means - A little dog!

Honey: Sometimes when we caused a lot of trouble, she'd say, I'll have to tell your dad! We were like, "Okay, okay, Mom, don't tell Dad!" We didn't want Dad to know because he could be stricter and she was much easier going.

One of mom's favorite things to do was to go downtown with her friends and sit and watch people go by. She always said, "People are the greatest show on Earth."

Mom supposedly had ulcers and God knows what else, so Dad was always very protective of Mom, overly protective. I remember going to the doctor with my mom to see…….

Corky: Dr. Francis Gerty, a psychiatrist.

Honey: I'd say, "Why are we going here, Mom?" And she'd say, "Oh, I have to see the doctors." Knowing that supposedly she had *ulcers, which later it turns out she didn't, I assumed maybe she had depression.*

Bill: How did you get around in Chicago in the 30's?

Honey: The IC (Illinois Central trains) and streetcars and buses.

I remember, we'd get on the streetcar for five cents with Margaret O'Conner and we'd ride it to the end and then back to 73rd Street. That would be a treat for us. The IC was tremendous because we could take that train straight downtown and you could go any old time and you didn't have to look at a schedule. You never waited more than five minutes for a train.

Bill: What went on during the depression years?

Honey: During the Depression our dad worked as a secretary. Ed Sweeney, Roger Mulcahy's uncle, told us this because our dad never told us anything.

Now, this is interesting. If you had a job, which was very hard to get during that time, and you wanted to get a better job, and you got the better job, then you told your friends so they could take your position. You didn't just go in and quit. The day you told your boss that you were leaving your job, you'd go out the door and your friend comes in to fill your position and get the job! So they protected each other!

Corky: It was the Irish mafia! They were tight, very tight! They were unbelievable!

Honey: Good friends! These weren't fair weather friends, they were very close. They had tons of close friends!

Corky: Dad drove us to church every Sunday because Ed Cabanski, who was daddy's personal driver, had the weekends off.

Honey: Our family always went to 11 o'clock mass on Sundays. After Mass, it was a social! Everyone gathered outside of Mass - everyone was there!

Bill: What was the name of the church?

Corky: St. Phillips Parish.

St. Phillip Neri. He was a happy saint, always laughing. His feast day was on May 26th. He was a happy saint! I was baptized there and married there.

Honey: Corky knows all the saints and their feast days by heart!

Bill: What can you tell me about my grandfather (your dad), Tom Callaghan?

Corky: Well Martin Thomas Callaghan married Frances Daugherty (Grandma Callaghan) and they had four kids: Tom (your grandfather), Kathleen, Emitt and Dennis. But the two youngest, Emitt and Dennis, both died at a very young age.

Our mom went to college, but Dad only went to high school because he quit college to take care of his grandpa Martin and his sister Kathleen, which I thought was utterly remarkable. He took night courses for a little while at Northwestern and worked as a secretary. He was really an interesting person. One of his favorite sayings was, "Don't be a fart in a windstorm – make something of yourself!

Bill: Tell me about your mom's (Mae Callaghan) family.

Corky: Mom had a sister named Florence.

Honey: Who became Florence Whalen.

Corky: And there was also George Coyne.

Honey: And Uncle Dan Coyne.

Corky: Dan was older than Mom.

Honey: Yeah, Dan was older. So was George. There was George, Dan, Mae and Florence - they actually had nine kids. I believe five died at birth. And my grandmother - - this is a funny story. Everyone was pleased with our Blessed Mother; everyone was naming their girls Mary this and Mary that. And once my Grandma Coyne said, "Ha, what's the big deal? Mary had only one child; I had nine!"

Corky: And we called her Minnie.

Honey: Grandma Coyne's maiden name was Minnie Crowley.

She was a character. For some reason Grandma Coyne was very hard on mom, which was very strange. We never totally understood why. And every single Sunday of his life, Dad put money under her plate at the dinner table, under Grandma Coyne's plate.

Bill: What can you tell me about my Grandmother Mae - your mom? Who I never met!

Honey: Everything about her was so special. I was very tight with her. When she died I wanted to die.

When Dad died, Mom was just lost without Dad. I mean, she really was. Dad and Mom shared a deep love – rare!

Tom, Coyne, Marty, Corky and I were all standing behind our mom at Dad's wake, which was held in our home. And we know people don't know what to say when someone dies, but a good friend of hers comes by and she shakes Mom's hand and says, "Don't you care, Mae we'll play a lot of bridge games together." At this time, Mom was so sad without Dad. We knew something was wrong with her and she only lived a short time after that - 15 months.

Bill: She died at the age of 53?

Honey: Yes! She was actually two years older than Dad, who was only 51 when he died.

We moved in on 7111 Paxton. Our folks were gone, and it's just the two of us. When our mom died, Corky was only 16 years old and I was only 20. Cork and I figured, we've got to be good, otherwise it'll reflect on Mom and Dad and people will think they were bad parents or something.

Bill: Was your brother Marty like my dad or was he more like Uncle Tom?

Honey: He was an individual, different from both of them. Cork and I always wondered, would he have gotten married or would he have been a priest? That's how the dichotomy was. He had a girlfriend and cared about her very much. But he also cared about the priesthood.

Remember, Cork, we'd say "I wonder what he would have been – I wonder what he would have done?" One thing that's kind of eerie is that the last snapshot that we had of Marty was him walking away. It gives me goose bumps to this day.

Corky: He was only 20 years old when he died fighting in the Battle of the Bulge.

Honey: "Marty was five weeks into his 20th birthday. On the 19th of February - -January 8 was his birthday. Tom's birthday was February 19. Marty was killed on February 19.

Our cousin Jack Coyne also died in the war. He was Uncle Dan's kid - we loved him too."

Corky: And mom died on Dad's birthday – November, 29.

Honey: Cork and I hated birthdays for a while. We had superb parents – and loved them dearly. But they both died at such a young age! So, for a time we hated birthdays. We were just sad.

Corky: And then our brother Tom leaves and goes to Washington D.C.

Honey: He really never came back home. Tom was Editor of the <u>Hoya</u>, the Georgetown University paper. And then he became part of the Navel Intelligence department during World War II.

Our dad had a will. And when he died naturally everything went to Mom. Then Mom dies a year later to the day and then everything goes to the kids. Then we lose Marty. So we lost our father, mother and brother all within 2 ½ years. Then all we had left were the four kids: Tom, Coyne, Corky and Honey. Birthdays were no fun! It was terrible, awful, absolutely awful.

While Marty was still living, and after Mom had died, we were all together at our home on Euclid, trying to figure out who was going to be our guardian (executrix). At first, Aunt Coe was assigned to be our guardian. Then Corky and I were saying "we don't need a guardian." So Marty suggested Mr.Feeley, who looked exactly like Popeye-the sailor man. He did our lawn and gardening.

Corky: Then there was Ms. Tousante; she used to go upstairs and sew for our family on occasion. "She was a strange one!" We were trying to figure out who was going to be our executors and our guardians and Marty suggested, "Why don't we just have Mr. Feeley and Ms. Tousante." And this was a serious moment and we all fell apart laughing.

Honey: Really burst out loud laughing! Marty was funny and sharp!

Corky: Back in those days, in the state of Illinois, girls reached the stage of adulthood at the age of 18, and boys, not until 21. So Marty, who was only 17 when he went into the service, still needed

*a legal guardian. Within weeks after that meeting, he was gone
and off to the war. But when Marty suggested Mrs. Tousante and
Mr. Feeley as our guardians, we couldn't stop laughing.*

Bill: How old were you, Aunt Corky, when you married?

*Corky: I was 20! I always knew Dick Hyland from Saint
Phillip Neri Parish. Being the youngest in the family, I had the
opportunity to meet older kids.*

*Honey: Back when we were teenagers, we dated many different
people. It's kind of sad today. I think the kids today miss out on
a lot because they lock into one person and never get to meet or
enjoy other people. It's crazy, I don't understand it. We would go
downtown and go dancing to the big bands of Glenn Miller on the
stand or Les Brown. We'd go to dinner and have a drink and we'd
go to the Drake Hotel or to the Edgewater Hotel and dance. They
had whole bands with drums and horns and all.*

Bill: Honey, how did you meet Roger Mulcahy?

*Honey: He also went to St. Phillips' Parish; he came from Holy
Cross. We were neighbors. We lived at 7236 Crandon and he was
at 7136 Ogalsby. We met in high school as Roger's sister Mary
Helen was a classmate of mine and we'd walk home from school
together. The first time I met him he looked at the two of us and he
just shrugged his shoulders and walked off. I thought, "What a
jerk." I'd go home and think boy, am I glad he's not my brother
and thank God for our brothers, especially Coyne, 'cause we're
close and he's so fun and nice. I thought, Roger's mean and nasty
and thank God he's not my brother. And he's the one I married!*

Bill: What was it like growing up in Chicago?

*Corky: I really enjoyed growing up on the south side of Chicago.
When I went to college, I took two streetcars and one bus to get
there. We did a lot of walking too! I'd get up early in the morning*

and walk to South Shore Country Club and ride horses and Honey played tennis. I loved riding the horses.

Honey: "They had outdoor dancing at night during the summer. It was located by Lake Michigan so if you wanted to go swimming you'd jump in the lake. The South Shore Country Club is now called the South Shore Cultural Center which is where the Chicago police keep their horses for the mounted police force. It's now open to the public and you can rent out the halls for weddings and swim at the public beach. But it's not the same!

I recall coming home with Coyne after going out with some dates and it was after curfew, although I didn't really have a curfew when I was out with Coyne. But our parents did expect us to be civil. So in we come and Coyne says
"I'm going to get a glass of milk Hon, I'll be up in a minute".
So I say, Ok, good night, and I go on up. And I get to the top of the stairs and my dad's standing there and says,
"Do you know what time it is, blah, blah, blah" and he chews me out. Then I finally caught on; Coyne knew I hated milk so he would wait in the kitchen drinking his milk and I would go upstairs and get chewed out and Coyne would never get in trouble. So the next time we came in late, Coyne said,
"Go ahead Hon, I'm going to get a drink of milk."
And I said, "Well, I'm going to get a drink of water.
He said "I thought you don't like milk." I said, "Water!" Then he just smiled at me. He knew I finally caught on.

Tell me about your neighbors the Dahmschitzes.
The Dahmschitz lived in the neighborhood and Mom would say to us at the dinner table, "Be nice, they are very proud of their name." And my dad would say, "Any Dahmschit would be!" And then we would just start laughing again!

Corky: Our parents both had a great sense of humor. They were fun!

Honey: I remember when we lived on Euclid and my parents were throwing a party downstairs and I would be up in my bedroom in bed and I could hear Mom and Dad's laughter, above everyone else's. I can still remember falling asleep listening to my parents laughter. It was a gift they gave to us!

Callaghan family photo taken at the 1933 World's Fair in Chicago, Illinois. From left to right: Honey, Tom, Mae, Corky, Marty, Coyne, Tom Jr.

The following interview took place in Northbrook, Illinois, on June 17, 2008, with my mom's sister, Aunt Anthy Martini.

Bill: Tell me about your mom, Mimi (Margaret Hayes).

Anthy: "Mimi always had full time help. We had a girl named Mary Friend, but she didn't stay overnight. Then we had a lady named Mick Habenstreit, who was from a small town near Stonington, Illinois. Mick had been training to be a school teacher and when she finally got the job to teach in Bloomington, she sent her sister Louise to work in our home. I was probably ten years old when Louise came into the picture. She was a saint!
My oldest sister Macie was born in 1919, I was born in 1922, your mom was born in 1925 and Catherine was born in 1928 – all three

years apart. We always had helpers at our house so Mimi could do whatever she wanted. She was a gifted singer and used to sing and play the organ at Moran & Sons funeral home in Decatur. My mother would take us to Moran's and she would say "You can sit in the back, but be still!" while she rehearsed with the other woman. Uncle Doctor would take us to school every morning and Mimi would bring us home.

Macie moved to Monticello and married Chuck Knapp and had five children. I eventually moved to Northbrook and have four sons – Jeff, Charles, Robbie and Dickie.

Bill: How did Mimi Muleady meet Ed Hayes?

Anthy: My mother and father met at St. Patrick's church in Decatur. She was singing in the choir and Daddy also sang in the choir. He had a great singing voice as well as speaking voice.

Bill: Did Mimi teach you how to play the piano?

Anthy: No. Aunt Irene, Leo Hayes' wife, taught us piano lessons, and I probably began learning the piano when I was six years old. Macie and I took lessons from Wilna Moffet; later she was the one who had me try out for a college scholarship.

When Daddy was National Commander of the American Legion, the three of us and Mimi all went along to Florida to the convention, and then we took a pontoon plane to Havana, Cuba. After that trip, I always felt like I had a little camaraderie with Cuba and knowing Jose Echaniz.

Let me get the map out again – Robbie gave me this map and you wouldn't know how much I've added to it. Here's Cuba and Guantanamo is here to the east and Havana is over here to the west.

Bill: What was your purpose in going to Cuba?

Anthy: Well, we took a train down to Miami. And on a lark, my dad heard that you could take a flight to Havana, so he decided to

289

take us to Cuba. I remember standing on this ledge and looking out at the barbed wire fence and everyone was saying, "That's Guantanamo Bay."

So just in the last few months, I wrote to my congressman because there was a lot of talk about closing the base and I didn't get it. So he wrote back and explained that in 1905 we signed a contract with Cuba to pay them $200/year for renting the land. It's worded that you can never break that contract unless both countries agree on whatever the new deal is. That's why the contract has never been broken. And guess what? Castro hasn't cashed one check. And now 100 years later, it's cost us only what - $ 20,000.00 to have a base there.

The following interview took place at the Plaza Hotel in Eau Claire, Wisconsin with my parents, Martha and Coyne Callaghan.

Bill: Tell me about the good old days.

Coyne: I spent nine summers as a kid at summer camp up in Clear Water Lake, Wisconsin—it was between Three Lakes and Eagle River. The first year I was there, I was six and a half years old. The athletic directors we had included Frank Greele, all-American quarterback Notre Dame, and Tommy Yarr, all American center. And the next three years we had Frank Lahey, a gifted kicker.

We had a wonderful time up at Camp St. George. It was built by a fellow named George Cardinal Mundelein—archbishop of Chicago. Family named Higgins donated the property to him. There were 2500 acres with virgin timber on it and three separate spring-filled lakes. Clear Water Lake was the big one. Then you had Peanut Lake and Coca Cola Lake.

When I was growing up in Chicago, a group of us owned about 17 Ford Model T's. They were mostly Junkers we accumulated for spare parts.

Back then, I was living on the south side of Chicago, about 7300 South and my dad insisted I go to Loyola Academy, which is 6500

North. It took me 2 hours to get there via the city bus and the L train – all told – 2 hours one way.

On the way back from Loyola, my friends and I would detour into Soldier's Field. The layout of Soldier's Field back then was a U shape and opened at the North end. The track inside was about a mile around. It was especially fun to go down there after a rain storm. There were various spots in the track where the water pooled and we would vie with one another to see who could make the biggest water geyser. We'd take the floor boards out of the Model T and take turns driving through the water. The guy that'd cause the biggest geyser to come up through the floor inside the car would win. We had fun!

We only used Model T parts for maintenance. We'd go down to State Street, which was really the old model T graveyard of Chicago. And let's say we need a new tire. We were willing to pay five bucks to get one. A lot of times the tire would be on the wheel, and the guy didn't want to take it off. We'd say how much for the combination? Eight bucks - we'll buy it! So while we were there, we would buy various component parts. We made this one car - called her Maude. Four door Phaeton, with Isinglass curtains you could roll right down in case there's a change in the weather. It was the best of times!

We wanted to test drive Maude, to see how fast she would go with just Model T parts. We decided to run on the Million Dollar Bridle Path in Chicago, pre-arranged with Park Police for an accurate, reliable time trial.

Our deal was to drive down the path as fast as possible and the police would chase us and then tell us how fast we were

going. That's what happened, too. We drove as fast as we could with the police following after us.

On one occasion, one of my many Irish friends, Laury Donahue, was pulled over for speeding. The policeman come over and says, "Laury, how fast do you think you were going?"

"Can't wait to find out," he says.

"You were going 63 miles per hour." We look around, Congratulations, that was wonderful! How about that, we were doing 63! With that, the policeman says,

"Go on, and get the hell out of here!"

In fact, my friend Laury Donahue later designed the layout for the O'Hare Airport.

During 1933-34, Ed Hayes, Martha's father, was National Commander of the American Legion. He was speech-making around the country, and he was bitter because Roosevelt campaigned on two basic issues to get elected. '32 was Roosevelt's first run against Al Smith, and he took office in March of '33. Hayes was elected in July of '33, and his term ran until July of '34. The American Legion is primarily dedicated to two things: one is the care of wounded veterans and their families; two is spreading Americanism, love of your country and what it stands for. Ed was the perfect guy for that; he was the epitome of an American patriot!

So Ed's at the American Legion Convention and Roosevelt says if you elect me we would stay on the gold standard, and we're going to support the veterans. So, Roosevelt gets elected! And the second thing he started doing was closing veterans hospitals and throwing these guys out in the street.

Martha: "And that's not helping the veterans."

Coyne: But first, Roosevelt takes America off the gold standard and closes the banks for six days, an effort to stop withdrawals and a run on the banks. It was a big crunch. But he thought that was the way to right it. But really it was a way for the government to control the money supply, by printing fiat currency.

The groundwork for it was in 1913 when America's big banks established the Federal Reserve System. It's all part of this deal when congress passed the XVI Constitutional Amendment to establish the Income Tax.

So Ed is out there in Boise, Idaho, making a speech. And newspaper man William Randolph Hearst liked Ed's Americanism, so he passed the word that whenever Ed Hayes was talking, give him lots of print.

Martha: In newspapers across the country.

Coyne: But Hearst liked Ed because he always spoke great things of America, why it was founded and what it stood for. It's one of the reasons he was elected national commander. He had that great voice, a tremendous speaker. So in a speech in Boise, Ed told his audience that their president was a congenital liar.

Martha: A congenital liar.

Coyne: He was reminding everyone what Roosevelt promised and what he's doing now since being elected. Immediately after that speech, Jim Foley, Post Master General and leader of the Democratic Party, sent Ed a letter, a wire saying that the President would like to visit with Ed at the White House and please indicate when you'll be in town. So, next time Ed was in Washington he went to the White House. He was scheduled to have a 15-minute visit with Roosevelt and it lasted 2 hours.

(Impersonating Roosevelt with his long cigarette holder)

President Roosevelt said, 'My dear commander, you know and I know that a lot of these boys that were in the hospitals were really not sick but they're on the public dole because of hard times. They are malingering." And Hayes says, "No, Mr. President, I don't know that. But if you do, you're negligent in your duty to allow it." That's the reason the elites didn't want Ed Hayes to be senator from Illinois. That's the reason Illinois Senior Senator Ev Dirkson appointed Hayes as Chief Counsel for the Senate Alien Property Custodian investigation to get Hayes off the campaign trail and out of Illinois and keep him busy in Washington.

Bill: "What was the Senate Alien Property Custodian Investigation about?"

Dad: "When you go to war and if there's property owned by the enemy in their country, that's alien property. And the government becomes custodian for the property.

So, after World War I, the two German properties, Bayer Fabricqen (Sterling Drugs) and AGFA Films were alien properties. But Morgenthau and the boys in the Treasury Department never returned those properties. They kept operating them and the proceeds didn't go back to Germany, they went to the Democratic Party to fund their activities. That's how it worked. So the Republicans in Congress were anxious to expose this and return the properties. They ended up doing that; they returned the properties to Germany. And of course they had to do it all over again when we went to war against Hitler during World War II.

Ed Hayes was running for the Republican nomination for the United States Senate seat from Illinois in 1954. Two weeks before the Senate election, Ed's campaign manager mysteriously disappeared. Ed was one of nine candidates who ran for the coveted seat. One of Ed's real supporters was Jesse Owens, the US Olympic runner. He said, "Ed, this is wrong, they should not abandon you."

I remember going with Ed one time down to a Chicago precinct. Ed had a great following because a lot of these guys were Legionnaires and they all loved him. During one visit a man says, "Ed, I know why you're here - but I'm committed to the Democratic side. Ed said, "Can't you get me some votes?" He said, "I know it's an insult, but I can get you two." And you know how many votes he got in that precinct? Two.

In Illinois the old joke about Election Day was – do your civil duty - vote early and vote often. Sleepy Hollow was a great precinct. Precinct workers would go to certain sections of a cemetery and take names off a required number of gravestones to make the vote quota. Chicago politics has been corrupt for decades! Just about every former Governor of Illinois ends up in jail.

Martha: You know Daddy died April 1, 1955, a year later, to the day, after he was defeated for Illinois Senator.

Coyne: Bob Taft died too. Ed was heartbroken when Herb Brownell, Attorney General of New York took charge of the Republican National Convention, unseated Taft's Ohio delegation and nominated Tom Dewey.

Martha: Daddy just went downhill after that. I remember visiting him in Chicago at the hospital and seeing him looking so frail.

Coyne: Ed Hayes was the kind of guy everybody liked … but one of the things people would say is that he would not compromise. In other words, if this is what the Constitution says, then this is what we need to do.

Bill: Tell me about Louise Habenstreit.

Martha: One of the most influential people in my life is Louise, our live-in help and dear friend. She grew up with simple means and appreciated everything she had. Her attitude and tone is something I longed to emulate. She would often say, "It'll be all right, Martha, don't you worry!" Louise Habenstreit, who today has to be a saint in heaven, never married, never dated, never went beyond a 7th grade education. But she lived in our house back in those days. She did all the cooking and cleaning and everything. Babysitting, whatever it was. Louise was the most giving person I have ever known.

Coyne: She used to say,"Mr. Hayes, you eat that, it's good for you."

Martha: He was always nice to her—nobody ever treated Louise like a maid.

Bill: I understand the friendship between the Hayes' and the Callaghan's go back to World War I.

Martha: That's right. The connection between Coyne and I is the fact that Coyne's father heard that his old friend from World War I and shipmate Ed Hayes was back in the Navy and in Washington. Coyne happened to be going to a naval prep school in New Jersey at the time and his older brother Tom graduated from Georgetown. He was studying law at Northwestern and would soon be eligible for service.

Tom Sr. called my father and said, "Could you help get my son Tom into the Navy?"

Coyne: He had a lot to offer because of his background in naval affairs.

Martha: So then Daddy made arrangements to have Tom Callaghan Jr. obtain a commission in the Navy and come to Washington where his knowledge of Naval history could be utilized in the Public Information Department.

Then Tom got married to Eleanor Lalley in Chicago. They came to Washington and lived in a hotel; I can't remember the name. It's the same place where Al Gore lived when Al's dad was in the Senate.

My mother, of course, dear friend of the Callaghans, was able to get Tom and his new bride an apartment in the same apartment building we lived in. At that point, you couldn't find a place to live in Washington. People were moving there by the thousands, but Mimi persevered and got them in. So the Callaghans, Tom and El, lived on the fourth floor, and the Hayes lived on the second floor.

We never imagined what was about to happen next! That we were about to enter into World War II – fighting two wars simultaneously – on the other side of the Atlantic against the Germans and in the Pacific against the Japanese.

Chapter 11
Assessing the Damage at Pearl

While working with my parents over the last 30 years, I have been fortunate to hear stories about their life as kids and teenagers, their involvement in WW II, and raising a big family together – not to mention religion and politics. Mom and Dad are like walking history books!

And I think that has a lot to do with why I have become exceedingly intrigued with our family's history and our nation's history, especially when the two collided with each other in December of 1941.

The following interview took place in the summer of 2008, at the Plaza Hotel in Eau Claire, Wisconsin, with my parents, Martha and Coyne Callaghan:

Bill: Let's go back to the year 1941.

Martha: To begin with, in May of 1941, my father, Ed Hayes, who was a lawyer and had his own law firm in Decatur, Illinois, could see the winds of war approaching and was very aware of what was happening in the world. This was the general attitude ... people wanted to go do something for their country, anything to help with the war.

As the years went along, Daddy remained very concerned about the course of our country because he was in the American Legion and was National Commander in July '33 to June of '34.

In 1936 he was Frank Knox's campaign manager when he ran for Vice President of the United States with Alf Landon from Kansas.

Coyne: The campaign slogan was "Land on the Rock with Landon and Knox." They should have won.

However, when Roosevelt was elected, he was trying to make peace among the political parties so he appointed Republicans to the Defense Department. Knox put his office together and his two executive assistants were from Illinois. One was Ed Hayes and the other was Adlai Stevenson.

Martha: Then lo and behold, he decided to give up his law practice for a year to go to Washington and serve his country with the Navy. He was in the Reserves all those years since World War I. So, off he goes to Washington.

Daddy would come home every three or four weeks. In those days you didn't get on a plane and fly home in an hour and a half. He had to take a train from Washington to Chicago and wait for another train to take him to Decatur.

When he came home in July of '41, I had just turned 16 and was madly in love with at least three boys. At that age, it's your life. What else is there?

Then a huge surprise happened. Out of the blue, my mother announced to my father and the family that she had sold the house and that we were moving to Washington because she wanted her daughters to have an opportunity to go to school in the East. There's no war yet! And the next thing you know, I have to leave anybody and everybody I ever knew.

So we headed to Washington D.C. in early August and moved into a hotel. We had to eat all our meals out because there weren't kitchens in those places then.

One month later, I was put into a Catholic girls school in

*Washington D.C. You had to wear black uniforms - long
sleeves and a stiff, white collar, no makeup and black old-
lady shoes with heels about this big around (showing a circle
the size of a tennis ball with her fingers). I had just turned 16
and was thinking, 'No, you don't do this to me.'*

*That was my war. But as time passed on, I began to have fun
meeting new friends.*

Bill: Where were you on December 7, 1941?

*Martha: I'll never forget it. We heard the news on the
radio. The Japs had bombed Pearl Harbor and President
Roosevelt immediately orders Frank Knox to Pearl to assess
the damage. Mrs. Knox calls my father tells him "Pack your
white uniforms and be at the west door of the White House
at 5:30 pm." In the meantime I had gotten my first driver's
license in Washington. My older sister could drive too, so
we drove Daddy down to the White House. You could drive
right up to the door back then; today you can't get any closer
than a couple blocks away. We dropped him off and didn't
know where he was headed. We just knew he was involved in
something special and helping the country.*

*The next day, Mimi got a call from the Navy Department
saying your husband has arrived safely at his destination.
There were no phone calls back and forth to say 'Here I
am' or whatever. And none of what Daddy was doing was
on the radio.*

*Back home at the apartment, nobody said anything about
where he went. The next day, my sister heard on the radio
that Roosevelt was going to ask Congress to declare war
on Japan and Germany. We jumped in the car and we drove
right down to the Capitol, parked, turned on the radio and
watched the building, imagining what was going on in there
as we listened intently on the car radio. We had no TVs.
After that we drove out to Embassy Row and passed the
Japanese embassy. The gate was wide open and there was*

a huge fire on the grounds. The Japs had burned all their papers. They were long gone.

The following Thursday, my sister and I went to the movies and they used to show news reels at halftime. This is how people got the news back then. And the news was Pearl Harbor! We're watching the big screen and lo and behold they show a picture of the secretary of the Navy and his staff on board one of the ships that was not sunk and there's Daddy.

I yelled out in the theater, "There's Daddy." And everybody said, 'Who? Which One,' and my sister Anthy and I ran out of the theater and drove home as fast as we could. We ran in the house and screamed the news, "Daddy is in Pearl Harbor." And we didn't know what was going to happen or if there was going to be more bombings.

Coyne: The investigating committee assigned by Knox to assist in preparing a special report to the President included Lieutenant Commander Ed Hayes, Captain Frank Beatty, Special Assistant Joseph Powell, Commander Leland Lovette and a shipbuilder …

Martha: The shipbuilder was from New England. They went over to inspect the damage.

Daddy didn't go to high school because there wasn't a high school in Decatur and his father couldn't afford to send him away. My father went to Browns Business Institute School in Decatur and learned shorthand typing. In fact, he won the state championship for shorthand typing.

On the way back from Pearl Harbor, Frank Knox dictated, or spoke out loud, to Daddy about the damage. Knox is talking out loud on the plane about what they saw and Daddy wrote everything down on the back of a bill that they had from the Royal Hawaiian Hotel. I think their room was something like $4.50/night. My Aunt Betty, Daddy's secretary, transcribed Mr. Knox's report from Daddy's shorthand that went to the

300

President. That's how Roosevelt heard the details about what happened that infamous day at Pearl Harbor. My sister Anthy has the copies of the hotel bill and the shorthand scribed on the back!

After the war broke out, they rationed gasoline and we only got three gallons of gas a month. Daddy was so patriotic, he wasn't about to say ask for a "B" card, which would allow him to get more gas. He took the least amount, which was three gallons a month.

Coyne: I don't believe that's right. I believe an "A" card allowed three gallons a week.

Martha: No. It's true - it was three gallons a month. There was a sign you put right on your windshield, an "A" card, or a "B" card, or a "C" card.

Coyne: Gasoline was 19 cents a gallon.

Martha: You were given an A or a B or a C on the sticker to let the gas attendant know how much gas you could get. Daddy drove one of those Road Master Buicks and with those cars it took that much gas just to turn the ignition on. The attitude of the people back then, who were genuine Americans, wanted to get involved and serve their country.

Coyne: I went to Great Lakes Academy and had a physical exam and they told me I was near-sighted in the right eye. The doctor and nurse said I didn't pass and they say, 'Don't feel bad.' They said the fella who was No. 1 in his class out of Annapolis that year wasn't commissioned. So because there was a possibility they'd have to buy glasses for him, they wouldn't commission him. That's how tight money was before the war.

Therefore, they said don't try and get in the Navy, but that didn't deter me. Dad said, "Where do you want to go?" And I said, "Let's go to Notre Dame." We used to go down there

301

when we were kids. I knew Frank Curdio, Tommy Arr, and Frank Leahy, all my buddies from camp up in Eagle River at Camp St. George on Clear Lake in Wisconsin.

The Navy came to Notre Dame and they had started an ROTC (Reserve Officer Training Core) there. So I decided to go to prep school at Notre Dame. That was great because I had just come from Admiral Farragut Academy, and I enjoyed training young cadets. When I was a sophomore at Notre Dame I joined the ROTC.

They signed me up and that's where I went. Once they were assured that I was going to be there, they put me in charge of the cadets. That's how I got my command experience.

I was in Chicago driving back to Notre Dame when Pearl Harbor happened (heard the news on the radio). The top brass wanted people who were in school to stay there. I had all that great training with the extra-duties squad, so they depended on me.

Martha: He got his Navy training while he was still at Notre Dame.

Coyne: I joined the Navy in September '41. Then all the Navy groups – like B1, B7 and so on – we all went on active duty in July of '43.

They accelerated our program and I was graduated as an ensign with my four years of engineering. Then I could proceed to report to the Naval Yard in Peugeot Sound, Washington. Big ships from Pearl Harbor were being repaired there and put back in the fleet. They assigned me to the USS Macon Island. I was in the pre-commissioning detail, which involved gathering the ship companies together. Our ship was being built in Astoria, Washington, at the Kaiser Ship Yard, and we were up in Seattle. We used to call them Kaiser's Coffins because the thickest hull was only an inch thick. But they were very good ships. Kaiser did a helluva job with them.

You have no idea how big this commission was. We were getting warrant officers from various other duties, guys who had their ships sunk from under them ... and we're building a ship's company.

We were sent to Astoria for training and we'd get together in a bus and go down there for firefighter school. The head of the firefighting school was a guy named Quinn, former commissioner of the Chicago fire department.

Martha: He was another smart-aleck Irishman from Chicago. The Navy had quite a few.

Coyne: He ran a great show. They simulated deck fires and engine room fires. They were tremendous. Quinn did a great job; he taught us how to handle that hose. You weren't afraid of anything after that. You had a guy behind you holding the hose and you'd hold on for dear life! We would go down there for a week, practicing putting out these fires.

Our ship was commissioned on May 9. We took a cruise down to San Diego, California, to get our arresting gear and all our air gear and also to pick up our squadron. The Makin Island was a jeep carrier.

I recall during one mission, we were in a group of six carriers with a screen of destroyers all around us. We were coming through Shiragoua Straights. And the Japs found us. They sent a Kamikaze to the bridge of the Louisville and they killed Admiral Sample and Dowd. Our ship was ahead of them and fortunately didn't get hit. I was at sea for over a year.

Interview with Aunt Anthy Martini (my mom's sister) in Northbrook, Illinois, on June 17, 2008:

Bill: Tell me about the time you and my mom worked at the Stage Door Canteen.

Anthy: A friend of mine suggested that we go there and volunteer. So I brought Martha with me, and we danced with the sailors and soldiers when they had shore leave. We were considered junior hostesses. Martha and I would just sit there and then these sailors would ask us to dance with them.

That was it. There was no dating or anything, except once in a while. I thought Martha was going to be bored, but she had fun too. We worked the 7:30 to 10:30 shift and then took the streetcar home. Washington D.C. was totally safe back then!

From left to right: Red, Martha, Jim and Anthy at the Stage Door Canteen in Washington, D.C.

Bill: Tell me about December 7, 1941.

Anthy: I worked for this group in Washington where we gave clothes away to the poor, and I had a meeting with them on

December 7. It was a Sunday night. One of the guys at the meeting said, "Did you hear about the bombings?" I didn't know much about it and we talked and they said the traffic around town was terrible. Our meetings lasted from 5:00 to 8:00 pm, and then some of us left in a car. And as we drove past the Japanese embassy, you could see a big bonfire in the back as they were burning all the important papers.

In the meantime, Mrs. Knox called my mother to say, "Have Commander Hayes bring white uniform." But, you see, we didn't hear this first hand right away, but she called because my father was going to travel with Frank Knox. He used to own the Chicago Daily news. Then he ran for President and my father campaigned for him all over the U.S. and made speeches, you know, in honor of Frank Knox; but of course he didn't make it.

So then Knox was appointed Secretary. Imagine, Roosevelt picked a man who ran against him for President to be his Secretary of the Navy. Then Frank Knox picked my father to be an Assistant to the Secretary of the Navy.

By Monday or Tuesday, we knew our dad was out of town, but we didn't know where he'd gone. We heard later that Mrs. Knox had called each night to tell my mother that Cmdr. Hayes had arrived safely to his destination. We were told that Daddy wore his white uniform on this trip, which meant he was going somewhere warm. Martha and I happened to go to the movies on Thursday, December 11. And back then there was no TV or anything, but they always had a newsreel that ran during intermission - showing the news of the day. It showed this big ship in Pearl Harbor and our dad and the Secretary of the Navy and two other men walking up the gang plank.

Then we heard later that Tom Hayes's son, Ted Hayes, who was named after his uncle Ed, and an Annapolis graduate, was standing there on the ship at attention. Rows of sailors

305

*in their whites were on hand to greet the landing party. And
Ted says under his breath "Gee that looks like Uncle Ed,"
and it was.*

*My husband Ro was in a group of the Navy called "The
Atlantic Fleet Camera Party." Being engineers, they
photographed from one ship to another ship and yet another
ship to see which naval group was the most accurate during
rocket test firing drills. He helped supervise the testing of
Weapons Fire Systems. Then they would take the information
back to the offices in Guantanamo and analyze the photos.
Once they determined who the best ship crew was, my
husband was selected to secretly bring target ship photos
to Washington; where I was, with Jeff, our new baby, and
Ro couldn't even call me. But when he got to Miami, on his
way back to Guantanamo, he called me. He couldn't tell
me he was going to be in Washington at the time because it
was confidential. But that information was critical because
the Secretary of the Navy sent that battleship group, which
proved to be the most accurate shooters, to the invasions of
both Iwo Jima and Okinawa; and they helped win the battle.
The firing was like this – up and over, because a lot of times
our men were landing on the beach and they had to land the
bombs over their heads with precision. The ship had rocket
platforms that would launch a barrage of rockets at the same
time. They sent the battle group through the Panama Canal
and out into the Pacific. Whenever I hear the words Iwo
Jima, I think of Ro's involvement to help them win the battle
in the Pacific.*

During my interview with Aunt Anthy, she handed me the
following letter which she received from Ted Hayes in 1991:

Dear Anthy,

*As you requested, I have put down in writing for your
records my memories of Uncle Ed's visit to us there in Pearl
Harbor right after "the bombing." I'll try to do my best.*

Recall, however, that this memory has to go back now some FIFTY YEARS!!! Little did I ever believe that I would be "remembering" things which occurred half a century ago!!!

The bombing, of course, was a terrible trauma. You may or may not be aware that a huge dance was held at the O' Club on Saturday nights. That night, my good friend from the class of '39 and I attended the dance as bachelors and had a wee of a time. After midnight sometime, "Benny" Benjamin said to me, "Hey, Ed, you don't have to be back on board until Monday morning, do you?" He then said that we ought to go to his "snake ranch" (we called the small apartments some of us rented by those names) for the night, attend Mass on Sunday morning, and then spend the rest of the day roaming around Oahu. I thought that was an absolutely capital idea, so we went back to his "pad" at about 0100 hours Sunday morning.

At 0700, we were resting comfortably in our beds and listening to the radio, when suddenly the music cut off and a sepulchral voice said, "Ladies and Gentleman, the island of Oahu is being attacked by a foreign power, but the attack is being repelled and all is well". Benny looked over at me, I looked over at him; we both said in almost the same breath, "Boy, oh boy! Orson Welles and the Men from Mars all over again." We continued to lie in bed as the Hawaiian music started playing again. In about another minute or so, the voice came on again and this time it said, "Ladies and Gentleman, this is no joke. Listen to those guns!!"

Well that got immediate results! Benny's place was located up on Wilhelmina Rise, which is sort of a highland area of development buildings, and actually looks down over Pearl Harbor itself. We jumped out of our beds and ran out to the lanai. Sure enough, the air was full of puffs of anti-aircraft fire! Both of us had enough experience firing PRACTICE runs to know exactly what all the stuff in the sky really meant. The two of us NEVER dressed faster! We jumped into

*Benny's little roadster and flailed our way down to the Naval
Base practically on two wheels around every curve. Now
that I think of it, fifty years later, I find myself wondering why
we weren't shot by the Marine Guard at the gate! We simply
flew past him, waving our caps out the window.*

*One bit of humor (somehow, the American GI can always see
humor in any situation, no matter how bad!) was that one
of the Jap torpedoes had "run wild" and ended up right on
the ground at the end of the sidewalk in front of the O' Club
at Merry Point. As officers and men would come running
at full tilt around the last turn, they were confronted by that
torpedo, just plain lying there, right in their path! You can't
believe how fast each one would grind to a halt, back down
full power, and disappear back around the bend! Those of us
who were "old-timers" by then simply laughed aloud, for we
knew the torpedo wouldn't go off. Then we waited for some
boat – ANY boat! – to come in and pick people up.*

*Boats were landing, filling up with passengers, and then
shoving off, while the coxswains called out, "What ship?"
There would be all sorts of yells then each one the name
of some ship or another which had received damage.
Benny and I managed to get "MARYLAND" (for me) and
"TENNESSEE" (for him) above the din. The boat coxswain
couldn't make either one of the two ships because of raging
oil fires around each one, so we "landed" at Ford Island,
from where we managed to make our way over to the great
concrete mooring piles to which the ships had moored. We
actually scrabbled our way over the mooring lines to get
aboard the ships.*

*By the way, that was the last time I ever saw, or heard from,
Benny Benjamin. God rest his soul.*

*There were several torpedo and bomb strikes over a period of
about thirty minutes or so and thunderous explosions going
off all around us! After it was all over, the MARYLAND had*

been hit by two of the big bombs, both on the forward end of the ship. Meanwhile, TENNESSEE had been hit at least twice, both times aft. The end result of all that was simply, that the MARYLAND was on the bottom by the bow, while TENNESSEE was on the bottom by the stern!

The USS Maryland alongside the capsized USS Oklahoma after the attack on Pearl Harbor, December 7, 1941.

Now, if you studied the holocaust that day, recall that OKLAHOMA was moored outboard of the MARYLAND, while WEST VIRGINIA was moored outboard of TENNESSEE. OKLAHOMA took probably six torpedoes, and rolled completely over in about eleven minutes, while WEST VIRGINIA took probably four "fish" or more, but it's rolling keel somehow caught beneath the rolling keels of TENNESSEE, and as a result, WEST VIRGINIA didn't roll over! It was another one of those "miracles" that happened that day which nobody could ever explain later.

So there we were in MARYLAND. Stuck in behind OKLAHOMA, down on the bottom at the bow, there were some twelve or fourteen men trapped in the forward compartment with NOWHERE to go!

I was standing JOOD (Junior-Officer-of-the-deck) watches at that time, and was still an Ensign USN. The main deck of MARYLAND was still somewhat above water, and the crew was doing its best to continue a "normal" routine. Believe me, it wasn't easy, what with all the water sloshing around with deep oil not more than a few feet below the deck. We managed somehow or other – I'll actually never remember how! – to get some sort of galley service going, and actually had some of food available for the crew.

That situation continued through several days, as far as I am able to recall. Then, we suddenly heard that SECNAV himself was coming to estimate the damage and the problem! Frank Knox was just a sort of vague chimera to us there in the Fleet at the time. Most of us had heard his name, but beyond that, we had precious little to go on. At any rate, the idea of Frank Knox, SECNAV, coming out to estimate the problem really meant precious little to me. I was much more interested in exactly what we could do on the MARYLAND to try to get her seaworthy again.

At any rate, I was standing the JOOD watch, when I looked over at the concrete pilings, and there stood someone who looked "exactly like my Uncle Ed"! It was hard to believe I wasn't hallucinating!! Uncle Ed was in his full khaki white uniform, and I was absolutely sure, after a second look, that it simply had to be him! He pretty much charged on board and the moment he arrived on the quarterdeck, it was perfectly obvious to me that he truly was my uncle, and to him, that I truly was his nephew!

We stood there on deck and hugged each other, and I will never forget how relieved I was to know that my Uncle Ed had come out, or how relieved he was to know that I was still alive! He was so tied up with Frank Knox and the study group that I just plain never saw him again. I wish I had had the opportunity, but it never developed. The first I knew, Secretary Knox, and the entire retinue had shoved off and returned to the States. That's my story of seeing Uncle Ed after the bombing of Pearl Harbor!

God bless, always

Ted

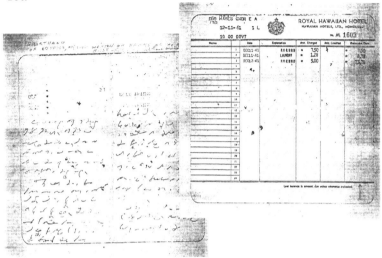

Copy of the original shorthand notes written on the back of the hotel bills from the Royal Hawaiian Hotel.

The following letter was sent in 1973 to Aunt Anthy from Aunt Betty Kearney, who was Mimi's sister and Ed Hayes's secretary for many years.

Dear Anthy,

At long last I am getting the shorthand notes typed and off to you and about time! Some of the words have eluded me, but you know how "cold" shorthand notes can get (32 years later). And then, the circumstances of taking these notes by your dad were certainly not the best – I seem to recall something about Ed taking them on the top of his briefcase – making them somewhat more illegible.

Lovingly,

Betty

The following transcript of shorthand notes were taken by Edward A. Hayes in route from Pearl Harbor after investigation by Secretary of the Navy, Frank Knox:

Upon innumerable occasions, as Secretary of the Navy, I have had evidences of this. These evidences will multiply from now on, and no war that the country, as a whole makes, or decisions, will fail to be honored, no matter how drastic the sacrifice may be.

I am just returning from a journey which took me clear across the continent and back and over the Pacific to our further out-post in the Pacific area. I feel we were met by great, determined Americans, angered and horrified by the treachery by which the war with Japan began, but we will see determined bullets in the field.

The crew that brings the freighter to the surface and reassigns it is as essential to victory and has the same part as a Jestroyer that feeds the oil into the portal of a ship on the Pacific front.

This is all-out war and to win it takes an all-over patriotism that doesn't count the cost but only seeks an opportunity for display in action.

At eight o'clock Sunday morning, Honolulu time, political personal feelings disappeared in America. There is only one class left and they are first, last, and all the time Americans. The President is no longer the leader of one political party representing dominant political division of the country. He is Commander-in-chief of the Armed Forces of the United States, and he commands the undivided loyalty not only of those men in the services but of each American in whatever walk of life.

War is no longer fought just by soldiers and sailors. Modern wars are fought by the people. The man making a shell case in a munitions factory is as important as a member of the gun

*crew that sinks that loaded shell into the breach of a gun. A
farmer who grows food stuffs to feed the men in our Army
and Navy, and the people of the countries allied with us, are
just as important to victory as the gallant boy who bears his
breast to the heel of the enemy.*

*That while Japan fired the first shot, the war should not end
until Japan is completely defeated and permanently removed
as a menace to the people and security of the whole Pacific
area and the Far East.*

*When I returned to Washington early Friday morning, we had
been at war with Japan only since Sunday. I came back to
find us at war with Germany and Italy and some of the other
satellite powers in Europe.*

*Note: The Secretary declined to make any statement whatever
concerning the investigation. He says his first report
naturally must be made to the President of the United States.*

Just recently, my first cousin, Marty Mulcahy, Honey's son,
made a surprise visit to the plant to say hello. Marty's father,
Roger Mulcahy was a great man and also a World War II
veteran. When Marty heard about this book, he sent me the
following email:

Bill,

*It was great stopping in Osseo and seeing Aunt Martha and
Uncle Coyne.*

*I know they went through hell when WWII was coming to a
close. I have been fortunate that Dad lived until 2001 and
Mom (Honey) is still with us.*

*I am still searching for my notes dictated to me directly from
Dad in the year 2000. I was trying to write everything down
that he could remember. I still recall telling him if he dies
– the information is lost forever. His shipmates were dying in
droves. 16 million men and women who served in World War*

II die at a rate of over 1,000 per day.

During his 22 months at sea, Dad had flown 310 Sorties, with 112 of them at night. The other squadron leader had most of the day flights. I remember Dad telling me that landing on a carrier at night was pretty scary.

He was assigned to the USS Savo Island, one of 48 – 50 ships assembled in a hurry by the Vancouver Shipbuilding Company in Canada. I think his squadron designation was CV-79. But they were called "The Saints."

They flew the F4F Wildcat and then the F6F Hellcat. He was also a Chuck Yeager test pilot. My dad flew some of the first fighter planes off the assembly lines. He was assigned to transport them to carriers being outfitted for sea duty.

Dad also flew reconnaissance missions along the Northeastern Coast out of Boston during the second year of the war. If they located enemy submarines, they dropped depth charges from their torpedo bombers.

In 1997, I spoke at a reunion in St. Louis for the remaining members of the USS Savo Island. The Navy wives were something special. I was the only son or daughter in attendance. I had brought the model of the Savo Island to the reunion as Dad drove in from Denver and I from Chicago. It was a big hit.

In my speech, I promised them that my children will know what they have done and what they have accomplished. I finished with a toast to all the Navy families and a review of the cost of WWII. I pointed out that the cost went deeply beyond those serving and affected family members for the rest of their lives.

Dad died in Denver. He went peacefully in his sleep. My brother Michael was with him when he died.

Captain Roger Joseph Mulcahy Jr.

United States Navy

Born May 11, 1920 - Died February 9, 2001

Losing a parent is a terrible thing. Another one of life's anchors ripped away.

Your cousin - Marty Mulcahy

The following interview with my dad's sisters, Aunt Honey Mulcahy and Aunt Corky Hyland, took place at my Cousin Mimi (Mulcahy) Cullnan's house on June 17, 2008, in Chicago:

Bill: Tell me about what was going on in Chicago during the war.

Corky: After Mom died in 1943, we moved out of our house on Euclid Avenue in '44.

Aunt Corky Hyland and Aunt Honey Mulcahy
during June 2008 interview

Honey: So in 1944, Marty was prepping for the war. Coyne's in the war on an aircraft carrier and Tom's in the Naval Intelligence Department.

In fact, Ed Hayes was instrumental in getting Tom in the Navy. Marty was nearsighted, I was nearsighted too. But by that time, Ed Hayes was unavailable and couldn't help Marty. So Marty couldn't pass his exam. We were all Navy; except Marty ended up in the Army.

Corky: Was Coyne in the ROTC?

Honey: Farragut is where I remember him.

Corky: Coyne was also Cadet Commander at Notre Dame.

Honey: During the war, I volunteered to work for the Red Cross. We worked in the churches and the ladies rolled bandages. We'd pick up the bandages and bring them the stuff to roll. Jack Benny, Mary Livingston, Phil Harris and Mom entertained the wounded servicemen at Hines Hospital.

Corky: I was 16 when Mom died.

Honey: I was 20. At that time, Tom was in Washington, Coyne was on a carrier, and Marty was on a Troop Transport. So we were only worried about Coyne. A girl on a bike came to our house on March 5, 1944, knocks on the door, and says, "I have a Telegram." I'll never forget it.

Corky: She had tears in her eyes.

And they have to stay and see how you react. That's how she was trained. She handed me the telegram and I saw, MIA and Cork and I both screamed, "Oh my God, Coyne."

Corky: So she stayed, and we opened it up, "Oh my God, it was Marty!

Honey: We couldn't believe it. Missing in action!

Corky: Imagine having the job to deliver that news. February 19, 1945, that was when he was killed. But we got the telegram March 5.

Honey: You understand that they couldn't get the news to us any sooner. They had to find the dog tags, all of that. The two of us said to each other, He'll be all right. I know he's going to be all right. Marty will be fine, he'll be ok. After all, he's on a Troop Transport. So then on March 8, the girl returned and handed us a second Telegram which stated Marty was killed in action! And we just couldn't believe it. It was just unreal! We sobbed - our youngest brother was dead! Cork and I were together at the time we heard the news, thank God!"

My visit with Aunt Corky and Aunt Honey lasted only three hours, but in that short amount of time, I was able to learn decades of information about our family's history. I never realized that they lost their parents and brother Marty at such a young age. Maybe that's why the rest of the family, Honey, Corky, Coyne, (my father) and Uncle Tom (who died in 2001) have been blessed with longevity.

Follow-up interview with my parents about the days following the war:

Martha: It was 1945. Coyne was back from the war and in Bethesda Naval Hospital. He had picked up pneumonia on his flight back from Pearl Harbor after the war was over, and we had moved to Chicago. My mother allowed me to go back to Washington for a week after Christmas. I went to see my old friends and stayed at my sister Anthy's apartment. She lived in the same apartment building as Coyne's brother Tom and his wife Eleanor. So I was down at the front door waiting for Bob Spain, my old boyfriend, to come and pick me up.

317

Tom and El came down to the front door and were about to take a cab to visit Coyne at Bethesda. They said, "Would you like to come with us?" And I said, "Oh, no thank you, Bob's going to pick me up so I really can't." I hadn't seen Coyne in two years because he was overseas - floating around the Pacific. But Tom insisted I join them, so I did. And I left word with the doorman to tell Bob as to why I left.

Coyne: Didn't I write you a letter?

Martha: Yeah, you wrote me. What was it you called it?

Coyne: Hope correspondence from the war. I told her I was going to swim across the moat and slay the dragons at Hirohito's Castle.

Martha: And then he signs it: Yours in Christ.

Cardinal Coyne Callaghan, Archbishop of Tokyo.

Coyne: That's me.

Chapter 12

Blessed Are They

A few years ago, I met a lab technician in Racine, Wisconsin, while testing some food ingredients with the Rollo-Mixer. He was a strong, smart-looking man who filled out his white lab coat. He looked like Secret Service. When I introduced myself to this kind, black man, I said, "How are you?" "I am blessed, how are you?" he replied. That was the best response I have heard yet to that popular question.

Religion is a fascinating subject, especially in America where we claim to be one nation under God and yet we are a country and a people made up of many religions: Lutheran, Episcopalian, Jewish, Baptist, Jehovah Witness, Catholic, Presbyterian and Muslim, to name a few.

Teaching religion is one of the most gratifying experiences of my life. As an eighth-grade Religious Ed teacher at Immaculate Conception, one of the subjects I am required to cover is the Nicene Creed. This special proclamation of the Holy Trinity is recited each Sunday at Catholic mass around the world and is the belief and definition of a Roman Catholic.

Last year's class included my daughter Meghan and some of her classmates from South Middle School, along with eighth-graders from Fall Creek, Altoona and Eleva-Strum – 17 students in all. The Nicene Creed is rather long - 32 lines total if you include the Amen at the end - so I decided to have each student write a line on the chalkboard. By the time we were done, we had filled the walls on both sides of the room. Once we had the Creed written out, we went through each line and discussed each belief:

We believe in One God,

The Father, the Almighty,

Maker of Heaven and Earth,

Of all that is seen and unseen. ...

With fifteen minutes left in the 75-minute class, I asked the kids to write on a yellow Post-it note why they believe in God the Father, God the Son and God the Holy Spirit. Here are some samples of the responses:

"I believe in God because all of the things that we have in this world couldn't have been just a coincidence."

"I believe in Jesus because of the great things that people tell about him and that it had to be written 4 times over."

"I believe in the Holy Spirit because how else was Jesus made?"

"I believe the Holy Spirit leads us to Heaven."

"I believe they are one in the same. They are our life and the reason we are here."

"I believe in all three because I was raised that way!"

I've noticed that eighth-grade kids are still at an age where they are pure of heart and still retain the mind of a child versus that of an adult. Once high school begins, all that begins to change. Their bodies go through so many physical changes and they become preoccupied with the opposite sex. Shows like Disney's "Suite Life of Zach and Cody" and "Hannah Montana" are replaced with "S" rated reality shows on MTV – I mean STV - such as "Next" and "Tila Tequila."

Honor Your Father and Mother

On December 28, 2008, my family and I attended mass at Immaculate Conception Church and were fortunate to sit just a few pews behind Dale Brunner, who sings like the seraphim and cherubim in Dolby digital surround sound - he really sounds professional. Dale raises his voice in praise to God like no one I've ever heard.

During that mass, I thought of my parents and Laurel's parents as I listened closely to the first reading from Sirach 3:2-6, 12-14:

God sets a father in honor over his children, a mother's authority he confirms over her sons,

Whoever honors his father atones for sins, and preserves himself from them.

When he prays, he is heard; he stores up riches who reveres his mother.

Whoever honors his father is gladdened by children, and, when he prays, is heard.

Whoever reveres his father will live a long life; he who obeys his father brings comfort to his mother.

My son, take care of your father when he is old; grieve him not as long as he lives.

Even if his mind fails, be considerate of him; revile him not all the days of his life; kindness to a father will not be forgotten, firmly planted against the debt of your sins – a house raised in justice to you.

Having been a lector at church for more than 20 years, I have had the opportunity to recite timeless readings from both the Old and New Testaments. These heavenly inspired writings from the Bible are thousands of years old and send a powerful message that is as relevant today as the time they were written.

As our parents get older, it is important that we help them and watch over them – just as they did for us. Treat them with honor and respect!

Although I attended eight years at St. Robert's grade school, I was fortunate to learn the majority of my Catholic faith from my parents. Mom would say, "If you claim to be part of something, you have to practice." To label yourself a Catholic and not take part in the practice of attending mass regularly on Sundays or partaking in the other Sacraments is not living your Catholic faith.

When I attend mass on Sunday mornings, I look forward to singing the timeless songs that still give my spirit chills. The first thing I do when I get in the pew is look at the song numbers posted in the front of church. Songs like "Here I am Lord," "Blest Are They," and "Gather Us In," take me out! They sound so heavenly in church.

"You are Mine," which I think is one of the top five church songs of all time, was written by David Haas (copyright 1995).

I will come to you in the silence
I will lift you from all your fear
You will hear My voice
I claim you as My choice
Be still, and know I am near

I am hope for all who are hopeless
I am eyes for all who long to see
In the shadows of the night,
I will be your light
Come and rest in Me

I am strength for all the despairing
Healing for the ones who dwell in shame
All the blind will see, the lame will all run free
And all will know My name

I am the Word that leads all to freedom
I am the peace the world cannot give
I will call your name, embracing all your pain
Stand up, now, walk, and live

Do not be afraid, I am with you
I have called you each by name
Come and follow Me
I will bring you home
I love you and you are mine

That song gives me comfort and goose bumps every time and makes me rejoice and be glad for all the gifts I have been given.

Beyond the songs, and the scripture readings from the Holy Bible, and Fr. Klink's well written sermons, I'm able to acquire food for my soul. The Bread of Life!

Did you know the Holy Trinity is present at mass every Sunday?

1. We give thanks to *God* in song and prayer.

2. We receive *Jesus*, the Body of Christ, during communion.

3. We observe the transformation of bread and wine, when the *Holy Spirit "comes upon these gifts and makes them Holy, so that they may become the body and blood of our Lord Jesus Christ."*

My favorite part of mass is when the priest says:

"We hope to someday forever enjoy the vision of your glory and the fullness of life, through Christ our Lord, from whom all good things come."

and

"Behold, the lamb of God, who takes away the sins of the world. Happy are we to be called to this supper!"

Where else on earth can you go to get food for your soul?

323

As parents and guardians of this wonderful gift called children, we are asked to do much more than care for and provide for them daily, although that in and of itself can be a constant challenge. It is our responsibility to teach them their faith. Parents seem to take this lightly these days or simply choose to avoid it all together. Maybe that's because *their* parents didn't teach them about religion, so they don't feel very knowledgeable or comfortable discussing a subject they know little about. If we don't teach our children their religion, who will?

After Meghan was born in 1995, the late Jesper Dinesen asked me what my goal in life was as a parent and I told him, "My goal is to see that my wife and kids get to heaven." And that I plan to help them any way I can. What else could be more important?

Mark 13 states:

People were bringing little children to him in order that he might touch them; and the disciples spoke sternly to them. But when Jesus saw this, he was indignant and said to them, "Let the little children come to me; do not stop them; for it is to such as these that the kingdom of God belongs. Truly I tell you, whoever does not receive the kingdom of God as a little child will never enter it. And he took them up in his arms. Laid his hands on them, and blessed them."

"Don't forget to show hospitality to strangers,
for some who have done this have entertained
angels without realizing it." Hebrews 13:2

A friend of mine from California, Bob Sjourgren, gave me a book written by J.H. Hunter titled "Saint, Seer and Scientist – The story of George Washington Carver." I worked with Bob on a project encapsulating biological insecticides, as we were creating a new mosquito growth retardant. Bob is a research chemist and formulations developer who is a joy to work with and extremely bright. I can see why he enjoyed the work of Dr. Carver. Here is an excerpt from the book:

His name is Dr. George Washington Carver. His position was director of research and experiment for the Tuskegee Normal and Industrial Institute in Tuskegee, Alabama. I heard of him being one of the three greatest scientists of the United States, a man who had done amazing things with peanuts, sweet potatoes and waste materials. His outlook is always humanitarian and progressive. He has a passionate love for his fellow man, particularly those of his own race and colour, and all his experiments have been directed towards the one end of ameliorating their lot and making life easier for them. … Never once has he sought to benefit by his discoveries. He owns no patents and maintains no claim over his amazing achievements. … It is my firm conviction that if Dr. Carver has been able to do so much with the things of the earth the secret lies first in the simplicity of his faith, and then in his amazing industry. He has the humble teachable mind of a child. He is the practical mystic, a saint, a seer, and a scientist. He is intensely "other worldly," and at the same time very practical. He sees visions, but the vision is transmuted into practical realities that will benefit his fellow man.

I believe instilling a strong faith in God will help your child make sound and wise decisions as they enter a world filled with unexpected problems. A strong faith will give your kids a solid foundation and help them weather life's thunderstorms, earthquakes and turbulent challenges. When the storms pass, they will still be standing strong.

John Lennon released "Instant Karma" in 1970, which sums up the way life can surprise you.

Instant karma's gonna get you
Gonna knock you right on the head
You better get yourself together
Pretty soon you gonna be dead
What in the world you're thinking of
Laughing in the face of love?
What on earth are you trying to do?
It's up to you - yeah you

Instant karma's gonna get you
Gonna look you right in the face
Better get yourself together darling
Join the human race
How in the world you gonna see
Laughing at fools like me?
Who in the hell do you think you are?
A superstar? Well, right you are

Well we all shine on
Like the moon and the stars and the sun
Well we all shine on
Everyone come on

Instant karma's gonna get you
Gonna knock you off your feet
Better recognize your brothers
Everyone you meet
Why in the world are we here?
Surely not to live in pain and fear
Why in earth are you there
When you're everywhere?
Come and get your share

I wonder if fear comes from stress or if stress comes from fear? No doubt they're related and it is really too bad that today's world is preoccupied with both.

The term "stress" is used a lot these days. It usually refers to the pressure, trauma, strain or tension associated with our daily lives and the accompanying anxiety, exhaustion and sorrow. Growing up in the 1960s and '70s, I only knew the word as an applied force to bend structural components or a designed strength-rating of steel members like I-beams, channel iron or angle iron.

So then what does "stressed out" mean? You're bending? When did "stress" become a national health issue? I believe it was in the '80s.

I know people who have physical and mental problems because of stress and I want nothing more than for these people to be comforted. But I think stress is oversold and misconstrued. What is stress? You have the option to make a problem as bad as you want and as a result you oftentimes bring undo pressure on yourself. What is a predicament for some people is not even a concern for others. Why is that? I think it depends on your attitude and how you choose to react to the unexpected. I heard that the true test of one's character is not how you act when all is well, but how you act under adverse circumstances. We all handle situations differently!

My parents raised me and taught me to make the most of every situation and constantly focus on the positive. Seeing things in a negative light is like a foreign language to me.

Charles R. Swindoll once said, "Life is 10 percent what happens to you and 90 percent how you react."

Winston Churchill wrote,"A pessimist sees the difficulty in every opportunity; an optimist sees the opportunity in every difficulty."

The headline in the Business section of the <u>Wisconsin State Journal</u> on February 19, 2008, read *"Work force under stress. Statistics show that the nation's work force is under the kind of stress not seen since March 2001."* Who are these stress experts? If you keep telling everyone everyday that they are under a world of stress, pretty soon they'll start to believe it. Almost like it becomes the norm! It seems like people without stress are a rare breed. A recent ad on the radio for skin care announced a new skin lotion with special anti-stress relievers. It sounds like we're living in the placebo world.

I'm sure you know someone or have met people who love to make their problems your problems. They live in what seems to be a constant quagmire of insurmountable dilemmas. Whoever coined the phrase "misery loves company" hit the nail on the head. If you're down or sad, the last thing you want to do is hang around someone who is happy or positive – heaven forbid, they might just cheer you up.

In 1976, Maurice White, Charles Stephney & Philip Bailey wrote this classic song that accurately describes how we wear our emotions.

Earth Wind And Fire – "On Your face"

Ain't it funny that the way you feel, shows on your face

And no matter, how you try to hide it'll state your case

Now a frown will bring your sprits down to the ground

And never let you see, the good things all around-

PB: My heart is feelin' glad
I'll take you with me when you're feelin' bad

MW: I start to wonder what's going down
In your life, is it safe and sound?
I start to wonder if your life's all right
Are you dealing with it every day or does it cause you strife?

In the Life section of the February 5, 2009, issue of <u>USA Today</u>, a poll addressed what health issues most affected the academic performance of college students. The top response was stress, the answer of 34 percent of the students.

Today's society is preoccupied with stress and how to combat it. We are reminded through radio, television, newsprint and the Internet to exercise more, get more rest, take medications, watch our diet, schedule downtime, etc., just to control our stress. Why don't the stress experts ever recommend humor as an antidote? Didn't someone once say that laughter is the best medicine?

The following article, "The Stress Management and Health Benefits of Laughter," was found on about.com:

Research has shown health benefits of laughter ranging from strengthening the immune system to reducing food cravings to increasing one's threshold for pain. There's even an emerging therapeutic field known as humor therapy to help people heal more quickly, among other things. Humor also has several important stress relieving benefits.

Stress Management Benefits of Laughter:

- *Hormones: Laughter reduces the level of stress hormones like cortisol, epinephrine (adrenaline), dopamine and growth hormone. It also increases the level of health-enhancing hormones like endorphins and neurotransmitters. Laughter increases the number of antibody-producing cells and enhances the effectiveness of T cells. All this means a stronger immune system, as well as fewer physical effects of stress.*

- *Physical Release: Have you ever felt like, "I have to laugh or I'll cry?" Have you experienced the cleansed feeling after a good laugh? Laughter provides a physical and emotional release.*

- *Internal Workout: A good belly laugh exercises the diaphragm, contracts the abs and even works out the shoulders, leaving muscles more relaxed afterward. It even provides a good workout for the heart.*

- *Distraction: Laughter brings the focus away from anger, guilt, stress and negative emotions in a more beneficial way than other mere distractions.*

- *Perspective: Studies show that our response to stressful events can be altered by whether we view something as a 'threat' or a 'challenge.' Humor can give us a more lighthearted perspective and help us view events as 'challenges,' thereby making them less threatening and more positive.*

- *Social Benefits of Laughter: Laughter connects us with others. Also, laughter is contagious, so if you bring more laughter into your life, you can most likely help others around you to laugh more, and realize these benefits as well. By elevating the mood of those around you, you can reduce their stress levels, and perhaps improve the quality of social interaction you experience with them, reducing your stress level even more!*

How To Use Laughter:

Laughter is one of my favorite stress-management strategies because it's free, convenient, and beneficial in so many ways. You can get more laughter in your life with the following strategies:

- *T.V. and Movie: There's no shortage of laughter opportunities from entertainment, both at the theater and in the aisles at the video stores, as well as at home with T.V. comedies. While wasting time watching something marginally funny may actually frustrate you, watching truly hilarious movies and shows is an easy way to get laughter into your life whenever you need it.*

- *Laugh With Friends: Going to a movie or a comedy club with friends is a great way to get more laughter in your life. The contagious effects of laughter may mean you'll laugh more than you otherwise would have during the show, plus you'll have jokes to reference at later times. Having friends over for a party or game night is also a great setup for laughter and other good feelings.*

- *Find Humor In Your Life: Instead of complaining about life's frustrations, try to laugh about them. If something is so frustrating or depressing it's ridiculous, realize that you could 'look back on it and laugh.' Think of how it will sound as a story you could tell to your friends, and then see if you can laugh about it now. With this attitude, you may also find yourself being more lighthearted and silly, giving yourself and those around you more to laugh about. Approach life in a more mirthful way and you'll find you're less stressed about negative events, and you'll achieve the health benefits of laughter.*

My parents both have a great sense of humor and a prevailing resolve to persevere. When times in our business seemed at their lowest of lows, Mom would say, *"It will be all right, this too shall pass."* Or Dad would say, *"We'll make it, all we need are some mixer sales!"* Hearing those words of encouragement from them, at their age, makes me only want to try harder.

Why am I a happy soul? Maybe it's because I get to laugh with my wife and kids at least once a day. Maybe it has to do with my pure Irish bloodline; blarney runs deep in my genes. Maybe it's because of my strong faith in God. Maybe it's because I get to work with my parents and brothers Coyne, Tom, Jim and John every day. And they, along with Marty, Margaret, Mary, Hayes, Muffie and Julie, are some of the most entertaining and enjoyable people I have ever met. Or maybe it's because I was raised with praise! Or maybe all of the above!

And although I carry major responsibilities as a father and husband - and I feel loads of accountability in our family business - one thing is for sure, I don't feel stressed! Like everyone in the world, I have difficult days. If I didn't, I wouldn't be human. I also wouldn't be able to appreciate the excellent days.

McCartney and Lennon were right when they sang: *"Boy, you gotta carry that weight, carry that weight a long time."*

Why don't we hear anyone suggest prayer as a remedy for stress? Maybe that's because we are afraid we might offend someone. I suggest praying to God as a form of combating problems and relieving life's pressures.

On May 2, 2009, the Eau Claire <u>Leader-Telegram's</u> front-page story in the Religion section was titled, "Faith at work – Impact of religious beliefs on personal well-being examined." It read:

Hilda Schau says it's a belief in God that carried her through divorce and job loss. Urologist Manual Padron says he regularly sees the power of faith at work in his patients.

Personal beliefs such as theirs drew millions to church on Easter Sunday. But are they quantifiably good for you?

They are, according to Michael E. McCullough, a University of Miami researcher who has been studying the relationship between religion and health for more than a decade. His conclusions are fueling the debate over the impact of religion on personal well-being.

"It's hard to find a downside to religion," says McCullough, a psychology professor and one of the top researchers in the field.

In a small lab on UM's Coral Gables campus, McCullough, 39, has conducted experiments with hundreds of people of many backgrounds, testing their ability to delay gratification, forgive and be thankful, and correlating those findings with health factors from drug use to depression. All the while, he has asked, "Do you believe in God? How much?"

McCullough's research suggests that religious people of all faiths, by sizable margins, do better in school, live longer, have more satisfying marriages and are generally happier than their non-believing peers.

My mother and father both possess a strong faith in God. And I would have to say they are very religious people. But never in an overbearing way! And they taught me *and* my brothers and sisters to have a strong faith in God as well. They always led by example and never wavered when it came to attending Mass on Sunday or praying as a family around the second floor railing.

If you were to apply the above research to my parents; you'll find two people who have been married for 62 years and have lived into their mid and late 80's. I would say they are both very happy souls!

I'm probably like most people who pray to God for many things that are going on in my family's life. Continually asking God to help me be patient and understanding and to watch over my wife and children, parents and extended family. What I find interesting is that many people seem to miss the follow-up. When our prayers are answered, we will forget to stop and thank God. I'm guilty of it all the time! We spend so much time asking God for everything to go well in our life that we don't often acknowledge Him when it happens. I would think our ungratefulness for the many gifts and blessings we've received disappoints God more than other things we do or don't do. God knows what is best for us and always works on His time schedule – not ours. Oftentimes He comes through in ways we never dreamed of. All we have to do is trust in His plan and ask for His guidance.

Reverence to God

I was golfing once at Hillcrest Country Club with two friends who worked in the clubhouse. On the second hole, one of the guys hit his ball to the right and out of bounds on a short par-3 and the first thing he did was curse God. "*JESUS CHRIST*" came spewing out of his mouth with disgust after his errant tee shot.

I said "You know, speaking of Jesus Christ, I went to my daughter's Confirmation the other day at St. Mary's in Altoona and I was in that church for almost three hours. It gave me time to catch up with the Lord while reviewing the past, thanking Him for the present, and downloading prayers for the future."

The guy looked at me somewhat surprised and didn't say a word. He knew exactly what I meant and never mentioned the Lord's name in vain the rest of the round. I wasn't mad at the guy. I was just trying to help him!

It bothers me to hear anyone take the Lord's name in vain – it's out of bounds. The Book of Exodus 20:7 states:

"You shall not take the name of the Lord, your God, in vain. For the Lord will not leave unpunished the ones who take his name in vain."

When my brother Hayes was employed as a Sports Broadcaster at TV 18 in Eau Claire, he worked with a news anchor from Iowa named Kevin.

Apparently Kevin would constantly say, "Jesus Christ" – or in his native Iowan drawl, "*G-Scrost,*" after something happened that was unexpected or undesirable. Hayes was getting tired of hearing Kevin repeatedly take the Lord's name in vain. So one evening after the 6:00 pm newscast, Hayes decided to help him out. While Kevin was gone from the station for an hour, Hayes left a note on his desk that read:

Kevin,

"While you were out, some guy named G. Scrost called for you."

Hayes

When Kevin returned to work, he grabbed the note, stood up and asked everyone in the room, "Who is G. Scrost?"

International Jesus

While our family was on vacation in Mazatlan, Mexico, we took a taxi to a cathedral on Sunday to attend mass. For the first time in my life, I was in a church that was filled with many devout Mexican Catholics and as I looked up at the statue of Jesus I saw an International Jesus. By that I mean, for the first time, Jesus appeared to me universal to all nationalities, which He is. He even had a tan. God is a variety master and has created a variety of people to inhabit the earth.

I received the following e-mail from my friend Jennifer, a fellow PREP (parochial religious education program) teacher, which I found most interesting.

Subject: 12 Days of Christmas- what does it mean?
Date: Mon, 15 Dec 2008

There is one Christmas carol that has always baffled me.
What in the world do leaping lords, French hens, swimming swans, and especially the partridge that won't come out of the pear tree have to do with Christmas?
Today, I found out.

From 1558 until 1829, Roman Catholics in England were not permitted to practice their faith openly. Someone during that era wrote this carol as a catechism song for young Catholics. It has two levels of meaning: the surface meaning plus a hidden meaning known only to members of their church. Each element in the carol has a code word for a religious reality, which the children could remember.

The partridge in a pear tree was Jesus Christ.
Two turtledoves were the Old and New Testaments.
Three French hens stood for faith, hope and love.
The four calling birds were the four gospels of Matthew, Mark, Luke and John.
The five golden rings recalled the Torah or Law, the first five books of the Old Testament.
The six geese a-laying stood for the six days of creation.
Seven swans a-swimming represented the sevenfold gifts of the Holy Spirit: Prophesy, Serving, Teaching, Exhortation, Contribution, Leadership, and Mercy.
The eight maids a-milking were the eight beatitudes.
Nine ladies dancing were the nine fruits of the Holy Spirit: Love, Joy, Peace, Patience, Kindness, Goodness, Faithfulness, Gentleness, and Self-Control.
The ten lords a-leaping were the Ten Commandments.
The eleven pipers piping stood for the eleven faithful disciples.
The twelve drummers drumming symbolized the twelve points of belief in The Apostles' Creed.

Now I know how that strange song became a Christmas carol. I wanted to share it with you. ... God be with you today and throughout the holidays and forever!!

My brother Tom loves to read whenever he gets a chance - everything from history, religion, and politics, to the <u>Tri-County News,</u> which chronicles the activities of the people of Trempeleau, Jackson and Eau Claire counties. He found the following short story squished between advertisements in the April 7, 2009, edition.

Squirrels had overcome three churches in town. After much prayer, the elders of the first church determined that the animals were predestined to be there. Who were they to interfere with God's will, they reasoned? Soon, the squirrels multiplied.

The elders of the second church, deciding that they could not harm any of God's creatures, humanely trapped the squirrels and set them free outside of town. Three days later, the squirrels were back.

It was only the third church that succeeded in keeping the pests away. The elders baptized the squirrels and registered them as members of the church. Now they only see them on Christmas and Easter!

On Easter Sunday In 1999, we were returning to Eau Claire after a long drive back from a family vacation in Marco Island, Florida, when my four year old daughter Meghan asked me, "Dad, does Jesus have two birthdays – Christmas and Easter?" I thought to myself, "How profound."

Laurel sent me an e-mail on July 18, 2008. Subject: God's Pharmacy. When I first read through it I was marveled at the unmistakable similarities between the human anatomy and the foods God made specifically for us.

It's been said that God first separated the saltwater from the fresh, made dry land, planted a garden, made animals and fish. ... all before making a human.

And God left us a great clue as to what foods help what part of our body!

1. *A sliced carrot looks like the human eye. The pupil, iris and radiating lines look just like the human eye and, yes, science now shows carrots greatly enhance blood flow to and function of the eyes.*

2. *A tomato has four chambers and is red. The heart has four chambers and is red. All of the research shows tomatoes*

are loaded with lycopene and are indeed pure heart and blood food.

3. *Grapes hang in a cluster that has the shape of the heart. Each grape looks like a blood cell and all of the research today shows grapes are also profound heart and blood vitalizing food.*

4. *Figs are full of seeds and hang in twos when they grow. Figs increase the mobility of male sperm and increase the number of sperm. They also can help in overcoming male sterility.*

5. *Kidney beans actually heal and help maintain kidney function and yes, they look exactly like the human kidneys.*

6. *Oranges, grapefruits and other citrus fruits look like the mammary glands of the female and actually assist the health of the breasts and the movement of lymph in and out of the breasts.*

7. *Celery, bok choy, rhubarb and many more look just like bones. These foods specifically target bone strength. Bones are 23 percent sodium and these foods are 23 percent sodium. If you don't have enough sodium in your diet, the body pulls itself from the bones, thus making them weak. These foods replenish the skeletal needs of the body.*

8. *Onions look like the body's cells. Today's research shows onions help clear waste material from all of the body cells. They even produce tears which wash the epithelial layers of the eyes. A working companion, garlic also helps eliminate waste materials and dangerous free radicals from the body.*

9. *A walnut looks like a little brain, a left and right hemisphere, upper cerebrum and lower cerebrum. Even the wrinkles or folds on the nut are just like the neo-cortex. We now know walnuts help develop more than three dozen neuro-transmitters for brain function.*

At the beginning of each new school year, I hand out and review the list below to my 8th grade students.

The following definitions were taken from "The Catholic Faith Handbook."

GOD: The infinite and divine being recognized as the source and creator of all that exists.

JESUS CHRIST: The son of God, the second person of the trinity, who took on flesh in Jesus of Nazareth. Jesus in Hebrew means, "God saves," and was the name given the historical Jesus at the Annunciation. Christ, based on the word for "Messiah," meaning "the anointed one," is a title that was given Jesus by the church after his full identity was revealed.

HOLY SPIRIT: The third person of the blessed Trinity, understood as the perfect love between God the Father and the Son, Jesus Christ, who inspires, guides, and sanctifies the life of believers.

TRINITY: Often referred to as the Blessed Trinity, the central Christian mystery and dogma that there is one God in three persons: Father, Son and Holy Spirit.

HEAVEN: Traditionally, the dwelling place of God and the saints, meaning all who are saved; more accurately, not a place but a state of eternal life and union with God, in which one experiences full happiness and the satisfaction of the deepest human belongings.

HELL: The state of permanent separation from God, reserved for those who freely and consciously choose to reject God to the very end of their life.

FREE WILL: The gift from God that allows human beings to choose from among various actions, for which we are held accountable. It is the basis for moral responsibility.

SOUL: The spiritual life principle of human beings that survives death.

VIRTUE: A good habit, one that creates within us a kind of inner readiness or attraction to move toward or accomplish moral good. The theological virtues are faith, hope, and love.

THANKSGIVING: A prayer of gratitude for the gift of life and the gifts of life.

Prospect of Peace

Ever since I became aware of international politics and the perpetual fight between Arabs and Jews, I have marveled at the impossibility of peace in the Middle East. When President Carter signed the Middle East Peace Accord in 1978, it turned out to be about oil – not peace.

As long as young Muslims and young Hebrews are raised to hate and kill each other, they will never give peace a chance. I wonder if they will ever figure out that they are related to each other. We are all God's children.

In my lifetime, the U.S. Government has spent billions of our dollars toward "peace" in this region of the world with military hardware, intelligence and behind-the-scene deals to somehow enact a solution to the ongoing war of hatred. Years ago, my brother Coyne suggested that we stop sending weapons that are used to kill each other and instead supply them with ships loaded with water balloons, sling shots and BB guns and let them have at it.

How are they related? Do you remember the story in Genesis 16 and 17?

"But Sarai and Abram had no children. So Sarai took her maid, an Egyptian girl named Hagar, and gave her to Abram to be his second wife."

It turns out Hagar became pregnant and gave birth to Abram's first son, Ishmael, which means God hears. Thirteen years later, at the age of ninety-nine, God made a covenant with Abram and changed his name to Abraham (meaning Father of many nations) and told him,

"I will give you millions of descendents who will form many nations! Kings shall be among your descendents!"

At the same time, God changed Sarai's name to Sarah (meaning Princess) and although she was ninety years old at the time, God told her that she will have a son and to name him Isaac. Abraham's two sons grew up together and were doing fine until one day Sarah looked out in the backyard and saw the two step brothers playing together and thought, my son Isaac shouldn't play with an Egyptian peasant like Ishmael, and chased him away. Although Abraham didn't want to see his son depart, he obeyed God and followed Sarah's orders. And unfortunately, the descendants of Abraham, Ishmael the Muslim and Isaac the Hebrew, have been tearing down each other ever since!

I have taught eighth-grade religion class for seven years and continue to learn so much about my faith in God. One of the lesson plans I developed a few years ago is a quiz that I give my students called "What Does God Think?" I ask my students to write an "A" or an "F" next to six worldly topics. The "A" is for "Against" and the "F" represents "For." Then I ask them, "What do you think God thinks of the following issues that are prevalent in our world today? Not what you think, but what you think God thinks of."

Abortion – euthanasia - homosexual behavior – the death penalty – same-sex marriage – teaching of evolution in public schools.

Take the test!

Chapter 13
Jackasses, Elephants and Sheep

Politics has been a topic of discussion in our family since I can remember. My grandfather, Ed Hayes, was the National Commander of the American Legion in 1933 and ran for U.S. Senator of Illinois in 1954.

I have noticed that it has become almost politically incorrect these days to discuss politics with most people. It is usually a brief discussion. In business, I'm told that the two subjects you never discuss are religion and politics! When the 2008 election was upon us, I remember talking to a good friend of mine about the differences between the two presidential candidates and his response was, "Bill, I don't engage in politics." I was actually surprised to hear him say that – but that's fine and I didn't press it and I didn't continue the political conversation. But later on I thought maybe we, the American people, should become more engaged in *our* government's every next move. Keep in mind; they work for us – and not the other way around!

Working in the political theater could be fun, except for the fact that it's an institution filled with deceitful, dishonest, power-hungry politicians who will tell you anything to get elected and then carve out their own agenda once in office. Therefore, as much as I enjoy discussing politics and debating our nation's strengths and weaknesses, I wouldn't want to participate in an arena that's driven by money and power. It's too bad because I know I would *pone face* (kick some ass) in Washington! Oh, I'm sure there are some good, honest, dedicated politicians representing us, but I think they are few and far between.

I think John Adams, George Washington, Jim Madison, and Tom Jefferson, would be shocked and disappointed at the way our government operates today. Only 235 years ago, they envisioned and crafted a Declaration of Independence, a Bill of Rights and a Constitution for the people of the United States of America. But today, my confidence in our government's ability to operate under those templates is at an all time low.

I'm not a fan of the two U.S. Senators from Wisconsin who represented me in Washington in 2009. Neither of these lifers reflected my position on a majority of the important issues facing our country. Their voting records show they lean heavily to the left and don't embody the beliefs I feel strongly about.

In my state of Wisconsin, Herbert Kohl has been our U.S. Senator since 1988. I remember seeing him come into his store in 1977, when I worked for Herb at Kohl's Food store on Oakland Avenue in Shorewood. I admire him for his successful change from selling food regionally to clothes nationally with Kohl's Department Stores; as a result he employees thousands of people around the country. He is the reason the Milwaukee Bucks are still in town!

But over 20 years in office is way too long!

It sickens me to think that both of Wisconsin's Senators plan to be in office for life. They both suffer from Senator Robert Byrd syndrome. The Democrat from West Virginia has served nine 6 year terms in Washington or 54 years! I'm sure neither Kohl nor Feingold are planning to step down anytime soon!

Journalist Ed Schieffer wrote a piece titled, "The Purpose of Government." He said, "Too many politicians have forgotten that government's only purpose is to improve citizens' lives. They've come to believe it's there to improve their lives."

Russell Feingold has been in Washington D.C. since 1992 and his re-election is coming up again in 2010. That means 18 years and counting if he wins re-election! I have never met Mr. Feingold, but I'm sure the man is a fine individual. I just never was a fan of Senator Feingold's politics. If I were to run for U.S. Senator, it would be his seat I would take. And I believe I would win. This is an excerpt from my fictitious campaign speech:

"My opponent, the BLM (Biased Liberal Media), will do its best to destroy me because I, unlike their guy Russell Feingold, disagree on many important issues."

For example:

I am for a small government, both at the state and federal levels. Less is better! Our government has grown so large in the last year alone - it's going to pop! Or maybe it already has!

I believe in term limits for all elected officials. No more of this, once a senator always a senator. Eight years or two four-year terms is plenty of time to spend in office.

I am for a strong military. The amazing men and women, who volunteer to defend our great country with their lives, deserve as much. Our way of life has been under attack and these brave souls answer the bell every time!

I am against Robin Hood economics; I want to lower taxes, not raise them. We already pay too many taxes to the government! We are being taxed to death and even after we die. Robbing the hard working citizens of America and giving hand-outs to people who don't work hinders the entrepreneurial spirit and the small business owners and employers of the United States. Runaway redistribution of wealth is socialism!

I would give our great state of Wisconsin a strong voice in Washington – and then when my term is up, I would get out of the way and let someone else try to mend these Divided into Red (Republican), White (Independent) & Blue (Democrat) States of America."

At least everyone voting would know where I stand on the issues!

This just in! The November 18, 2009 Milwaukee Journal Sentinel headline reports,

"Feingold's re-election war chest open wide." 3-term Democrat in top 2 for spending, top 5 for fund raising."

Washington – Three-term Sen. Russ Feingold, who won his last election by 11 percentage points, has already spent $6.6 million on his next re-election bid – the second highest total spent by any senator on the 2010 ballot.

Feingold, one of 29 senators up for re-election next year, also ranks in the top five when it comes to fund raising, bringing in roughly $9 million for his next election, according to his latest filing with the Federal Election Commission.

Sounds to me like Russell Feingold can't afford to lose! Apparently he will pull out all the stops (your money) to assure himself of a fourth term! His insatiable appetite for power has no limits!

My Governor, Jim Doyle, decided not to seek a third term in 2010 in the "no-limit" state of Wisconsin. He reasoned that the Governorship should be limited to two terms and decided to lead by example and step away after eight years. Doyle added, "I know that I will regret this decision many times over the coming year, but I am not going to pull a Brett Favre on you."

According to www.wisegeek.com:

The laws about term limits for governors in the United States vary from state to state. Each state determines its own system, and the rules can get a bit entangled and complex, at least in the view of outsiders. Before delving into the mysteries of term limits by state, it may help to know that for the most part, a given term lasts four years for a governor, unless he or she is impeached, except in New Hampshire and Vermont, where governors serve for two years only. If a governor steps down or is removed from office, the Lieutenant Governor usually steps in.

Term limits are designed to keep the political system fresh, and to ensure that people do not have an opportunity to consolidate power. Governors can be tremendously influential in their states, making term limits rather critical, as a governor can easily become more like an emperor than an elected official if there are no limits on service. This is especially true in the case of large and powerful states such as New York, California, and Texas.

I'm not a fan of abortion on demand. The Fifth Commandment simply states: "Thou Shalt Not Kill." I can't understand how people find those four words from God so difficult to understand. Since the passing of <u>Roe vs. Wade,</u> the number one cause of death for African-Americans is abortion.

A headline in the Leader Telegram's October 25, 2007, "Voice of the People" section states: "Abortion backers' logic is puzzling." The article, by Dale Nehring, reads:

"Apparently, abortion supporters who value their compassionate view towards woman, relish the idea of empowering woman by giving them the legal right to 'play God' and have the ultimate say in which babies live and which ones are aborted without the chance to live in our world. If a pregnancy is planned or wanted, it's a baby; if it's unwanted or unplanned, it isn't. This is strange, puzzling logic for justifying the legal abortion of healthy fetuses and determining the value of human life."

Abortion is the ultimate form of materialism. Pro life is the "pro" choice.

Did you know that John the Baptist and Jesus are cousins? Do you remember reading about what happened when Mary (pregnant with Jesus) went to visit her cousin Elizabeth (pregnant with John) in the town of Zacharias?

(Note: When I reached for my Bible (which has 1,437 pages) to find the following scripture passage, I randomly opened the book to page 1,127 – which just happened to be Luke chapter 1. The exact page I was looking for! That gave me chills.) Luke 1:41-44

At the sound of Mary's greeting, Elizabeth's child leaped within her and she was filled with the Holy Spirit.

She gave a glad cry and exclaimed to Mary, "You are favored by God above all other women, and your child is destined for God's mightiest praise. What an honor this is, that the mother of my Lord should visit me! When you came in and greeted me, the instant I heard your voice, my baby moved in me for joy!

Notice how back then they refer to their unborn as a child and a baby!

I recall seeing a news clip of former President Clinton leaving the Vatican after a brief meeting with Pope John Paul. As Clinton is smiling and saying his goodbyes, the Pope was looking at him in disbelief and shaking his head in disappointment. It looked so odd! I was embarrassed for Bill Clinton – and every American! The Pope couldn't understand Clinton's pro abortion attitude.

I'm not a fan of the death penalty either. Thirty-six states have the death penalty on their books, along with the U.S. government and military. Wisconsin, fortunately, is not one of them.

Once again, man is playing God and determining the timeline of someone's life.

Flying home from a business trip, I read an article dated Dec. 21, 2006, written by Jim Anderson in the "Letters" section of USA Today. The piece was titled: "End Death Penalty: Florida's macabre execution of Angel Diaz demonstrates that our Constitution and judicial system must be amended to exclude execution as a penalty in the USA." It read:

Diaz was subject to two rounds of lethal injection, likely because of botched execution practices by those individuals given the job to end the life of a human being.

That Diaz received two doses of lethal drugs does not make the execution any "more cruel." Regardless of the methodology, execution is a barbaric form of justice. Diaz was killed, and we as a society are responsible for his death, just as if we physically inserted those needles and poisoned him ourselves. It is irrational to take a human life to demonstrate that taking a human life is wrong.

Humans do not have the right to kill each other. The existence of such an erroneous right is established only in the corrupt minds of those who fear and allow their fear to govern their twisted ethics."

Who do we think we are, fogging around with God's precious gift of life?

Two years ago (10-09-07), my oldest brother and Godfather Marty sent me the following email:

I always thought that we were pretty normal growing up until I met so many boobs, lounge lizards, saps and fops as life moved on. Only then was I able to reflect back and really appreciate our unique upbringing.

By the way, here's an e-mail I recently received:

A United States Marine was attending some college courses between assignments. He had completed missions in Iraq and Afghanistan. One of the courses had a professor who was an avowed atheist and a member of the ACLU.
One day the professor shocked the class when he came in. He looked to the ceiling and flatly stated, "God, if you are real, then I want you to knock me off this platform. I'll give you exactly 15 minutes." The lecture room fell silent. You could hear a pin drop.

Ten minutes went by and the professor proclaimed, "Here I am God. I'm still waiting." It got down to the last couple of minutes when the Marine got out of his chair, went up to the professor and punched him, knocking him off the platform. The professor was out cold.

The Marine went back to his seat and sat there, silently. The other students were stunned and sat there looking on in silence. The

347

professor eventually came to, noticeably shaken, looked at the Marine and asked, "What the hell is the matter with you? Why did you do that?"

The Marine calmly replied, "God was too busy today protecting America's soldiers who are protecting your right to say stupid shit and act like an a-hole. So, he sent me."

Bill, I'll reach back in my grey-matter archives and see what interesting, or not, anecdotes that I can come up with. I'll be in touch. - Martin T.

Note: Marty's son Michael is Major Callaghan with the U.S. Marines. He served three tours in Iraq piloting C-46 twin-prop helicopters. Michael now lives in Texas training future Marine pilots and was recently recognized by his superiors as Outstanding Instructor of the 4th quarter, 2009.

Fear Not

I believe fear is the biggest disease we face as a people today. It's no wonder the most repeated phrase in the Bible is "fear not." And the remarkable thing about that phrase is that not only is it mentioned throughout the Bible, it was primarily spoken by Jesus within just a three-year period from the time of his ministry at age 30 to the time of his death and resurrection. For the phrase "fear not" to be the most-often recited in the Bible is evidence of how aware Christ was that he was teaching a people preoccupied with fear.

And ever since it became evident that December 21, 2012, is labeled by Mayan and Chinese (manmade) calendars as the end of time, man (and Hollywood) has found another opportunity to wallow in fear.

Just last week, during my 8th grade religion class, one of my students asked me what I have planned for 12-21-12. I asked, "Isn't that the Winter Solstice – marking the first day of winter? She said, "I don't know about that, but I heard it might be the end of the world." I replied, "Wow, who said the world will end on that day?" She replied, "I don't know, but what if it's true? "What if it's not?" Then she asked me, "Have you seen the movie 2012?" I asked, "What do you think would happen if God made it known to man that December 21, 2012, will be our last day on earth? "People will live without hope and dwell in fear," she answered. As far as I know, nobody knows when the end of the world will be - except for God, who made it!

President Roosevelt was dedicating a bridge in Chicago when he shared his famous saying to a crowd of thousands after World War II broke out:

"We have nothing to fear but fear itself!"

Millions of people live with fear. If allowed, fear can drive and destroy the human mind.

The following list is for anyone who forgot the Ten Commandments or have never read them before:

THE TEN COMMANDMENTS: Author – God

Copyright 1550BC

I.	*I Am the Lord Your God, Thou Shall Have No Other Gods Before Me*
II.	*Thou Shall Not Take The Name Of The Lord Your God In Vain*
III.	*Keep Holy The Sabbath Day*
IV.	*Honor Your Father And Mother*
V.	*Thou Shall Not Kill*
VI.	*Thou Shall Not Commit Adulter*
VII.	*Thou Shall Not Steal*
VIII.	*Thou Shall Not Bear False Witness Against Your Neighbor Your Neighbor*
IX.	*Thou Shall Not Covet Thy Neighbor's Wife*
X.	*Thou Shall Not Covet Thy Neighbor's Goods*

When Moses came down from Mount Horab with the Ten Commandments (over 3,550 years ago), people were engaged in lawless sexual behavior and building a golden idol for all the godless to worship.

These laws handed down from God were designed to help us live our life according to *his* design – not ours. All we've been asked to do is follow these basic rules of life, be kind to one and other, and remember that the glory and honor belong to Him – not us.

Speaking of idols to worship, the 2007 Emmy Awards showed the epitome of an industry gone awry with many anti-Christian remarks and rampant profanity that was bleeped over throughout the night. Comedian Kathy Griffin made amazing statements, including, "A lot of people come up here and thank Jesus for this award. I want you to know that no one had less to do with this award than Jesus.... This award is my God now." She had just won a creative arts Emmy for Bravo's *My Life on the D-List.* I couldn't believe she said that out loud! What does she gain by proclaiming her profound God-less beliefs to millions of people tuned in around the country?

More Americans voted during last season's No. 1 TV show, "American Idol," than any presidential election ever held. That speaks volumes about America today! But now that I think about it, the presidential election has sadly become a show that resembles "American Idol."

I received an e-mail a couple years ago from my good friend, Bill Dixon, who now lives on the island of Maui. The e-mail was a "Did You Know" piece written by Andy Rooney that pointed out some interesting facts about the U.S. government and the Ten Commandments I had not known before.

1.   *As you walk up the steps to the building which houses the U.S. Supreme Court you can see near the top of the building a row of the world's law givers and each one is facing one in the middle who is facing forward with a full frontal view. ... It is Moses and he is holding the Ten Commandments.*

2. As you enter the Supreme Court courtroom, the two huge oak doors have the Ten Commandments engraved on each lower portion of each door.

3. As you sit inside the courtroom, you can see the wall, right above where the Supreme Court judges sit, a display of the Ten Commandments.

4. There are Bible verses etched in stone all over the federal buildings and monuments in Washington, D.C.

5. Every session of Congress begins with a prayer by a paid preacher, whose salary has been paid by the taxpayer since 1777.

6. James Madison, the fourth president, known as "The father of Our Constitution," made the following statement: "We have staked the whole of all our political institutions upon the capacity of mankind for self-government, upon the capacity of each and all of us to govern ourselves, to control ourselves, to sustain ourselves according to the Ten Commandments of God.

7. Thomas Jefferson worried that the Courts would overstep their authority and instead of interpreting the law would begin making law – known as an oligarchy – the rule of few over many.

Rooney concludes: "How then, have we gotten to the point that everything we have done for 220 years in this country is now suddenly wrong and unconstitutional? It is said that 86 percent of Americans believe in God. Therefore, it is very hard to understand why there is such a mess about having the Ten Commandments on display or "In God We Trust" on our money and having 'God' in the Pledge of Allegiance."

Lawyers, Guns and Money

Have you noticed that many politicians in Washington today are lawyers? I wonder why that is? Don't get me wrong, I've met some great lawyers in my time and I don't have everything against lawyers, but a majority of the over-educated politicians in office today with law degrees are a troublesome breed. Try implementing Tort Reform to a room full of lawyers and see how far you get! Today's politicians are like stealth hybrids that have infiltrated our national political network and corrupted our once precious system of government. Having someone who knows how to dissect and distort the letter of the law and possesses the influence and power to dictate the course of our great nation worries me. What a dangerous combination!

These wordsmiths, or lawticians, are capable of saying amazing things like, and I quote former President Clinton, "That depends on the definition of what 'is' is."

How ridiculous *is* that? Many of these politicians have proven to be false-witness- bearing champions. I wonder how many politicians are lawyers.

Isn't President Obama a lawyer?

This is just one glaring observation and problem that we have in Washington. Another is that I believe Congressmen and Senators should adhere to the same two-term limits that presidents and some governors face. Many elected officials go into "public service" to change the way things work and end up being changed by the way things work. And we pay for their All-Inclusive ego trip. Unfortunately, the perks and the spotlight have made it impossible for these fork-tongued champs to walk away. It seems the power and glory is too intoxicating for the average politician and fogs with their purpose and judgment and behavior.

According to CNN.com - 2008 was not lacking for political scandals.

"Most recently, Illinois Governor Rod Blagojevich has been in the spotlight for allegedly scheming to sell Obama's vacant Senate seat, among other things. Just one day before he was arrested on federal corruption charges, he proclaimed, 'there's nothing but sunshine hanging over me.'"

Another governor who got in trouble this year was New York's Eliot Spitzer. "Client No. 9" had to resign because of his involvement with a high-priced call-girl service.

Former Detroit Mayor Kwame Kilpatrick also resigned amid a sex and perjury scandal.

And after months of brushing off what he called "tabloid trash," former presidential candidate John Edwards confessed to having an extramarital affair.

Florida also saw a sex scandal this year when Rep. Tim Mahoney confessed to "multiple affairs." In 2006, he defeated Florida Rep. Mark Foley after it was revealed that Foley had sent sexually suggestive messages to congressional pages. Mahoney lost his bid for re-election.

Somehow we have allowed these self-absorbed representatives in Washington to become career politicians. How did we let that happen? With all the years these jokers spend in office, it amazes me that the result is an inefficient, overspent, unhealthy system of government. You would think most of them would have enough gumption left in their hollow suits to step down and resign out of shear embarrassment. Ron Kind, Dave Obey, Russell Feingold, Herb Kohl; how can you run for re-election with a straight face?

What was once "We the People" has become "We the Sheep" of the United States of America, and these permanent politicians have proven to be (in my view) shitty shepherds!

My dad refers to them as "international hooligans."

Animal Kingdom

I always wondered why the donkey and the elephant were the symbols of the Democrats and Republicans. During the 2008 presidential election, I happened to be watching the History Channel, my favorite on television, and I learned that in 1828 when Andrew Jackson became the seventh President of the United States, his opponents and some in his own party thought he was a jerk and referred to him as jackass. Jackson liked the nickname so much; he adopted the jackass as a symbol for the Democratic Party. What about the Elephant? I researched the donkey and elephant as the symbols of the Democratic and Republican parties and found the following on www.infoplease.com.

The Donkey – Presidential candidate Andrew Jackson was the first Democrat ever to be associated with the donkey symbol. His opponents during the election of 1828 tried to label him a "jackass" for his populist beliefs and slogan, "Let the people rule." Jackson was entertained by the notion and ended up using it to his advantage on his campaign posters.

But cartoonist Thomas Nast is credited with making the donkey the recognized symbol of the Democratic Party. It first appeared in a cartoon in Harper's Weekly in 1870, and was supposed to represent an anti-Civil War faction. But the public was immediately taken by it, and in 1880 it became the unofficial symbol of the party.

The Elephant - Nast was also responsible for the Republican Party elephant. In a cartoon that appeared in Harper's Weekly in 1874, Nast drew a donkey clothed in lion's skin, scaring away all the animals at the zoo. One of those animals, the elephant, was labeled "The Republican Vote." That's all it took for the elephant to become associated with the Republican Party.

I recently heard a guy on the radio say, "The only thing these two parties agree on is keeping a third party out of government."

What four-legged animal would best symbolize the Independent Party?

The fact that we have irresponsible jackasses and elephants in the Beltway Zoo that have been running up an enormous debt that our children and grandchildren will undoubtedly get stuck with is deplorable. For this reason alone, we should fire anyone who voted for these disastrous spending bills!

The "Deficit Express" is a dangerous runaway spending train that has to be slowed and brought to a stop. This blatant neglect by our elected representatives is totally irresponsible, and why we allow it to continue is beyond me. The last time I heard a presidential candidate discuss our national debt crisis with any seriousness was Ross Perot in 1992.

There are three jackasses currently in Washington that in my opinion are destroying our great country, one bill at a time. They are Majority Leader Harry Reid, Speaker of the House Nancy Pelosi, and President Barack Obama. Because of their utter incompetence and pathetic leadership as public servants, I have no confidence in their ability to steer our nation in the right direction. I really wish I could rally around them – but because of their warped vision of America – I can only look forward to the day they are voted out of office.

If these elected officials only knew what it were like to be an employer and the enormous pressure that comes with making payroll every week, they might understand how creating economic stimulus can be easily accomplished. Payroll taxes and federal and state income taxes must be reduced so companies and their employees can take home more money each week and thus reinvest and grow the economy. Small businesses like ours, which employ local folks, are the backbone of our great country. America was built by entrepreneurs like my dad.

On February 12, 2009, the day after the senate approved the $789 billion "stimulus/deficit" bill, I found this sidebar to the cover story in the <u>Milwaukee Journal Sentinel</u>:

Record Deficit

The recession and massive costs for the financial bailout have pushed the federal deficit to an all-time high for the first four months of the budget year.

The Treasury Department reported Wednesday that the deficit for October through January totaled $569 billion, more than six times larger than the imbalance during the year-ago period.

The deficit for January alone totaled $83.8 billion, worse than the $78 billion economists expected. The government had run a surplus of $17.8 billion in January 2008.

With eight months left in the current budget year, the deficit already has surpassed the deficit for 2008, an imbalance of $454.8 billion that is the full-year record.

The Congressional Budget Office has forecast that the deficit for the current budget year will hit $1.2 trillion, but that estimate does not include the costs of the economic stimulus plan that President Barack Obama is pushing Congress to pass quickly to combat the recession.

The Leader-Telegram's February 2, 2009, "Voice of the People" section included a letter written by Bob Martin:

A real stimulus

As a nation we are facing an uncertain, unstable and unsustainable economic future. The current income tax system has significantly contributed to this, leading to the failure of the financial systems and businesses, from small companies to domestic automakers.

While many in Congress from both parties concede that change is absolutely necessary, they also understand that any meaningful change, such as the FairTax, would lead to a loss of their power to decide the winners and losers in our economy. Congress would approve almost any scheme for economic recovery, except one that diminishes their power.

The system has also led to an explosion in the number of registered lobbyists on Capital Hill. Their numbers have doubled over the last eight years, from approximately 1,900 to nearly 4,000. Their influence over Congress and our tax dollars has led directly to many of the problems we now face; Fannie, Freddie, the mortgage crisis, bailouts, stimulus spending packages and a tsunami of debt.

Congress and lobbyists have held these powers over us for far too long. We have lost control of our government. But a solution exists to regain some control and create a lasting stimulus program. This solution would allow us to take home our entire paychecks, stimulate job growth and untax the poor completely, while still collecting enough federal revenue to run the government. The solution is the FairTax, HR-25, a bill that was reintroduced recently in Congress. It would take power away from lobbyists and Congress and give us real economic stimulus in the short and long term. Check it out at www.FairTax.org.

Which of the definitions below best describes President Obama's vision for America's economic future?

According to the online version of the Merriam Webster's Dictionary*:*

Capitalism *– An economic system characterized by private or corporate ownership of capital goods, by investments that are determined by private decision, and by prices, production, and the distribution of goods that are determined mainly by competition in a free market.*

Or

Socialism *– Refers to a broad set of economic theories of social organization advocating public or state ownership and administration of the means of production and distribution of goods, and a society characterized by equal opportunities for all individuals, with a fair or egalitarian method of compensation. From* Wikipedia*.*

Washington – we have a problem! With this administration at the helm, our freedoms and liberties are evaporating before our very eyes. Our enormous debt is growing to a point of no return. Simply put - Our country is undergoing a major change for the worse.

You can probably tell that I didn't cast my vote for President Obama. He did overcome some amazing odds to become our President, and I admire his determination for that. But I really don't care for someone who speaks to me and my fellow American's in a condescending tone, and often times with a scowl on his face. As smooth as he sounds with a teleprompter, I couldn't see voting for someone who was so unqualified and has accomplished so little. As a State Senator from Illinois, he cast 130 "present" votes – which equals zero! But to me, it exposed his lack of commitment and leadership skills. And *now* he is our Commander in Chief! Someone like Barak Hussein Obama, Jr., who possesses such profound socialist skills, would be the last person I would consider putting in the White House. Maybe it's just me, but I get the impression he thinks we (the American people) are kind of stupid.

Here is a snapshot of the history and characteristics of our great country:

According to: encarta.msn.com/encyclopedia

"United States People, human population of the United States today and the characteristics of that population."

These characteristics include the information on the growth of America's urban and suburban society, the history of religion in the United States, and changes in the American family over time.

The population of the United States has grown continuously, from 4 million at the first national census in 1790, to 76 million in 1900, to 282 million in 2000. Its natural growth rate in 2008 was a moderate 0.6 percent compared with a 1.25 percent growth rate for the world. This U.S. growth rate reflects the 14.2 births and 8.3 deaths per 1,000 people that were occurring yearly in the United States. At this rate of growth, it would take the United States 79 years to double in population, while the world population would double in 55 years. These growth rates, both nationally and internationally, are likely to change, however, as birthrates were declining in developed and developing nations at the turn of the 21st century, and death rates were rising in parts of Africa and the former Soviet Union.

Although America's culture is becoming more uniform, its society remains a diverse mix of ethnic, racial, and religious groups. The United States is a pluralistic society, meaning it is composed of many nationalities, races, religions, and creeds. Some of the people who immigrated to America embraced the opportunity to leave old cultures behind and to remake themselves unencumbered by past traditions and loyalties. Others found that the liberties promised under the Bill of Rights allowed for distinctiveness rather than uniformity, and they have taken pride in preserving and celebrating their origins. Many Americans find that pluralism adds to the richness and strength of the nation's culture.

The diversity of the U.S. populace has been a source of friction, as well. Throughout the nation's history, some segments of American society have sought to exclude people who differ from themselves in income, race, gender, religion, political beliefs, or sexual orientation. Even today, some citizens argue that recent arrivals to the United States are radically different from previous immigrants, can never be assimilated, and therefore should be barred from entry. There are very different understandings of what makes a person an American.

The nation's motto, E pluribus unum ("From many, one"), describes the linguistic and cultural similarities of the American people, but it falls short as a description of the diversities among and within the major groups— Native Americans, those whose families have been Americans for generations, and more recent immigrants. This diversity is one of America's distinguishing characteristics.

Until the late 19th century, immigration to the United States was unrestricted, and immigrants came freely from all parts of the world. However, the areas of the world contributing the largest share of immigrants have shifted during the course of America's history. In the 1790s the largest numbers of immigrants came from Great Britain, Ireland, western and central Africa, and the Caribbean. A hundred years later, most immigrants came from southern, eastern, and central Europe. In 1996 they were most likely to come from Mexico, the Philippines, India, Vietnam, and China—indicating a recent increase in Asian immigration.

America's political history has shown that senators are rarely elected to the highest office in the nation. Before Obama, the last was President Kennedy in 1960. Maybe that's because most senators have little experience running anything. Some Governors have made good presidents because they at least have experience leading people and managing an economy on a state level. I believe the owner of a proven successful business would make a good president of the United States because he or she would run the nation's government more like a corporation, which must operate efficiently and within budget in order to grow and prosper.

We the shareholders of the United States want results. We need less politics and more progress.

You may have heard this classic saying:

Vision without action is only a dream!

Action without vision is only passing time!

Action with vision can change the world!

From the Washington (CNN) Web site:

For a candidate who won the White House on a mantle of bringing the country's two political parties together, Washington could not be more divided on Obama's initial weeks in the Oval Office and the policies he has put in place.

Depending on who you ask, in 30 days the new president has either rescued the nation's economy from financial ruin or set in motion the most liberal government in a generation, and one that's likely to prolong -- perhaps even prevent -- the country's economic recovery.

There have also been heated debates over a string of executive orders and bill signings that have fundamentally reversed several policies of the Bush administration -- including the closing of Guantanamo Bay, a firm decree against torture, the extension of children's health insurance, and the lifting of a ban to give funds to international groups that perform abortions.

"Hillary Clinton's earlier critique of change has quickly become very valid," said Julian Zelizer, a professor of history and public affairs at Princeton University. "The Washington of George Bush is the same Washington of Barack Obama. The promise of bipartisanship and hope in Washington is difficult to actually achieve."

It's the massive $787 billion stimulus bill that has drawn the most criticism -- and praise -- in the president's first month. To be sure, while former President Clinton famously declared an end to the "era of big government" 13 years ago, Obama will herald its return in his speech to a joint session of Congress on Tuesday.

Congressional Democrats and Obama supporters argue the new president has admirably taken bold action in response to the dire conditions he inherited, swiftly accomplishing a string of dramatic reforms in a town known to operate at a sluggish pace.

Obama has also enacted dramatic Wall Street reforms, salary caps on CEO pay, and a wide-ranging plan to stem the ongoing foreclosure crisis.

"This is a presidency on steroids," wrote Eugene Robinson, a liberal columnist for the <u>Washington Post</u>. "Barack Obama's executive actions alone would be enough for any new administration's first month. That the White House also managed

to push through Congress a spending bill of unprecedented size and scope ... is little short of astonishing."

But scorn from the right is equal to admiration from the left: He championed a new way of doing things in Washington, but Obama went about shepherding his stimulus bill in a very old-fashioned partisan way, Republicans said.

That Obama signed the historic measure into law 1,500 miles away from Washington in Denver, Colorado, was a symbol to some of just how much animosity it had stirred up in the nation's capital.

"If this is going to be bipartisanship, the country is screwed," Senator Lindsey Graham, R-South Carolina, declared last week. "I know bipartisanship when I see it."

One area that bothers me about politics is the enormous fundraising effort during a presidential election and the hefty flow of money that is generated to put one of these elected officials in the White House. I can't think of a bigger waste of money. According to the Center for Responsive Politics, if you combine all of the funds generated by all of the political races, you are looking at over $5.5 billion spent every four years. It's enough money to unravel some big problems that exist in our country.

The media loves it because it cashes out and drives the political frenzy to compete for ratings. And now that the corrupt and powerfully manipulating media have abandoned the creed of unbiased journalism, major TV corporations and some newsprint companies now posses the power and budget to sway the outcome of an election. The Land of the Free has become the Home of the Greed.

In the past, the national media's role was, among other things, that of a governmental watchdog. If any of the three branches of government; Executive, Legislative and Judicial, had overstepped their power, the major networks could be counted upon to be our check and balance and thus expose the corruption to the electorate. When did their role change? With perhaps the exception of Fox

News, our national news organizations have now morphed into a monster of persuasive partiality and have become a pawn for the like-minded liberal mindset.

Can you believe this last presidential election lasted almost two years? Before 2012 comes around, we should adopt Canada's simple approach to a presidential election, which starts only 36 days before the big vote.

Imagine if Americans came together and donated those dollars toward noble causes like feeding poor children in the United States and around the world or helping low-income families with basic necessities like clothing, food and medications: essential things most of us take for granted. Organizations like Food for the Poor in Florida, Feed My People in Oklahoma or the local Hope Gospel Mission in your hometown could benefit greatly from these campaign funds. Those donations could certainly go to a worthy cause and it's something we as a nation could all be proud of. We could eradicate a problem that faces our own citizens every day.

Why do we spend millions of dollars to elect our politicians? Because in today's world of power politics, it seems enough money can buy the White House, the coveted 100 seats in the Senate and a place in the house of Congress. How sad. To be an elected official in the U.S. government, you either have to be independently wealthy or have some financial backers with deep pockets. Either way, without the money train, your campaign won't make it out of the TV station or in the newspaper or on CNN.com.

We the people have the ability to make wholesale changes throughout our government and vote in a fresh outlook in Washington. The last time the United States of America was run "by the people" or "for the people" was probably over 150 years ago in the days of Lincoln.

Many of today's politicians are short-term artists and seem to lack any long-term vision for our nation's future. They seem to accomplish little, waste big money (our money) on questionable programs and spend half their time focused on getting re-elected.

363

I'm not impressed or well represented. And I'm not a sheep!

One thing that gets a politician's undivided attention is when they lose their bid for re-election. It has a lasting effect!

Since we the people are the real zoo keepers, I suggest we clean both houses, and as my good friend, Andrzej from Atlanta once said. "Start over from scratches."

Chapter 14

Circle of Life

Growing up on Menlo was so much fun because I always had family and neighborhood kids to play with. And of all the rooms in our house, the Big Room was most unique. It was like having a mini indoor gymnasium inside your house that allowed me to run around and play, and create unlimited adventures. I wanted my kids to enjoy the same fun possibilities that I felt when I was a kid, so in 1999, I decided to add a big room to my home in Eau Claire, and drew up the plans with a T-Square and drafting board. My brother-in –law, Bob Duffy (Mary's husband), brought his construction crew up to Eau Claire from Milwaukee and spent the summer months building the new big room. Bob is one of the finest gentlemen I have met and is a gifted carpenter as well. Today, this great utility room is used for many events, including Laurel's branch meetings, Meghan's dance practices, and Christmas and Thanksgiving celebrations. In fact, I spent the last two years in the Big Room, listening to my favorite music, and writing this book.

Ageless Music

Since 1938, with the release of "Snow White and the Seven Dwarfs," Disney has been creating classic animated features for the world to enjoy.

In its first five years, between 1938 and '42, the company also came out with "Pinocchio," "Fantasia," "Dumbo" and "Bambi." It was a pretty good start as Disney Studios set the standard for animated films. During the 47 years that followed, between 1942 and '89, Disney produced 22 animated movies, including award winners "Cinderella" (1950) and "Sleeping Beauty" (1959). But in the '60s, '70s and most of the '80s, Disney seemed to scale back its production of animated classics.

All that changed in 1989 when Disney's reawakening in animated movies seemed to parallel the arrival of our children. Elizabeth was born in 1987 and "The Little Mermaid" opened in 1989 (the year Joe was born) with the magical music of Alan Menken and Howard Ashman. Those two teamed up again on "Beauty and the Beast" in 1991 (the year Michelle was born) and again in 1992 on another masterpiece, "Aladdin." In 1994, "The Lion King" featured classic music from Elton John and Tim Rice and in 1995 (the year Meghan was born) "Pocahontas" arrived in theaters.

To this day, my niece and Godchild, Tricia Callaghan, reminds me of Ariel, Belle, Jasmine, Pocahontas and Mulan – all wrapped into one.

One of my favorite CD's is "Disney's Greatest Hits Vol.1," which includes songs from the aforementioned feature films. I think my memory banks and music are directly wired since these timeless songs continually take me back to a time when my kids were young and I was a new dad.

In the mid-1990s, the city of Eau Claire built a beautiful facility not far from our home called Fairfax Pool. I remember the day I took our four little kids to the new pool for the first time. Laurel was working as a registered nurse at Sacred Heart Hospital that weekend, and I was in charge of the young ones.

I was sitting by the pool watching my children running in and out of a mushrooming waterfall and cooling off in the hot June sun. My friend Patty happened to be watching her two young daughters swimming close by, and I said, "This place is missing something! – I'm going to get the Disney's Greatest Hits cassette out of my car and have them play it loud on the outdoor speaker system."

She laughed and said, "That won't work, they'll never let you do that – I wouldn't even bother trying!"

So with that encouragement, I told Patty I'd be back in five minutes and asked her to please keep an eye on my kids. I ran to the car, grabbed the tape and ran to the office inside the pool pavilion. A pretty girl was sitting at the manager's desk, and I asked if she would play this great music on the loudspeaker for everyone to enjoy.

"I love this music," she said. "Sure, I'll put it on right now."

When I walked back out to the pool and sat down, Patty looked at me with a Grinch-like grin and said, "I told you they wouldn't let you play your music here!" I just looked at her and smiled!

The next thing we heard was: (Circle of Life - Music and Lyrics by Elton John and Tim Rice)

From the day we arrive on the planet
And blinking, step into the sun
There's more to be seen than can ever be seen
More to do than can ever be done

Some say eat or be eaten
Some say live and let live
But all are agreed as they join the stampede
You should never take more than you give

In the circle of life, It's the wheel of fortune
It's the leap of faith, It's the band of hope,

Till we find our placeOn the path unwinding, In the circle, the circle of life

Some of us fall by the wayside
And some of us soar to the stars
And some of us sail through our troubles
And some have to live with the scars

There's far too much to take in here
More to find than can ever be found
But the sun rolling high
through the sapphire sky
Keeps great and small on the endless round

The kids, parents and lifeguards loved it and were singing along to the timeless music as they frolicked in the water. Patty wasn't sure how to react. My kids were jumping around in the water and singing "I Just Can't Wait to be King," "Whole New World," and suddenly Fairfax Pool looked and sounded like Walt Disney World.

When someone tells me, "That won't work," it only motivates me to find a way to make it work.

As human beings, we experience many wonderful feelings and a whole spectrum of emotions, but my dad was right when he told me at a young age:

Billy, there is nothing like the feeling of accomplishment. It is something you create out of doing, and no one can take it away from you.

In 2004, when I turned 44, my friend Paul gave me the book Finishing Well, by Bob Buford. This book helped me to realize that there is so much more to accomplish in the next 40 years, and so many exciting challenges ahead to look forward to. I'm just getting started!

Laurel and I were invited to Vern and Denise's annual Christmas party a couple of years ago with a bunch of other good friends. I was standing in the crowded kitchen telling my good friend Dick about my plans for the future. Dick looks like General Petraus, with the voice of Larry David and the same great sense of humor. I explained to him that by the time I turn 60, I will have been in the mixer business for 40 years and at that point in my life, I may want to change it up a bit by working part-time, educating teenagers at Memorial High School in Eau Claire.

Maybe teach two classes. The first would be a Material Science class that would teach Solids Processing and Project Engineering and interesting stuff like particle size distribution, surface tension, low coefficient of friction, insipient wetness and about liquid viscosities and spraying velocities. Cool stuff like that!

The second class would be called "Advanced Broken English: The Study of Domestic Language Arts." We would explore the vast range of English languages spoken throughout America. And Memorial is a large high school with more than 1,700 students. I told him it would be the most entertaining class in the school and it would be held in an auditorium filled with hundreds of students. Dick thought I wasn't seeing the big picture and suggested I take it to another level by teaching a Life's Studies AP course with Advanced Broken English and Material Science as part of the curriculum. What a great idea!

Music to my Soul

Have you ever noticed that many songs could be sung as though God is singing to you or you are singing to God? If you place God's name into most love songs, you won't believe how well it fits. The Beatles song "Eight Days a Week" is a good example.

Ooh I need your love "God,"
Guess you know it's true.
Hope you need my love "God,"
Just like i need you.
Hold me, love me, hold me, love me.
Ain't got nothin' but love "God,"
Eight days a week.

Billboard's Hot 100 chart turned 50 in September 208. To celebrate, the magazine set up www.billboard.com/hot100, which chronicles a list of Hot 100 record holders each week, culminating with the top 100 songs of all time. The top five artists with No.1 hits:

1. The Beatles, 20;

2. Mariah Carey, 18;

3. Michael Jackson, 13;

4. The Supremes, 12;

5. Madonna, 12.

The amazing staying power of Beatles music speaks volumes of the band's greatness. The Beatles changed the music world forever between 1964 and 1970, the year they went their separate ways. Thirty-nine years have passed since the Beatles were a band and yet their music is still alive and well today.

One of my favorite songs – "Give Me Love" (Give Me Peace on Earth) was composed by the late Beatle, George Harrison. Written in 1973, three years after The Beatles broke up; it seems to be a love song written to God.

Give me love

Give me love

Give me peace on earth

Give me light

Give me life

Keep me free from birth

Give me hope

Help me cope, with this heavy load

Trying to, touch and reach you with,

Heart and soul

Oh My Lord ....

PLEASE take hold of my hand, that

I might understand you

Won't you please?

Oh won't you!

When I hear the horns in Parliament's "Do That Stuff" or the guitar riff in The Rolling Stones song "It's All Over Now" or the piano in Supertramp's "Bloody Well Right" or the grand-finale jam in The Beatles farewell song "The End," my soul is moved with memories and emotions that are hard to describe.

As you can see, music is a big influence in my life. So much so, that I had to create a soundtrack and weave it throughout the book!

I am fortunate to live in a town with a deep musical tradition that includes the nationally known UW-Eau Claire jazz program as well as Eau Claire Memorial High School's outstanding music program under the direction of Bruce Hering and Eric Dasher.

But it all starts in grade school. For the students who attended South or North Star middle schools, they and their parents have been fortunate to have Lori Wolf and Bill Simon as music teachers. These people devote their time and talents to hundreds of kids each year and are the ones who help launch many children's music careers. They taught our four kids the oboe, tenor saxophone, clarinet and trumpet with remarkable results. The reason Eau Claire will continue to have a deeply rooted and richly talented music program is because of the passion and dedication of teachers like Wolf, Simon, Hering and Dasher.

In May of 2005, when Elizabeth was a junior at Memorial, her jazz band qualified as one of the top 15 in the country. They had the privilege of flying out to New York City to compete as a finalist in the Essentially Ellington Festival and perform at Lincoln Center in the heart of Manhattan. Laurel and I brought the rest of our family out to see Biz play tenor saxophone on a grand scale. It was a wonderful, educational family trip. Biz loved knowing that her family was there to share in the experience.

Live from New York. Eau Claire Memorial High School
Jazz Ensemble I. (Elizabeth is front row, second from the left.)

While going through high school in the mid '70s, there was one musical group that touched my soul more than any other.

Supertramp was one of my favorite bands. In 1974, I was fortunate to go with my good friend Dave Haugh to see the group's American concert debut tour promoting their 'Crime of the Century' album. The momentous event was held at the Riverside Theater in downtown Milwaukee.

Roger Hodgsen and Rick Davies wrote one of my favorite songs in 1977 titled, "Even in the Quietest Moments." These are just two lines taken from a very pretty and powerful song:

The music that you gave me, the language of my soul,

And Lord I want to be with you, won't you let me come in from the cold.

Patrick Snyder summed up the band's unique sound on the inside cover of the CD "Supertramp Classics – Volume 9."

If ever a band was meant for CD technology, it is Supertramp. Their meticulous engineering, explosive dynamics and iridescent swirls of sound take on breathtaking depth and precision. This is their best, better than you've ever heard before.

Supertramp occupies a unique place in popular music, a well-upholstered niche festooned with sly wit, catapulting rhythms and baroque melodic richness. Their genius is one of juxtaposition: buzzsaw dervish guitars whirl and spin but never quite splinter their veneer of English calm. High tragedy, low humor, and vice versa all find shelter beneath the band's bemused yellow umbrella. Supertramp's music has a timeless shimmer and these songs have never lost their freshness of emotion and ability to delight. Lean times combined with new enthusiasm to create 1974's Crime of the Century. The album and the single, "Dreamer," both topped the British charts and Supertramp were on their way to what was to become truly global success.

Few bands have enjoyed the worldwide attention Supertramp earned with their succession of brilliant albums. From Vancouver to Vienna, from Melbourne to Milwaukee, their music cast its spell and struck a responsive chord. The band has sold over 35 million albums around the world! They worked aesthetic ground first broken by the Beatles but cultivated a hybrid sophisticated rock undeniably their own. The sensibility was tart, thoughtful and expansive; the music joyful, intricate and uplifting.

When the Beatles wrote "All You Need is Love," they were right on! This is another great example of a song that sounds like God is singing to all of us:

There's nothing you can do that can't be done.

Nothing you can sing that can't be sung.

Nothing you can say but you can learn how to play the game

It's easy.

There's nothing you can make that can't be made.

No one you can save that can't be saved.

Nothing you can do but you can learn how to be you

in time - It's easy.

All you need is love, all you need is love,

All you need is love, love, love is all you need.

There's nothing you can know that isn't known.

Nothing you can see that isn't shown.

Nowhere you can be that isn't where you're meant to be.

It's easy!

Love is all you need!

I recently attended our next-door neighbor's poolside wedding for their daughter Tiffany. Greg and Carol Brandrup are two of the most giving souls I have encountered. Judge Benjamin Procter, a friend of the family, was the Justice of the Peace. Tom and I had golfed with Ben at Hillcrest Country Club in one of the President Cups a few years back. He is an excellent guy and a steady golfer. When the ceremony was over, I asked the judge if I could have a copy of the vows; I especially loved the paragraph he recited about love:

"Love is the strongest and most fulfilling emotion possible; it lets you share your goals, your desires, and your experiences. … It lets you be yourself. It lets you speak your innermost feelings to someone who understands you. It lets you feel tenderness and warmth – a wholeness that avoids loneliness. Love lets you feel complete."

I'll be doggone

I never grew up with a dog in our house and generally had bad experiences with dogs as a kid and as a teenager. I can recall three times in particular that I was bitten by a dog for no reason at all. And because of these dramatic occurrences, I didn't trust dogs and couldn't understand how people could have such affection for these four-legged power sniffers with a mouth full of teeth. So much so, that every time a dog barks at me, I hear vulgar swear words!

Like the time I was walking through the Oakwood Mall parking lot on my way to Scheel's Sports. I'm strolling past the parked cars and pick-up trucks, minding my own business, when suddenly out of nowhere this German Shepard appeared in the rear window of a Suburban and launched into this loud, abrasive foul mouth tirade that was totally uncalled for! This monster startled the "S" out of me and immediately put all my defenses on high alert. The raised glass window was the only thing keeping the crazed canine from ripping me apart. He really pissed me off! To the point where I wanted to bark back at him – which probably would have looked kind of strange. So instead of causing a scene, and swearing back at him, I maintained my composure and walked into the store.

Laurel grew up with dogs and would tell me how wonderful they are to have around the house and around the kids. I just couldn't see it until 2004 when Laurel and Michelle picked up a new puppy, a Bischon Frazee to surprise Meghan on her 9th birthday. This little ball of white fluff was unlike the dogs I had come across in my past and slowly grew on me to the point where I now understand what people are talking about when the speak of the joy they receive from their pets. Our dog actually has two names; his Spanish name is Jorge, but his American name is Colby Sno-Cone, Budda Thumper, Oshi-Maru, Cutie Pie, Packerfan, Jumper, Butter Finger, Tootsie-Roll-Maker, Cody, Callaghan. He answers to both!

Full Circle

The raised with praise approach has now moved on to the next generation. I recently received the following email from my daughter Michelle, who is a freshman at Minnesota State University in Mankato, Minnesota.

Hey Dad,

Things are going well at MSU. But today is a rainy one here at Mankato; my shoes got all wet and my hair is a frizz ball. Despite all of that, I still have hope that today will be a great one!

I can't believe the world we live in sometimes – people seem to find the negative in everything! And I can't tell you enough how glad I am that you taught me how to have a positive outlook on life. It makes me a happier person. Really! And when I say something positive, people look at me, surprised. A good surprised, though! You can see them thinking about it. But I hope you have an awesome day at work; sell some mixers!

I love you the most,

Michelle

Elizabeth, Joseph, Michelle and Meghan put together the following thoughts about their childhoods.

Setting the pace

Elizabeth, the oldest of the Callaghan clan, was working 40 hours a week in Minneapolis as a bartender at a steakhouse and attending Argosy University in pursuit of an associate's degree in Echosonography in 2009.

Her common-sense approach to life was beyond her years and set an example for her siblings, as did her you-can-do-it attitude. If Elizabeth wanted something done, it got done, yet she still had time and energy for a bevy of friends.

"When I think of my dad, he has been nothing but the best role model any child could ever ask for," Elizabeth said. "When things are stressful at work, he never brings it home and is always happy to be with his family."

"My dad has always had a positive outlook on life and very rarely looked at the negative. He even took our housework to the positive-outlook level, which at times irritated the hell out of us," she joked.

"Clean your room because then you can see the floor," dad would say or, "You'll be able to find clothes you didn't know you had if you organize your closet."

"He is the funniest person, and I think people enjoy being around him because of his positive outlook," Elizabeth said. "I think most of his stories are from people's reactions when he threw a positive curveball their way."

Being "raised with praise," however, occasionally was a challenge for the oldest child.

"I know there have been times when he would try to make me feel better about a situation, and I would have to make sure he knew the (whole) picture before jumping to conclusions," Elizabeth said. "For me, before I see the positive, I see all points of view, and there have been times where he has given 'hope' but realistically there's not a chance.

But it's a small price to pay for a confidence-boosting upbringing, Elizabeth said.

"One thing that has had a huge impact on me is when my dad says, 'Life is nothing but a ride, so don't sweat the small stuff,'" she said. "I know there have been times when I'm in a social setting and people are just drawn to me because I love to dance and laugh and tell stories and enjoy being in the present. If there is anyone who knows how to enjoy the present, it's my dad."

The end result was a nurturing childhood.

"My mom and dad are the best parents I could ever ask for," Elizabeth said. "Not only do they play off each other, but they laugh together, love each other, and would do anything for their children and then some."

Joseph, Elizabeth, Michelle and Meghan at the IMTA
Awards Banquet in Los Angeles, California - January 2009

The Entertainer

Joseph Callaghan, an entertainer adept at acting, dancing and voice impressions, boasts a serene yet energetic disposition. By all accounts, he wears his heart on his sleeve and exudes positive energy. He also has a strong faith in God and isn't shy about sharing that aspect of his personality with his friends.

Joseph, a full-time student at Chippewa Valley Technical College in 2009, fondly remembered his father's parting words each day as he dropped his children off at school during their formative years. Joseph also worked at the Metropolis Hotel, which provided high-end accommodations in Eau Claire, and did voiceover work in the Twin Cities at the time.

"Today's a new day," dad would say. "Go in and make the most of it. See how many people's day you can brighten."

The words left a lasting impression with Joseph.

"He didn't say, 'Get an 'A' on that test, Joe, your future depends on it,' Joseph said. "Instead, my dad taught me that being a light in my classmates' and teachers' day is what life is all about."

"I was raised with praise absolutely, and I'm very proud of my mom and dad."

Faith also played a key role in the Callaghan household, said Joseph, who added that he learned kindness, humor and trust because his parents were masters of the traits.

"I also noticed my mom and dad were never mean to anyone so I was never taught how to be mean to others," Joseph said. "They had a whole new approach at handling problems or unexpected change.

"Stress doesn't mess with my dad because it never wins. Life's too short, and when times are tough my dad taught me to be thankful that my sword's getting sharpened and it's making me a stronger person."

The "raised with praise" label accurately describes his upbringing, Joseph said. It's about treating your kids and others like you'd want to be treated and can start at any age, he said. It's about self-sacrifice and controlling emotions.

"For example, in God's eyes who looks more immature?" Joseph said. "The kid crying because he's not getting his way, or the parent who's screaming at his kid, reacting like a dumbbell and punishing him for crying?

The parent, at the same time, is teaching his child that the way to handle an awkward situation is to overpower the kid with physical, verbal or harsh discipline.

'Raised with praise' to me is living with patience, wisdom and compassion on a day-to-day basis. I plan to instill these same virtues in my kids."

Empathy Important

A joy to be around, kind and giving accurately describe Michelle Callaghan. She consistently is aware of - and sensitive to - the needs of others. She is a generous listener, deep thinker and a keen conversationalist. She also has a gift for artistic creativity.

Michelle, the third of the four Callaghan children and a student at the University of Minnesota-Mankato in 2009, also had fond memories of school days during her childhood.

"Every day before school, I would walk downstairs to say goodbye to my dad," she said. "No matter how tired I looked, he would tell me I was beautiful and to go kick some (Eau Claire) Memorial ass that day.

"As I walked out the door, he would say 'See you when it's over!' That phrase can be taken many ways. I always figured he meant after the school day, but it could also mean in eternity up in Heaven."

And the praise didn't subside over the course of the day.

"My parents are constantly telling me how great the things are I'm doing," Michelle said. "There is just not one example to describe it; it comes with everyday living. No matter what the situation, my parents will get the most out of it."

One surprise trip to a fast-food restaurant for ice cream illustrated her parents' perspective on life.

"While we were waiting in the drive-thru lane, a man walked past our car when one of my siblings said 'Jeez, look at that guy; he looks tough,'" Michelle said. "Instead of agreeing with the comment, my dad said, 'Isn't it cool how God made everyone?

"The meaning was not to judge other people; no person is better than another."

Not dwelling on the past, looking forward to the future and looking at life in a positive light were valuable lessons, Michelle said.

"Giving people the benefit of the doubt goes a long way," she said. "Not to judge people, but to understand why they may look or be acting in a certain way.

"Talking bad about people will get you absolutely nowhere, complicate your life and will add unnecessary stress."

And stress is not welcome in the Callaghan household, Michelle said. "Stress is completely overrated and completely stuck between your ears," she said. "Find time for God in your life and everything is easier.

"Who cares what other people think. To complain about something is worthless; you are only making everyone else in the room miserable."

As far as the "raised with praise" mantra, Michelle said it has several components.

"(It) means my parents are proud of me and support me," she said. "Not only will they act proud, but they will tell me about it too."

Communication is also critical.

"When I do something wrong, they relate it to me in a way I understand," Michelle said. "My parents can come down to the same level I am on. Not always having to be the superior. They talk to me like a friend or teacher, giving advice instead of yelling, finding the fault, and putting me down.

"They don't concentrate on the negative but go the positive route to fix the problem."

Trust also comes into play, Michelle said.

"My parents trust me with what I say; we communicate everything to each other," she said. "I never find the need to lie. Most fights begin between parents and kids because the parents don't believe what their kid is telling them.

"Don't try to mold your kid into someone you wish they were or expect them to be. Instead, look at the positive and see all the great they have done."

The result can be harmonious.

"My parents are the happiest people I know," Michelle said. "We were affectionately known in some circles as the 'happy family.' I wonder what gave them that idea. My parents have the gift to brighten rooms at every entrance."

Dancing queen

As the youngest Callaghan, Meghan was wrestled with, knocked down, helped up and loved every minute of it. The positive attention and support her brothers and sisters gave her resulted in an easy-going and humble disposition. She also developed meticulous organizational skills and a passionate interest in dance.

Meghan was a freshman at Eau Claire Memorial High School in 2009. She was a member of the varsity dance team at the time with gainful employment as a babysitter when her schedule allowed.

A painful bowling accident that resulted in a broken thumb reminded Meghan of her parents' compassion.

"I knew I was going to be fine because my parents were always there for me," she said. "My parents drove me to the hospital, helped me, nurtured me, and did everything they could to help me."

Sledding outings to Northstar Middle School were a welcomed annual event. The parents would join the kids for a day of tubing down a mogul-filled track. Dad would blow up the tubes and mom would make sure the kids were bundled up from head to toe.

"We have a jolly time," Meghan said. "My parents are always working on ways to help us. They are always on my side."

Religion also has been influential.

"My parents have always been very spiritual," Meghan said. "I mean, I go to church every Sunday and they have me go to prep class. My parents have taught me to always try hard in life, try and follow the Ten Commandments and keep a positive outlook on life. I have tried to do that."

The results speak for themselves.

"My parents have made me happy," Meghan said. "When I grow up, I hope to teach my kids the same lessons.

Such as being "raised with praise."

"To me, it means that I have grown up in a positive light," Meghan said. "I have been nurtured to the fullest. As a result, I am a happy kid."

Chapter 15

Faith - The Final Frontier

My fascination with space exploration has captured my imagination ever since I was seven years old, when the early Apollo missions were shown on our black and white TV.

(CNN) Forty years ago, three men in a tiny spacecraft slipped their earthly bonds and traveled where no one else had before, circling the moon 10 times and bringing back an iconic image of a blue-and-white Earth in the distance, solitary but bound as one against the black vastness beyond.

Host Nick Clooney and astronauts Frank Borman, Jim Lovell and William Anders answer questions in October 2008.

The voyage of Apollo 8 from December 21-27, 1968, marked humans' first venture to another heavenly body.

"We were flying to the moon for the first time," said Jim Lovell, one of the three astronauts aboard the historic flight. "Seeing the far side of the moon for the first time. Coming around and seeing the Earth as it really is -- a small fragile planet with a rather normal star, our sun."

But beyond the monumental aspects of such a scientific achievement, the feat was a major psychological and emotional boost for many Americans at the end of a particularly bad year in U.S. history.

The Tet offensive in January 1968 had left many Americans shocked and doubting that victory in Vietnam was possible. In April, the Rev. Martin Luther King was assassinated, and streets throughout the nation erupted in fire and fury. Sen. Robert F. Kennedy was gunned down two months later.

That summer, the nation watched in horror as police and anti-war protesters battled in the streets of Chicago during the Democratic National Convention.

The launch of Apollo 7 in October was a major victory for NASA, putting the space program back on track after a 22-month interruption because of a launch pad fire that had killed three astronauts in January 1967.

Then came Apollo 8.

"Providence happened to put everything together at the end of the year to give the American public an uplift after what had been a poor year," Lovell told CNN on Monday.

The mission produced one of the most famous photos from the space program, showing a large chunk of gray moon in the foreground and a dappled blue-and-white, three-quarter Earth rising in the distance.

Apollo 8 also produced what to many was one of the most inspirational and soothing moments in history when Lovell and crewmates Frank Borman and William A. Anders took turns reading from the Book of Genesis. It was Christmas Eve and the whole world was watching. NASA said at the time it was expected to be the largest TV audience to date.

The astronauts signed off with these words: "And from the crew of Apollo 8, we close with good night, good luck, a merry Christmas and God bless all of you, all of you on the good earth."

The timing could not have been better, Lovell said.

"It happened that it all jelled," he said by telephone. "The fact that we circled the moon on Christmas Eve. A screenwriter couldn't have done a better job."

The success of the mission also gave the United States a major boost in its race against the Soviet Union to see who would get to the moon first. The United States would land two men on the moon in the summer of 1969 on Apollo 11, beating the Soviets and fulfilling a goal set by former President John F. Kennedy at the beginning of the decade.

Lovell went on to fly another historic mission, Apollo 13 in April 1970. That flight, which he commanded, became famous when an oxygen system aboard the craft blew up and the three astronauts had to limp around the moon and back to Earth using makeshift and improvised systems. Their triumph over adversity was immortalized in the movie "Apollo 13," in which Tom Hanks played Lovell.

Lovell was supposed to land on the moon that time, but did not make it.

"Twice a bridesmaid, never a bride," he said with a laugh, admitting that for years he harbored resentment that the mission had been a "failure."

It was only in later years, Lovell said, that he fully realized what a success that mission had been, as he and his two crewmates returned safely to Earth.

"It is mind-boggling in some respects."

Although I've always been enamored with space exploration, I don't believe in the existence of aliens or other creatures from outer space spying on our primitive planet. I just can't see how they fit into the belief that God created all living things. It's impossible to imagine the will of our creator, but why would God create an alien? Certainly not to put fear in our lives while we hang out here on this planet.

That doesn't sound like something God would do. He's not a fan of fear. He knows all too well that our time living on earth can be scary enough as it is, without the fear of aliens. If aliens do exist, do they have souls like human beings or are they part of the animal kingdom?

In the past 15 years, you would think we would have seen many photos of aliens, especially on YouTube, which covers the world's latest pictures and videos for all to see. In that short time span, the earth's population has seen a tremendous growth of amateur photographers and the ability to instantly capture, record and send digital images to anyone anywhere using cell phone cameras, cameras that record video, and hand-held digital video cameras. Yet we haven't seen any pictures of aliens.

(CNN) -- As NASA prepares to hunt for Earth-like planets in our corner of the Milky Way galaxy, there's new buzz that "Star Trek's" vision of a universe full of life may not be that far-fetched.

Pointy-eared aliens traveling at light speed are staying firmly in science fiction, but scientists are offering fresh insights into the possible existence of inhabited worlds and intelligent civilizations in space.

There may be 100 billion Earth-like planets in the Milky Way, or one for every sun-type star in the galaxy, said Alan Boss, an astronomer with the Carnegie Institution and author of the new book "The Crowded Universe: The Search for Living Planets."

• The Milky Way is believed to be more than 13 billion years old.

• It is just one of billions of galaxies in the universe.

• The Milky Way has a circumference of about 250,000-300,000 light years.

• It is about 100,000 light years in diameter.

To illustrate, Boss said the fastest rockets available to us right now are those being used in NASA's New Horizons mission to Pluto. Even going at that rate of speed, it would take 100,000 years to get from Earth to the closest star outside the solar system, he added.

"So when you think about that, maybe we shouldn't be worried about having interstellar air raids any time soon," Boss said.

People in general and Hollywood in particular, usually portray aliens as scary, mysterious, bizarre creatures with superior intelligence who bring destruction to the earth. The alien that Sigourney Weaver encountered in the movies was not nice. With the exception of "E.T.," "The Last Star Fighter," "Starman" and a few other light science fiction movies, aliens typically are portrayed in a negative light.

One of my favorite movies is Star Wars - actually all six of them. I'm such a fan of "the force" that the name on the identity tag on my golf clubs is "Obi-Wan Kenobi," a famous Jedi. It should come as no surprise that I prefer to play the Titleist "Pro V1 Kenobi" golf ball. I can hit that brand further off the tee than any other on the planet.

I was 17 when the first Star Wars movie came out in 1977. I love how George Lucas wrote six screenplays and started with a trilogy of movies, four through six chronologically, and finished the story with a trilogy, one through three, that tied it all together. Brilliant.

In the movie "The Empire Strikes Back," Luke Skywalker flies off to the Dagobah system in search of Yoda, a Jedi Master. While Luke was learning the ways of the force, Yoda tells him "anger, fear, aggression – the dark side are they." "And worry you should not – for my ally is the force and a powerful ally it is – life creates it – makes it grow. Its energy surrounds us." Yoda tells Luke, "luminous beings are we, not this crude matter," as he pulls on his arm. That phrase really caught my attention. He's referring to our bright spirits, our souls living inside these carbon-based bodies. "Luminous beings are we!"

Let There Be Light

Did you know that the colors of a rainbow coincide with the days of creation? I was taught in grade school how to remember the bowed colors as ROYGBV, but I found out later that I had it backwards. My father gave me a copy of an article some years ago that was written by Gary Stearman titled "Before Creation, There Was God's Primeval Light."

In this fascinating piece, the author describes, among other things, the account of the days of creation in the book of Genesis and how they perfectly match the colors of the rainbow.

Genesis 1: 3-5 "And God said, Let there be light: and there was light. And God saw the light, and that it was good: and God divided the light from the darkness and God called the light day, and the darkness he called night. And the evening and the morning were the first day."

The writer adds, "The light called into existence by God, and called by him "good," is seen well before the creation of the Sun, Moon, planets and stars on the fourth day of creation. Where did this light come from? Man falls far short of even being able to imagine it, let alone describe it. Nevertheless, it seems to be the very material of creation. Apparently, it is a creative energy: a force that may be used to forge particles that fit together as atoms, molecules and finally, of the created beings, man, the earth, planets and stars.

It came from God – Elohim – as He spoke the words, "Ye-hee Ohr." Since the verb "to be" in not expressed as such in Hebrew, God's command is really an expression of his person: "Me … come into existence … light." Thus the light is only an expression of His own radiance. In a sense, God's Creation is a reflection of His Primeval Light. When the light of the sun is divided into six spectral colors, the six days of creation are illustrated.

On the first day, God said, "Let there be light!" This can be illustrated at the highest point of the color spectrum by ultra-violet and violet – the color of royalty. God is King of the universe.

On the second day, God divided the waters, illustrated by the color blue.

On the third day, God called forth the grass, illustrated by green.

On the fourth day, God made the sun, illustrated by yellow.

On the fifth day, God made cold-blooded animals, illustrated by orange.

On the sixth day, God made warm-blooded animals – plus man, illustrated by the color red. "Adam", the name of the first man, means "the red one".

Note that the progression down the color spectrum matches the successive days of creation in perfect order. Furthermore, God created the universe from the top down, not from the bottom up. God is not lower, but higher than his creation. Finally, the seventh day – the Sabbath – recombines the separated colors, producing white, the light of righteousness.

The Bible promises eternal life in a world and a city ablaze with the unfailing light of God. Revelation21: 23-25 offers a brief description of the holy city - Heaven; the New Jerusalem.

Its magnificent setting is bathed in a brilliant light. But it is not any form of artificial light. Nor is it the light of the sun. It is the pure light of God: "And the city had no need of the sun, neither of the moon, to shine in it: for the glory of God did lighten it, and the Lamb is the light thereof. "And the nations of them which are saved shall walk in the light of it. "And the gates of it shall not be shut at all by day: for there shall be no night there."

I believe we are all spirits cruising around earth in these bodies and that God put us on this earth to accomplish a certain number of things. Our bodies become like old run-down cars with cracked windshields, leaky transmissions and blown tires that end up in the junkyard or graveyard after many miles of use - but our spirits move on.

The challenging part is that we don't know what it is that God wants us to do unless we make ourselves available to hear His word and act on it. God brings us into the world and God takes out.

We have to make the most of the gifts and talents He has blessed us with in the finite amount of time we are each allowed, so we can give Him a sound report when we check out of earth and our souls check into the infinite world to come - Heaven!

A strong faith in God will trump the daily stress in your life. To worry all the time, live in fear and be anxious about things you can't control, means you are putting the entire load on yourself and not relying on God to help you through your problems. God wants you to believe in him and trust in him. That is the definition of faith. Don't try to go it alone!

I have found that positive energy is uplifting, contagious and has a magnetic effect on those around me. It is a force that enlightens everyone within its presence. Negative energy, not surprisingly, has the exact opposite result. It spoils the human spirit, invites fear and often dwells on problems – not solutions.

This story is taken from the book of Mark 4:35-41.

On that day, as evening drew on, Jesus said to his disciples: "Let us cross to the other side." Leaving the crowd, they took Jesus with them in the boat just as he was. And other boats were with them.

A violent squall came up and waves were breaking over the boat, so that it was already filling up. Jesus was in the stern, asleep on a cushion. They woke him and said to him, "Teacher, do you not care that we are perishing?"

He woke up, rebuked the wind, and said to the sea, "Quiet! Be still!"

The wind ceased and there was great calm. Then he asked them, "Why are you terrified? Do you not yet have faith?"

They were filled with great awe and said to one another, "Who then is this whom even wind and sea obey?"

I was taught as a Catholic that the reason God made us is to know him, serve him and love him in this world so that we may be with him in the next world - in the kingdom of Heaven.

We have all seen at one time or another, these three numbers - 3:16. When I was growing up, I remember seeing a tall white guy on TV with a rainbow afro at NFL and NBA games and Golf Tournaments, holding up a sign that simply read 3:16. This guy would show up out of nowhere, always within camera view, promoting the following sacred scripture from the Bible.

"For God so loved the world that he gave his only son, that everyone who believes in him shall not perish, but may have eternal life." (John 3:16)

(John 8:51) "Very Truly, I say to you, whoever keeps my word will never see death."

(John 11:25) "I am the resurrection and the life; whoever believes in me, even if he dies, will live."

When former White House press secretary, Tony Snow, died from relentless cancer at the young age of 52, one of his close friends said, "One of Tony's favorite sayings was 'God doesn't promise tomorrow, but he does promise forever."

All You Need Is Love

The Beatles' Abbey Road album was No. 1 on the album charts on November 1, 1969. This was to be their last album. It contains some of my favorite Beatles songs and some of their best work. The last song on the album and the last song ever composed by Lennon and McCartney is titled "The End." What a fitting name for a song that would bring closure to the band's brilliant music career. They wrote:

Oh yah, all right,

Are you going to be in my dreams tonight?

And - in - the end,

The - love - you take,

Is equal to the love - you make.

In December 1999, my wife and I were on vacation with Longaberger in London, England, enjoying a cruise down the Thames River on a dinner boat. Sandy Pond, one of the sales directors on the trip, told us that while attending Harvard her professor asked his students to explain on a final exam what the words to that classic Beatle's song meant.

She said most of the students missed the meaning and failed the assignment. Then she asked me what I thought Lennon and McCartney were saying. I told her,

"And in the end - *of your life*, the love you take - *with you to heaven*, is equal to the love you make – *here on earth.*" I told her it was along the same lines of "you reap what you sow." She said I would have aced the Harvard exam.

Get In The Zone!

I've been in the end zone with a football for a touchdown and I've been in a zone on the golf course when I'm putting unbelievably well and can see an imaginary Hot Wheels track on every putt. But of all the zones I've been in, the spiritual zone is unlike anything I have felt or experienced. Have you ever been in a zone with God or Jesus or the Holy Spirit? Yes! They are one in the same – The Holy Trinity!

I was driving home from work one day - a 20-mile commute from Osseo to Eau Claire - and I was talking to God and thanking him for a productive day at the plant. The radio was off and it was just me and the Lord recapping the day. All of a sudden a feeling of indescribable comfort and joy was flowing through my body. It was as though my spirit was radiating and glowing so bright inside me that my human flesh was doing its best to contain the ecstasy and restrain the light from overflowing. My body tingled and felt almost weightless as I could feel the hairs on my toes, my legs, my arms and my head shimmering. It was powerful! I was temporarily in a heavenly zone of eternal bliss. It was the nexus!

The feeling lasted only a mile before fading away. But for that mile and that minute in my life, I experienced something out of this world! "Luminous beings are we, not this crude matter!"

Borrowed Time

The late, great John Lennon composed some of the most beautiful music and love songs ever written. His work as a Beatle along with the music he produced during a brief solo career is legendary. On December 8, 1980, Lennon's life ended abruptly when he was shot to death outside the Dakota, a high-rise apartment building directly across from Central Park in downtown New York. Lennon was just getting back into writing and producing beautiful music when he was gunned down by a delusional "fan." His life was short-lived and when he died at the young age of 40, he took his unique sound and creative songwriting with him.

Like most of the nation, I found out about his death from Howard Cosell while watching Monday Night Football. And like everyone else, I was shocked at the news!

The cover of the Dec. 22, 1980, issue of Time Magazine showed an artist rendering of John Lennon and the headline read: "When the Music Died."

In 1984, Yoko released an album in honor of John titled "Milk and Honey" containing songs he wrote and fabulous music he produced leading up to his unexpected death. The song "Borrowed Time" was written just before his time on earth came to an end. John Lennon was truly ahead of his time.

John Lennon and Yoko Ono, Milk and Honey, 1984

Borrowed Time

When I was younger
Living confusion and deep despair
When I was younger ah hah
Living illusion of freedom and power

When I was younger
Full of ideas and broken dreams (my friend)
When I was younger ah hah
Everything simple but not so clear

Living on borrowed time
Without a thought for tomorrow
Living on borrowed time
Without a thought for tomorrow

Now I am older
The more that I see the less that I know for sure
Now I am older ah hah
The future is brighter and now is the hour

Good to be older
Would not exchange a single day or a year
Good to be older ah hah
Less complications everything clear
Living on borrowed time
Without a thought for tomorrow
Living on borrowed time
Without a thought for tomorrow

Fountain of Youth

One of the gifts God gave me is the ability to find the kid in anyone I meet. I feel age exists mostly between your ears and people are really just grown-up kids once you really get to know them. I see a world filled with children of many ages.

When adults slough off their sophisticated persona or professional demeanor, you're left with kids in grown-up bodies who want to enjoy life to its fullest but somehow have forgotten what it was like to think and feel like they did in their younger days.

I have met many adults who are so preoccupied and impressed with themselves, their possessions, their wealth, that they are a bore to be around. They are so caught up in being important and "professional" people that they don't remember how to laugh or simply enjoy life. Those are the people I go after; the ones who know everything and aren't happy about anything. When meeting people, I can tell when I've made it past all the years of age that have dulled their youthfulness because I hear laughter coming from their soul and see a smile in their eyes that is unmistakably young.

From The Kinks "Percy" original soundtrack, 1971

God's Children

Man made the buildings that reach for the sky
And man made the motorcar and learned how to fly
But he didn't make the flowers and he didn't make the trees

And he didn't make you and he didn't make me
And he got no right to turn us into machines
He's got no right at all

'cause we are all god's children
And he got no right to change us
Oh, we gotta go back the way the good lord made us all

Oh, the rich man, the poor man, the saint and the sinner
The wise man, the simpleton, the loser and the winner
We are all the same to him
Stripped of our clothes and all the things we own
The day that we are born
We are all god's children

My parents are the ones who taught me how to have a positive attitude about life and how to approach people in a complimentary way. And that was the example I followed when it came time to raise my family.

Coyne and Martha Callaghan at John's wedding - September 2003.

The essence of the book is simply this: Be kind and understanding to your children during the brief time they live under your wing. Be their teacher – Not their boss! And learn to appreciate every day you have together.

Bert sang it best, when he was explaining that very thing to Mr. Banks at the end of Disney's "Mary Poppins".

You've got to grind, grind, grind at the grindstone,

Though childhood slips, like sand through a sieve,

And all too soon they're up and gone,

And then they've flown,

And it's too late for you to give!

Treat your children as God as treated you – with kindness, compassion, unconditional love, and understanding.
Raise them with Praise!

About the Author

Bill Callaghan was born in Milwaukee, Wisconsin, in June of 1960. He and ten brothers and sisters grew up in the village of Shorewood, along the shores of Lake Michigan. Bill attended grade school at St. Robert's Catholic School and spent the next four years at Shorewood High School, graduating in 1978 as the senior class president. Bill attended UWEC (University of Wisconsin-Eau Claire) before joining the family's mixing business in 1980. He has spent the past 30 years working with his parents and four brothers, manufacturing blending and coating equipment. Bill and his wife Laurel were married in 1986 in Eau Claire, Wisconsin, and have four children, three in college and one in high school. Bill is a father, husband, teacher, an inventor, and now an author. Above all, he is just a kid at heart!

Acknowledgements

The stories and people I have encountered, and the help I
have received was beyond my imagination. Writing and
self-publishing a book are both major undertakings. When I
started this adventure nine years ago, I never knew how much
support God would send my way. I thank my wife, Laurel, for
professionally editing my work and especially her support and
patience with me, as I spent many nights and weekends in the Big
Room writing. Big thanks to my mom and dad for taking the time
on ten separate occasions, to sit down with me and record decades
of stories. I am grateful for the encouragement that I received
from my oldest brother Marty and my sister Mary and for their
positive feedback when I first announced to the family that I
was writing a book about the way we were raised. My brother
Tom's input was most helpful throughout the writing process,
as I would constantly bounce ideas off of him. We had some
good laughs! I also want to thank my youngest brother John,
whose technical support was priceless. He was instrumental in
converting photographs for the book and the website, as well as
helping me complete the digital formatting process. And Tricia
Callaghan, my niece and God child, who helped transcribe some
of the original recordings into word documents, and developing
the original "Family Tree."

Special thanks to my "stellar support team" including Liam
Marlaire, who was key in the book's structuring and polishing
phases. Thanks to all the wonderful people, including Katie
Cataldo, who were part of the study group, for sharing their

insightful comments and suggestions. I want to thank Kathy O'Leary for creating the cover art work, designing and building the website, and her eleventh hour effort making this book a finished product. My sincere thanks to my friend Shelley Ayres for meticulously proof-reading the entire text. She could teach teachers English grammar.

Finally, I thank God for inspiring me to write this book and keeping me focused and on task. I'm so grateful to you for sending all these special people my way.

4298630

Made in the USA
Charleston, SC
26 December 2009